A Said
Dictiona

A Said Dictionary

R. Radhakrishnan

WILEY-BLACKWELL

A John Wiley & Sons, Ltd., Publication

This edition first published 2012
© 2012 R. Radhakrishnan

Blackwell Publishing was acquired by John Wiley & Sons in February 2007. Blackwell's publishing program has been merged with Wiley's global Scientific, Technical, and Medical business to form Wiley-Blackwell.

Registered Office
John Wiley & Sons Ltd, The Atrium, Southern Gate, Chichester, West Sussex, PO19 8SQ, UK

Editorial Offices
350 Main Street, Malden, MA 02148-5020, USA
9600 Garsington Road, Oxford, OX4 2DQ, UK
The Atrium, Southern Gate, Chichester, West Sussex, PO19 8SQ, UK

For details of our global editorial offices, for customer services, and for information about how to apply for permission to reuse the copyright material in this book please see our website at www.wiley.com/wiley-blackwell.

The right of R. Radhakrishnan to be identified as the author of this work has been asserted in accordance with the UK Copyright, Designs and Patents Act 1988.

Library of Congress Cataloging-in-Publication Data

Radhakrishnan, R. (Rajagopalan)
  A Said dictionary / R. Radhakrishnan.
    p. cm.
  ISBN 978-1-4051-8378-9 (cloth) – ISBN 978-1-4051-8377-2 (pbk.)
  1. Said, Edward W.–Criticism and interpretation.   2. Said, Edward W.–Language–Glossaries, etc.   I. Title.
  PN75.S25R33 2012
  801′.95092–dc23

                                                                    2011047215

A catalogue record for this book is available from the British Library.

Set in 10.5/13pt Minion by Aptara Inc., New Delhi, India
Printed in Singapore by Ho Printing Singapore Pte Ltd

1   2012

The book is dedicated, with affection and abiding gratitude, to Edward Said and his impeccable and imaginative legacy of critical, humane, and inclusive worldliness.

Contents

Terms

Preface

Edward Said has been in the general international eye for a number of years now as a public intellectual steeped in a very specific sort of academic scholarship; and the purpose of this book is to explicate and explain the public salience of Said's work for our times without in any way dumbing down the conceptual or the polemical complexity of Said's perspectives and positions on a variety of worldly issues: positions that could not have been reached without the help of erudition achieved rigorously within the walls of academia. It is intended to be of use to specialists, non-specialists, Edward Said aficionados as well as those who have a general awareness of Said and his prominence, and particularly students, both graduate and undergraduate, as well as professors in the humanities who will seek this book out as a text for their courses.

Since the publication of his *Orientalism* in 1978, Said had built up a tremendous reputation as a visible and audible public intellectual who was unafraid to contaminate and politicize the hoary chambers of scholarship with the clamor and urgency of worldly, political issues. At the risk of dire misrecognition, even death threats, Said continued to espouse causes that were anathema in the West and did so on the basis of his formidable expertise as a humanities scholar steeped in the tradition of the West. It is precisely because he cared for the West that it was important for him to be the ambassadorial voice of the so-called non-West to the West; and of course, his real objective was to break down the falsity of the Occident–Orient, or for that matter, any putative civilizational divide that disavowed the reality of shared and coeval histories. Precisely because of the richly ambivalent nature of his subject position as well as politics of location, Said was vulnerable to hostile criticism from both sides. He was of the West, academically and disciplinarily speaking; and yet, how could he, how dare he bite the very hand that had fed him? He was a spokesperson of the Palestinian and the Arab cause, but he was neither a Middle Eastern Studies scholar nor a gung-ho Arab (nor any other kind of) nationalist; moreover, he was more interested in finding an ear in the West rather than in being the authentic representative of Arab or Palestinian identity. He was no defender of nationalism *per se*, and yet he was a member of the Palestinian National Council in exile and was vilified as the "professor of terror" because of his support of the Palestine Liberation Organization and the *intifada*. But as an eternal oppositional critic, he was as much a critic of Arafat and his cronies as he was of the state of Israel and Zionism. Political activists of a certain color found his commitment to Western humanism irrelevant, even offensive; whereas the pure scholars of literary humanism found his politics obstreperous and reprehensibly partisan. He was always talking about the significance of representation; and yet he meant by representation something other than identity politics, insiderism, and the politics of authenticity.

Was he academically political or politically academic? It would all depend on who your interlocutor was. As a distinguished humanities professor at an Ivy League institution in the United States, his position was clearly secure and privileged; and yet within academia, his reputation was hotly contested. In many circles he was so much *persona non grata* that he would even say that in those unpopular contexts a letter of reference from him would be tantamount to the kiss of death. Whereas he was after all an academic and a professor, he had indeed rendered the academic department a different kind of place by openly acknowledging and embracing an interested rather than a disinterested mode of scholarly enquiry. While on the one hand there is a chorus of voices maintaining that postcoloniality was nothing but an aseptic metropolitan, academic, diasporic formation fraught with no peril whatsoever, there is ample proof on the other hand that area studies that have been influenced by *Orientalism* in particular, and Edward Said's work in general, have been targeted for patriotic nationalist-American surveillance, even more so after 9/11 and the American Homeland Security Act. Whatever he wrote about, and his range was indeed impressive; and wherever he wrote, and indeed he published in a wide spectrum of sites, he brought to his writings a sense of worldly urgency. In other words, whether the reader agreed with Said or not, she could sense that there was always something at stake behind the essay or the article, and that whatever was at stake was open to multilateral argumentation. In other words, whatever Said wrote was intellectual and public at the same time, in the same breath. It was in this spirit that he would exhort those who came under his influence to write, whatever their immediate area of specialized focus, firstly, for a large audience that would transcend their specialist argot, and secondly, for a range of constituencies, from the narrowly academic to the broadly populist. What he preached, he clearly practiced all his life as he strove tirelessly to make sense of the world he lived in through passionate, lively, partisan but contrapuntal dialog with other voices and perspectives.

Like the work of all public intellectuals, Said's work too was richly and deeply symptomatic of the times he lived in. His was an intensely situated life, in Jean-Paul Sartre's sense of "situatedness," and Said endeavored, till the very end when he collaborated with Daniel Barenboim (*Parallels and Paradoxes: Explorations in Music and Society*), in the field of music, to bring about some real conversation between the state of Israel and an emerging Palestinian state, to produce critical-oppositional meaning from the symptoms of historical existence. There are three particular aspects of Said's life and career that make him particularly readable and attractive to the lay reader. Firstly, Said tried the best he could to bridge the so-called professional gap between life and career. His goal was to render the one intelligible in terms of the other and vice versa. What were his considered opinions on identity politics, representation, authenticity, the two-state solution to Israel–Palestine, Bach's or Wagner's music, anthropology, colonization, self and other, truth and power, democracy, intellectualism, professionalism, the West and the Rest, civilizational clash, cosmopolitanism, and nationalism? His responses were simultaneously those of Edward the Palestinian-American citizen with a cause and those of the dazzlingly brilliant critic and distinguished Columbia University professor Edward Said. What his ongoing work tried to dramatize was the truth that these issues and the passions that they engender are to be lived through critically and self-reflexively; and that criticism and self-reflexivity are to be practiced and performed both qualitatively and democratically, that is, both in the name of a restless individual critical consciousness that dances to the tune of scholarship and erudition, and in the name of the inclusive All. In other words, for Said, to understand the world and to understand the more selective world of music and literature and literary scholarship were flip sides of the same coin.

Secondly, in the pursuit of his objective, Said was unafraid to declare that the object of his critical analysis was not just Culture (this would be the choice of apolitical theorists) or just Imperialism (this would be the preference of reductive agitprop polemicists), but Culture *and* Imperialism. He was not daunted by contradiction, complicity, the abject asymmetries of guilt and blame, the realities of what he so eloquently termed "discrepant but overlapping experiences," histories that had not lived up to their theoretical promise, and theories that in their utopian haste had chosen to become post-historical. Instead, he lived in the tensions, in the glaring gaps and contradictions of our times, and actively *chose*, intentionally and agentively, to make sense of these symptoms. It was by exercising a mercurially oppositional critical consciousness, between Culture and System, that he tried both to understand and to go beyond the given, the status quo.

Thirdly, he did not seek, philosophically or systemically, to produce a grand theory of reading or of the text that would result in some massively monolithic universal understanding of the world and its significance. Much more humble than the grandstanding theorists or the pure ethicists who were his contemporaries, he was more than satisfied to be syncretic, eclectic, non-systemic, partial and non-totalizing, and pragmatically contingent in his thinking. What was important to him was to make conscious choices rather than be spoken for, in a formulaic manner, by culture or by professional system. It was equally crucial for him to announce his agenda; he was no immaculate theoretical rebel without a cause or a rebel looking for the birth of the perfect cause or the Cause of all causes. He was also quite happy to declare "where he came from" and where he was headed. He might stumble in the process, perhaps make strange and inconsistent choices, or, as I found myself saying wistfully a number of times during the course of this book, not be a philosophic enough thinker as he addresses the crises and problems of humanism and essentialism; but what he did consistently, and with rigorous integrity, was to compile, in the Gramscian sense of the term, an inventory of the historical traces that lead him to the present. It is quite easy to hoist Edward Said with his own petard for the very simple reason that his criteria are transparent, and easy to read by all. What makes Said interesting are the choices that he made: choices that win him a number of fellow passengers as well as opponents who are on different trips altogether.

Said was a pragmatic literary and cultural critic who used and borrowed from existing vocabularies to create his own non-standard usages. His phrases and locutions are for the most part directly available to anyone with a degree, say in English literature. Even when he avails extensively of terms for literary and cultural criticism, his discourse is never dense with its own ponderous materiality. His language is much more explanatory and explicatory than self-referentially theoretical. As he maintains time and again, particularly in the context of Vico, the world and reality are already complex and theory-laden; and the task of the critic is to do justice to the heterogeneous and multi-layered richness of what he called "worldliness," rather than pretend that theory manufactures its own autonomous meaning. He is interested in explaining to the reader why he finds a text rich and significant, what he finds in the text, how he finds it, how the text is put together and towards what objective. His prose takes on a clear responsibility of representation, demonstration, and critical paraphrase. In light of this, we may wonder: why would such a critic who explains so lucidly need further explanation? Clearly, Edward Said is not a Samuel Taylor Coleridge "explaining metaphysics to the nation," of whom Byron famously quipped, "I wish I could explain his explanation." Nor is he "difficult" in the manner of a Jacques Derrida: an out and out theoretical thinker deeply invested in the priority of philosophical reading. The answer to the question is: to explain to the reader Said's critical position on issues, the reason he takes these positions, and the ways in which he justifies the taking of these positions; and in particular, how he uses his expertise as a reader of texts to clarify issues and problems in the real world. Said was always committed to knowledge both as a way of knowing and a way of being, a way of being and a way of doing. In other words, this book aims to account for Said's way of being worldly: for example, not so much defining concepts or ideas that he might have formulated (he was not an original thinker in that way), but rather to explain how and why he related to certain ideas and formulations and not to others, and how in the making of these choices within his professional world he had also invited the world out there into the narrow rooms of scholarly erudition. It was his way of occupying a certain terrain that needed explanation. His most impressive achievement was his ability to bridge the gap between worldly reality and the excitement of books, of scholarship, of cultural enrichment. The meanings, valences, and inflections that he chose on behalf of scholarship, that is, on behalf of the text and the critic, were the same, representatively speaking, as the ones that he valorized on behalf of the world. If there are special words in a Said dictionary, they are special by democratic usage, and not because they are esoteric *mantras* that warrant exclusive initiation.

In writing this book, it was important to find the balance between making Said available in a reader-friendly way to the general reader, and at the same time making the reader aware of the delicate and nuanced complexity of Said's democratically oriented erudition. Said lived democratically, but all the while pushing it towards greater inclusiveness and higher levels of qualitative appreciation without turning such a project into one of paternalistic aristocratization. There were two important challenges here: first, to deal with each of the entries on a double register with the objective of telling the reader that these terms have a take and a bite both in the world of scholarship and the world out there. Terms like "identity," "theory," "representation," "secular criticism," and "nationalism," resonate both for the common lay reader and the humanities scholar. In fact, the lay reader and the scholar are often one and the same person. Said's contention was that these terms are in fact lived realities which are then subjected to professional and scholarly analysis, but only to be brought back to the terrain of lived life on a heightened level of critical awareness. In other words, there always is a representative connection of meaning and meaning-making between life and literature, life and scholarship. After encountering the travails and vicissitudes of "representation" in a novel, the reader returns to her life with a meaningful exclamation of "Wow, so that is what representation is all about," and on the basis of that insight understands more critically what it is to be an American, a Palestinian, a literary scholar.

The second challenge was how to find some credible equilibrium between presenting Said's thought objectively and providing the reader with an appreciative critique of what Said was all about. The method that has been used for each entry is to begin with the concept, locate it in Said's context, and offer an explanation or definition from Said's perspective without quoting too much directly from Said. Then a few questions are raised around the entry by way of suggesting to the reader the significance of the concept or the term. I thus introduce to the reader a brief history of the term in the field, including the debates and polemical confrontations occasioned by the concept. I then focus in particular on Said's own specific participation in these argumentative conversations, and differentiate his take from those of others in the conversation. I have also been keen on accounting for the reasons why Said sometimes abandoned a certain path to go in a different direction. Said made a number of choices as a critic, and I have attempted to show what these choices were and how Said went about shaping and styling his own trajectory as a critic as a cumulative function of these choices. My hope is that in doing so I have been able to elucidate Said's freewheeling relationships and affinities with a number of theories, theorists, and schools of thought. Wherever possible, without being too intrusive, I have also outlined criticisms of Said or briefly indicated the limitations of his mode of enquiry.

In addition to having been a general and long-distance student of Said for a long time, I had also had the privilege of having been his actual student during the summer of 1982 at the School of Criticism and Theory at Northwestern University. (This was the summer of catastrophe in the Middle East and I distinctly recall how Said would travel under great pressure to London, Cairo, and Lebanon, during that period and dash back and forth and still be available to us, his eager and demanding students.) He was kind and attentive to my presence and my contributions, even though I was a mere senior doctoral student on the verge of completing my dissertation under the direction of that magnificent teacher William V. Spanos. Despite the uneven and asymmetrical nature of this relationship, he empowered me, made me feel like a potential equal, and most important of all, he pushed and pressured my thinking with tough suggestions and critical comments.

I would like to thank my editors Emma Bennett and Ben Thatcher for their patience and support all along. A special "thank you" goes out to Kathleen McCully, my copy-editor, for her critical rigor, care, and her unerring eye/ear for any kind of infelicitous phrasing. I am also grateful to Shalini Sharma for her patient technical help during the final stages of proof reading. I also wish to acknowledge, in profound friendship and solidarity, a whole family of critics and theorists who have all endeavored to keep the Said legacy alive critically and meaningfully in their own projects: William V. Spanos, Paul Bove, Donald Pease, Aamir Mufti, Neal Lazarus, Jonathan Arac, Bruce Robbins, Gauri Viswanathan, Timothy Brennan, Anne McClintock, Rob Nixon, Asha Varadharajan, Ibish Hussein, Satish Kolluri, Ling-Yan Yang, Marian Aguiar, Giovanna Covi, Mina Karavanta, and Robert Marzec, Steven Mailloux, and many more. I thank Edward Said for his brilliant and humane critical intelligence and for having opened up a path for us to follow, each in his or her own way, as we keep the conversation going with the world, contrapuntally, in the hope that the world to come will be meaningfully and critically "out of place," forever dedicated to the project of admitting the all in the name of the All.

And as always, I thank my wife Asha for her unconditional support and inspired and inspiring partnership, and my son Surya for his deeply caring and rigorous friendship. My warm and affectionate greetings also drift out to my parents in distant Chennai.

affiliation   This is a classic example of a simple and non-technical word that Said inflects imaginatively to produce a critical semantic range. First of all, rather than define the word or fix its denotation in isolation, Said makes it a point to differentiate "affiliation" from "filiation." Whereas filiation, as in "filial duty or piety," represents a genetic, dynastic, familial, natal, na-tivist, or natural-biological order, affiliation is a mode of belonging based on secular and historical choices that an individual makes: choices that may or may not re-validate or re-recognize the pattern of filiation. Thus, in a *Bildungsroman*, the protagonist may be born Irish or Sephardic-Jewish, but may reject, problematize, deconstruct, or redirect or re-channelize her "given" identity in response to other pressures, calls, passions, and impera-tives that emanate from elsewhere and from other histories that are not part of her "given" birth-identity. Questions like "What is my history?," "Which 'we' am I part of?," and "Which community is more binding: family, class, gender, nationality?" could be answered from a filiative or an affiliative point of view. A vibrant example of a character in fiction who downplays filiation and valorizes affiliation is the nameless narrator in Amitav Ghosh's eloquent novel, *The Shadow Lines*, who asserts on the very first page of the text that he "did not *want* to think of her as a relative: to have done that would have diminished her and her family – I could not bring myself to believe that their worth in my eyes could be reduced to something so arbitrary and unimpor-tant as a blood relationship." Affiliation plays a major role in Said's theatre of thought for the simple reason that it mediates effectively in the interplay

A Said Dictionary, First Edition. R. Radhakrishnan.
© 2012 John Wiley & Sons, Ltd. Published 2012 by John Wiley & Sons, Ltd.

between identity politics and the politics of **representation**, between **exile** and belonging, between so-called authenticity and the inauthentic, between racialized, essentialist, and stereotypical modes of communal belonging and secular and open-ended ways of constituting community, between "blood and guts" rhetoric and secularist discourse, and finally between solidarity and critique. It is significant that Said reads filiation diagnostically as a "failed idea" and understands affiliation as "a kind of compensatory order that, whether it is a party, an institution, a culture, a set of beliefs, or even a world-vision," that is capable of providing "men and women with a new form of relationship" ("Secular Criticism," in *The World, the Text, and the Critic*, 19). Affiliative moves can be kept trace of and accounted for immanently, that is, from within themselves, unlike filiative reiterations that resist diagnostic or symptomatic accounts in the name of natural self-evidence. Also, affiliations are like chapters in an ongoing **narrative** of "becoming" whereas filiations promote a notion of "completed being" from the very beginning and thus come in the way of subsequent relationships and solidarities. Born a Hindu always a Hindu, born American always American, and so on, are examples of dogged and non-porous filiation.

An affiliative genealogy has no place for an *a priori* essence such as "Jewishness" or "Arabness" which could then be seen to instantiate itself in every Arab and every Jew. Take, for example, phrases like "a filial daughter," "filial piety," and "filial propriety or correctness": in these phrases, the implication is that mere filial belonging to a family, group, nation, or tribe automatically and unquestionably provides a normative template for the historical process and growth that is still to come. Thus in the diasporic context of Maxine Hong Kingston's *The Woman Warrior*, the protagonist, given her physical as well as symbolic distance from China, her country of origin, will agonize over whether she is a filial daughter or not, and ponder if the truth of the Chinese legend of Fa Mu Lan will work only for true filial Chinese women and not for the diasporic Chinese daughters such as herself. In organic terms, filiation begins to resemble a kind of umbilical fidelity to the origin. In the context of affiliation, relatedness and relationality are not exemplified or defined with reference to a pre-existing relationship within a natural bond or natural forms of authority. Instead, relationships and connections are understood and acknowledged in response to histories that overlap and intersect. Said makes the point that the "filiative scheme belongs to the realms of nature and of 'life,' whereas affiliation belongs exclusively to culture and society" ("Secular Criticism," 20). Through affiliation, mankind chooses and makes its own history or histories rather than merely repeating and reinforcing forms of parochialism based on birth, blood, and origin.

Affiliation plays a crucial role in Said's definition of secular **humanism**. To Said, being human is in fact a becoming human; that is, being human is not just a natural fact. To be human is not to be filial, for the simple reason that humans are not animals or flowers that naturally belong to nature and to life. It is in the realm of culture and society, the realm of the Freudian "second nature," that the human becomes actively human. In the domain of affiliation, belongings and solidarities are neither natural nor self-evident: they are the result of an active historical performance. Said is keen to celebrate the human as affiliative and not as naturally filiative for the simple reason that the filiative scheme tends to reduce the broadly historically human into umbilical containments such as Hindu, Arab, Muslim, Christian, and so on. In valorizing natal schemata as "natural," the filiative mindset undervalues the human as such that does not belong, as an essential property, to any one group. The human dimension, to Said, is a relational possibility that is forever in the making in the interactions and movements among different histories, none of which is completely coextensive or synonymous with the human condition. There may well be a human nature in the ultimate analysis; but such a nature is never a given, but rather, a precious multilateral finding and a discovery undertaken non-denominationally by all human beings. What is at stake for Said in the affiliative enterprise is the possibility of a human home that will be more than just a Jewish or a Palestinian or an Arab or a Christian or a male or a female or a Eurocentric or an Afrocentric home. That is exactly what Said has in mind when he thinks of filiation as a failed idea and affiliation as compensatory. The entire history of mankind, in so far as it has been an attempt by a dominant group to naturalize and nativize the entire world within its own filiative schemata, has been a sorry history of violence, exploitation, alienation, and colonization. As such, it is a failed idea.

Affiliation provides possibilities for new forms of human relationship that demonstrate the poverty of rigid historicisms that trap people into vertical destinies that are prey to the specious thesis that histories are mono-radical and incapable of movement. Whereas filiative accounts of history covet history as one's own and in the process either deny or play down the contribution of "others" in the elaboration of one's own history, affiliative accounts of history tend to be dispersed, disseminative, and horizontal whereby the seeds cast in one place could grow into a vital tree in another place. It is how we understand history that matters most to Said. An affiliative mindset does not debunk or recant filiation; but rather it argues that filiation is not sufficient by itself. The filial needs to perceive itself both as a starting point and the lack thereof. To put it simply, no starting point, however sacred it may feel to the person who has started there, is correct or complete in and by itself. It is only when filial arrangements understand themselves as a form of "lack," that they will be willing to displace themselves and learn from other histories and other starting points and origins. After all, no history is an island by itself. What do they know of England who only England know? Or to put it differently, filial histories such as, say, Chinese history or Indian history, can only belong to those people who come under that particular filial jurisdiction. But what about an affiliative history, such as secular history? Said would respond that such a history belongs and pertains to all and every one, despite their particular provenance.

Had Edward Said been more of a philosophic thinker, he would perhaps have glossed more on the semantics of "the compensatory order" of affiliation. Here are a few questions that Said leaves unanswered. Is the compensation real or metaphorical? Is there an originary lack, in the Lacanian sense of the term, that can never be compensated for? Or is the compensatory order, that is, the symbolic process by which human beings create their own history, the only order that pertains to the human? Is the filial lost forever, or is it recovered, in a transformed mode, in the compensatory order? Once we are in the realm of compensation, do we ever look back furtively, nostalgically, or in bad faith, towards the failed idea? Said's pragmatic understanding of the term "secularism" gives us an idea of how affiliation works. Are we born secular, say, the way we are born female, Syrian, Coptic Christian, or Californian? Or, does "secular" belong to the affiliative compensatory order? If yes, then, what happens to one's born identity? Has it been left behind once and for all, transcended, compensated? Can one be a secular Jew, a secular Muslim, a secular Christian, or a secular Hindu? Said is not interested in putting down filiation absolutely and substituting it forever with affiliation. His objective is to enable movement and flow between the two orders. He is rigorous enough to worry that even affiliation could create a naturalized orthodoxy of its own. His affiliative intention is to loosen up the filiative bind so that the human can become human in the name of the all, rather than be stifled, provincialized, and denominationalized in the name of exclusive and exclusionary identity regimes.

Auerbach, Eric   Along with **Joseph Conrad** and **Giambattista Vico**, Eric Auerbach plays a formative role in Said's development and self-recognition as a scholar and critical **intellectual** (Auerbach, "Philology and *Weltliteratur*"). It could perhaps be said that these three figures are Said's implicit, and sometimes explicit, role models. When in doubt, or when in need of a telling example, Said turns to them again and again, and for the most part persuasively. All three of them provide Said with a sense of credible location and a range of empathetic and elective affinities. Among the three, it is Auerbach who resonates, for Said, both epistemologically and existentially, that is, both at the level of knowing and at the level of living. Said identifies with Auerbach the individual as well as the intellectual: in fact, in Auerbach's predicament Said sees the becoming intellectual of the individual, the individual exiled from his homeland. Indeed, **exile** is the theme that links Auerbach and Said in intellectual brotherhood and solidarity.

So, what makes Auerbach's *Mimesis* an unforgettable classic? Surely its content and insightful erudition. But what makes it unique and priceless is its perspective, its orientation to its own subject matter, and in particular, "the circumstances of the book's actual writing." He was writing his book in Istanbul as a Jewish refugee from Western Europe. He was not home; he was not at home while writing this book. Moreover, he was producing this classic of scholarship not from a plenitude of academic resources, but from a situation of impoverishment where he had no access to libraries or specialist material. Here is the profoundly ironic situation. He was writing about his own culture from a position of double estrangement. He was, geopolitically speaking, sundered (umbilically or filiatively, one might say) from his home; and moreover, he was also alienated from all those rich scholarly resources that would have restored him his existential loss in the domain of scholarship. It is the fact that the classic emerges from a genealogy of double dispossession or dislocation that leaves a deep impression on Said's critical consciousness ("Reflections on Exile").

We turn now to the implications of Auerbach's exile for his scholarship. For one thing, his work cannot be self-assured. Unlike a work saturated with scholarship and therefore impregnable, Auerbach's *Mimesis* is incomplete, imperfect, and contingent. We might wonder why this is a plus and not a minus. It is precisely because it is not fully backed by the privilege of **professional** erudition, that it is inventive, risky, and imaginative. Unlike the perfect scholarly tome that is a mechanical instantiation of what it already knows, Auerbach's work is a risk taken against heavy odds. (Here we might be reminded of Neville Cardus' movingly insightful characterization of the batting technique of Sir Donald Bradman, the opposite of Auerbach: a technique that is so hopelessly perfect and consummate that it tends to become boring and predictable. Cardus says something to the effect that Bradman is imprisoned by his immaculate technique. Bradman's predicament, in Cardus' view, is that of an acrobat who actually wants to fall and perhaps immolate himself, but just cannot do so since her technique rules out any possibility of contingency, of failure, of falling.) What is indeed heroic is that not having the necessary resources did not paralyze or prevent Auerbach from undertaking his daunting task. It is as though Auerbach, who could have been the consummate and immaculate spokesperson of his culture, is forced into a kind of amateurish ad-libbing, full of inventive courage and entrepreneurial audacity. Auerbach, who could have turned out to be a proper professional scholar, thanks to the adversities of history, becomes a make-shift maverick composer: a *bricoleur* in the structuralist sense of the term, as well as, to borrow from Ralph Ellison's perennially magnificent work, *Invisible Man*, a "thinker-tinker," that is, a hands-on fixer who is also capable of abstract philosophical thought. What makes Auerbach's work even more urgent in a way that enables "the existential to tangle with the epistemological" (Guha, *History at the Limit of World-History*, 87–8) is the fact that it is written during crisis, during loss. Unlike a self-assured work that is confident of its genealogy and its anchorage in its own proper domain, here is a work, much like the fiction of Franz Kafka, written from the very heart of crisis, the abnormal. Auerbach, to use the terminology formulated by Gilles Deleuze and Felix Guattari, is doubly "de-territorialized" both from his native location and his subject-positional privilege as a scholar backed unconditionally by academic resources. Auerbach does not "belong." In other words, he is neither at home in his native-natal Europe, nor is he in his affiliative home, the library, as he writes his master work.

In what seems *prima facie* a situation of loss, deprivation, and victimization, a critical sense of perspective is enabled. Now, because of his profound dislocation, Auerbach does not just understand his own Western European culture: he is enabled and empowered to understand it perspectivally – a perspective made possible by exile, by physical as well as symbolic displacement. Auerbach's critical evaluation of his own culture does not take the form of an acquiescent, non-diagnostic, celebratory reading from the heartland of identity. Instead, it becomes critical mimesis. In a way, even though Said himself does not put it this way, Auerbach's reading of his own culture takes the form of a phenomenological "return to things themselves." It assumes the geographical and cognitive contours of a phenomenological world as well as a phenomenological way of knowing, before (and here I am paraphrasing the great phenomenological philosopher Maurice Merleau-Ponty) such a knowing was formalized into a philosophical system. In such a phenomenological discovery, Auerbach both loses and re-finds his culture. He loses what would have been comfortingly and comfortably identical as his culture, and literally re-cognizes it in difference: it is the same and at the same time not the same. What remains is precious knowledge, not sovereign knowledge, which is to say, a kind of knowledge always already baptized as a form of official rectitude. As Auerbach himself acknowledges in his brief epilogue to his book, he might have missed or overlooked a number of details and nuances that should have been the concern of his scholarly gaze, or for that matter, he could have made interpretive or analytic truth claims that might not have been *au courant*, or stood the test of contemporary scholarly standards. And yet, Auerbach observes, it is precisely because of these flaws and shortcomings that he has been able to compose an "other," a different kind of book. Paradoxically, the very conditions of deprivation that could well have killed even the possibility of book production have turned into enabling conditions of an unorthodox composition. What animates and informs Auerbach's *Mimesis* is not method or system, or the imper-sonality of a serene, indifferent, or aseptic scholarship, but rather the voice of a lost individual critical consciousness forced to rely on a creativity, an inventiveness that has little to do with the marmoreal and hermetic closure of official scholarship.

It is easy to see what exactly Said valorizes passionately in Auerbach's "situation," to use the word in the Sartrean sense of the term. For starters, Auerbach's scholarship in the very act of elaborating itself also genealogizes itself; that is, unlike official scholarship, it is only too happy to avow where it is coming from. It does not pretend to have any fundamentalist, essentialist, nativist, or primordial relationship of correctness with its object. To put it somewhat simply, had Auerbach written his work sitting in a library in his European home, there would have been no need for him to divulge where he was writing from. The circumstances of his scholarly production would have been too normal, axiomatic, and transparent to warrant special avowal or disavowal. It would have been a dominant, "un-marked" performance: a *tour de force* of authentic representational **virtuosity**. Quite to the con-trary, and much in the spirit of a Nietzschean–Foucauldian–(and up to a point) Chomskian genealogist who looks for history in lowly, humble, and unconsecrated sites and venues, Auerbach's interpretive account of his own culture opens up another frame of reality, and in the process challenges

Europe's Eurocentric version of itself. In Auerbach's version, Europe becomes an exilic perspective; a perspective that cannot reach home in a gesture of supreme self-adequation. Just think of an American in foreign soil, forced to think of himself from a different point of view. He is not the same American any more.

Said's reading against the grain of Auerbach's authorial intervention paves the way for his coordination of the space "between Culture and System." Auerbach's scholarship is exemplary neither of his culture nor of a professional system. Thank God, we can hear Said saying, that Auerbach was an exile in Istanbul as he was writing his masterpiece. Had he been comfortably home in his home town library, he would have produced a suffocating treatise that would have remained true to its culture and obedient to a particular system of scholarship: a stillborn work, in whose lack of pulsation, emergence and rigor mortis could have been seen as flip sides of each other.

beginnings "Well begun is half done." "I can't even begin to tell you."
"It all began that rainy morning." "Where shall I begin to tell my story?"
"In the beginning is the end." "It was an auspicious beginning." Despite all
these commonplace and transparent usages of the word "beginning," do
we really understand what "beginnings" are conceptually, philosophically?
What begins? Who begins what? What begins whom? Are beginnings transitive or intransitive? How do we know that something or some moment or
gesture is indeed a beginning? If indeed beginning is something that has to
happen anyway, how can anyone, anybody take charge of a beginning, as if
it was of their making? Isn't every beginning acknowledged as a beginning
only retrospectively, after the fact? Who is the proper and viable subject of a
beginning: an individual, a group, a class, a people, a mood, a thought? Here
is a word that is almost a cliché in our human lives, and yet theoretically or
philosophically speaking, the meaning of a beginning, or what it means to
begin, is hardly clear. "Beginning/s" is a simple word that is in fact a fraught
and profound concept that is not always reducible to simple practice.

Edward Said's first major book (right after his doctoral thesis on Conrad)
that announces the author's arrival as a brilliant, original, major voice in
critical theory is indeed a long meditation on the concept of *Beginnings*.
The book has a subtitle, *Intention and Method*. The subtitle makes it very
clear that Said's objectives are both phenomenological, that is, intentional
with and from a point of view and in the world, and structural/formal.
To begin is to declare an intention and at the same time make certain

A Said Dictionary, First Edition. R. Radhakrishnan.
© 2012 John Wiley & Sons, Ltd. Published 2012 by John Wiley & Sons, Ltd.

methodological choices that will help in the materialization of the intention. The epigraph to the book is a quotation from **Giambattista Vico**, a major and abiding presence in Said's critical consciousness: "Doctrines must take their beginning from that of the matters of which they treat" (*The New Science*). No knowledge is immaculate: every doctrine has to avow, as we say colloquially, "where it came from." Not merely that: even doctrines that sound so mighty and axiomatic as though they were transcendent truths independent of context emerge from specific historical beginnings, and these beginnings have a profound connection to the world of which they speak. To put it in overtly Saidian terms, with beginning, begins **representation**. The avowal of a beginning places the project of knowledge making entirely in the field of history. Said's theme is "beginnings" in the plural, and not a singular "Beginning." In Said's world, there is no room for sacral beginnings that take on the magisterial status of an *a priori*. As Said shrewdly observes, beginnings are acknowledged as "beginnings" only retrospectively: in other words, beginnings are contingent and historical undertakings that do not contain within themselves any spiritual essence or trans-historical teleological guarantees.

Much like Nietzsche and Foucault, Said warns the reader that beginnings are not origins, and most certainly not Origin, with a capital O. In other words, to begin is not to initiate a chosen and secure destiny or invoke providential resolutions pre-contained in the beginning as a promise. Beginnings are meant to be made and unmade, in the course of history and in the course of **narrative** development. One of the most important questions that Said raises in his philosophical meditation on beginnings is the question of authority. A number of questions arise here. Is a beginning a break from a prior temporality? Whether it is Wordsworth in *The Prelude* constructing by way of poetic anamnesis a beginning and then building on it didactically towards a thesis, or a Sterne in *Tristram Shandy* spoofing, relativizing, the very notion of a stable beginning towards an infinite regress, *ab ovo*, *ab initio*, the question remains, what is a beginning a beginning of?

Beginnings have as much to do with authorial intentions as with systemic or discursive possibilities, and indeed, with the relationship between the two. It is important to note that Said poses beginnings as an issue to be confronted and resolved both practically and theoretically. Throughout his long and tangled career, Said made it a point never to let **theory** realize its autonomy in separation or in secession from practice. For Said, beginnings are inextricably linked with choice. The beginning as a choice is both "given" and "taken" by the writer who in making the choice assumes a certain historical responsibility. This responsibility is mediated linguistically, but is not exclusively linguistic. Said does not ascribe an ontology or a "being" to language. Language is what human intentionality does, just as intentionality requires the medium of language to embody itself historically. Said is a pragmatist when it comes to language.

It is also worth observing that even during those heady days when it was fashionable to talk about epistemological breaks *à la* Derrida (especially in *Of Grammatology*), Gaston Bachelard, Michel Foucault, and Thomas Kuhn, Said is careful enough not to privilege discontinuity as its own autonomous cause. Beginnings could be symptomatic of continuity, or antagonism, or some admixture of both. What is important, however, is that beginnings initiate and partake in inter-textual relationships with other **texts**, with which the new text creates some common formal and systemic ground. Whatever their other differences, in this limited negotiation with beginnings and traditions, Said and T.S. Eliot, otherwise unlikely partners, do share a common perspective. No new work is so new as to be utterly maverick, or so new that it is new *ex nihilo*. To Eliot, it is a matter of reconciling "individual talent" with "tradition," and to Said, it is matter of aligning the historicity of every beginning with an already existing world and its many constituent histories. Said's intense advocacy and defense of **humanism** against assault by high theory is posited precisely on such a reading of history: a history that is forever being begun from some perspective or the other, and in conversation with other overlapping beginnings from elsewhere, and their imaginings on behalf of their own stories and narratives. In the final analysis, beginnings carry great significance for Said because beginnings dramatize and enact the rich double-ness of history: it is both a given and the possibility for a new start, both an already constituted horizon and the excitement of something new and different that is going to take place within the horizon, both the possibility of meaning as a historical *a priori*, as well as the constant unsettling of the formal *a priori* by the unpredictable pulsations of life and experience.

between/between-ness   Not being a philosophic thinker, Said does not offer his readers anywhere in his vast works anything like a definition of "between," or "between-ness," but there is no denying the fact that the term works for Said pragmatically as his preferred preposition of placement. It is indeed typical of Said's strategy to show something at work in a range of contexts rather than offer a theoretical definition or *expose* of the phenomenon of "between-ness." The first time the word/preposition enters

Said's corpus in an obvious and self-proclaiming manner is in the title of one of his most influential essays, "Criticism Between Culture and System" (in *The World, the Text, and the Critic*). It is to Said's everlasting credit that he endows the spatiality of the "between" with a positive and productive connotation. It has always been customary to think of being between as an untenable and unpleasant situation: either sandwiched with no breathing room, or suspended in painful ambivalence, or stranded in a state of perpetual waffling and indecision, stuck in perpetual liminality, a state of precarious becoming with no guarantee of effective arrival. The difference, of course, is that Said creates his "between." In other words, he does not merely and passively occupy a given position that is between A and B. Quite to the contrary, he creates, or perhaps discovers, the space of the between in a situation where such a position does not exist in mainstream topography.

It must be noted that it is in the context of locating or mapping criticism that Said uses the preposition "between." He is not talking about the diasporic condition, ethnic hyphenation, Du Boisian double consciousness (as explained in Du Bois' monumental work, *The Souls of Black Folk* where he expresses and theorizes the agonizing condition of the African-American torn between Africa and America in a horrible double bind): in other words, the between is not a special historical condition that is germane to certain populations that are the product of racialization, minoritization, immigration, and so on. He is talking about an **intellectual** condition, about the position of criticism within a field called literary studies. It is characteristic of Said to braid together two independent thought strands to create a new polemic. Here the questions raised by Said's work are: Who cares about the between? If criticism is the particular practice that is to be performed between Culture and System, should the lay human being even care or take notice? Who is a critic and what is her relationship to this precious activity known as criticism? Is this activity professional, amateurish, organic, specialist, elitist, democratic? The space of the between is not just any indeterminate or allegorical between. By dangling Culture and System on either side of the between, Said is able to interrogate both the absolutism of identity (by way of culture) and the authoritarianism of **professionalism** (by way of system). Criticism becomes the pivot that democratizes professionalism even as it claims intellectuality in the name of the "all." Said also demonstrates that criticism has a double disjunctive, rather than conjunctive, relationship with Culture and System. His thesis is as simple as it is profound. Our capacity to be critical is constrained, held in check, preempted, bounded by the culture into which we are born.

Culture becomes a rigid and un-crossable boundary: our culture right or wrong. Criticism, however radical, transgressive, and **oppositional**, has to stay within the cultural fold. In the final analysis it has to remain an exemplary spokesperson of, if not an apologist for, its native culture. America, Islam, Hinduism function as boxes that decide what is inside and what is outside, what is permissible and what is not. Americans are taught not to think un-American thoughts not because such thoughts are erroneous, but just because they are un-American. Culture, as in religious or ethnic or national culture, performs as the *imprimatur*, the official seal, that sanctions criticism: there is no place for the "between" here. One has to be an insider or an outsider: again, there is no room for being "between."

The other orthodoxy, Charybdis if you will, is the thing called System, to which all professionals are expected to genuflect. If constriction and censorship by Culture can be called macro-political, boundedness by System is a micro-political form of privation. Who, then, is a system-bound critic? Take, for example, poststructuralism, deconstruction, New Historicism, Structuralism, Structuralist-Marxism, Cultural Studies, French feminism, Lacanian psychoanalysis, Freudian criticism. Each of these functions as a system, each with its own protocols, rituals, and credentials, each with its own set of master concepts and argot or technical vocabulary. The systematic critic has to belong, body and soul, to her sovereign system and, in order to be true to her professional faith, has to stay within the "dos" and "don'ts" of her system. A deconstructive critic is obliged to find a moment of indeterminacy in any **text** and use that moment to destabilize the architectonic as well as the ideological integrity of that text, or for that matter, any text. Compulsively, helplessly, choicelessly, the deconstructive critic is obligated to demonstrate, by any means necessary, that no text is or can be sure of its meaning. Take away terms like aporia, indeterminacy; and the deconstructive critic is a fish out of water. The Marxist critic would be looking for class, contradiction, overdetermination, false consciousness, ideology, while the psychoanalytic would be seeking the Unconscious, certain forms of latency, the irruption of a chronic lack in the midst of a seeming plenitude. The feminist would be searching for determinations of gender, the ubiquity of patriarchal structures, while the gay and lesbian critic is aiming to do a symptomatic reading of sexual heteronormativity everywhere. All these professional critics are ensconced in orthodoxy within their respective systems: by definition they cannot be "between."

In finding the "between" between Culture and System, Said is opening up a vital space of creative and critical knowledge that cannot be blithely predetermined by who we are or what we do professionally. The spatiality of the "between" allows for a non-dogmatic, non-binding, non-prescriptive, non-exemplary relationship to both Culture and System. In other words, Said will not disavow that he is a Palestinian Arab American citizen, and that indeed he is deeply and indelibly marked by the culture or the cultures of filiation as well as **affiliation**. At the same time he does not have a problem with acknowledging the various theories, theorists, epistemologies, philosophies, and schools of thought from which he has learned. He is only too happy to make an inventory, *à la* Gramsci, of all the traces that have made him who he is. What matters is not "who" but how we produce critical knowledge about ourselves. Let us take a simple example. If someone asked me where I lived, chances are that I would give that person a specific, determinate location with a street name and an unambiguous house or door number. Instead, I could also have said that I live between Elm Street and Main Street, which in fact is where my home is located. Such an answer may be poor and suboptimal in terms of providing directional clarity to my interlocutor (who would then have to look at all the spaces between Elm Street and Main Street), but it is in fact not an erroneous answer. Instead of nailing my address down as if my address were something in and by itself, what I have done is to provide a more fuzzy but relational topography. The insight here is that there is not a mutually exclusive relationship between being somewhere in a normative sense of the term, and understanding that very normative somewhere as a relational space between two other locations or *topoi*. Thus, to be in the United States could be parsed as being between Canada and Mexico. When the "between" is acknowledged and valued as a term that constitutes the identifiability of all locations, then what follows is a different practice as well as understanding of who we are and what we do. Gone is the *hubris* of natural knowledge whereby a German claims a privileged relationship to "truth as German": gone also is the *hubris* of professional certitude whereby the critic names truth exclusively as capitalist, Marxist, and psychoanalytic. What is enabled in the space between Culture and System is an "other" kind of worldly knowing that is simultaneously amateurish and critical.

Beyond all this, the fundamental insight that Said leaves us with is that we all, (whether we call ourselves Americans, men, feminists, poststructuralists, Africans), live, theorize, and make sense of our lives, literatures, and cultures *between* different languages, peoples, histories, cultures, and locations. There is no escaping the "between," and no reason why we should even attempt such a silly and fatuous escape.

centrism   The English language is full of "centric" words: Eurocentric, Afro-centric, logocentric, anthropocentric, Indo-centric, Sino-centric, gyno- and andro-centric. Take expressions like: "thinking you are the center of the universe," "taking center stage," "being the center of attention," not to mention, of course, the famous Yeatsian lines about the center not being able to hold, and mere anarchy being loosed upon the world. Or, think of typical parental advice that exhorts the son or the daughter to find a meaningful center for her developing life.

Let us take the term "Eurocentric." Let us imagine a situation where I introduce George, my European friend to you, the third party, as my Eurocentric friend. What exactly am I doing here? Did I just describe my friend neutrally, or was it an evaluative description? If evaluative, was it pejorative? Why not just say European, instead of Eurocentric? Would calling a European friend European be an inane tautology? Just because George is European by origin, is he condemned to be Eurocentric? Is it not possible for a non-European to be Eurocentric by choice and not just by virtue of birth and natal filiation? Is centrism the automatic and inevitable result or function of a certain origin, or is it a deliberately cultivated attitude that transforms the point of origin into a mighty organizing center? Unlike, say, Jacques Derrida, who devoted a major chunk of his oeuvre to the philosophical critique of various forms of centrism, such as logocentrism, phallocentrism, phallogocentrism, photocentrism, phonocentrism, Eurocentrism, and eventually of "centrism as such," Edward Said deals with the issue of the center and centrism tangentially and episodically. Unlike

A Said Dictionary, First Edition. R. Radhakrishnan.
© 2012 John Wiley & Sons, Ltd. Published 2012 by John Wiley & Sons, Ltd.

Derrida, to whom "centrism" is an important philosophic and discursive formation, to Said, the term "centrism" as such does not carry that much weight. And yet, Said deals with the practical and worldly effects of centrist and centric thinking in much of his critical output. Centrism, to Said, is no more and no less than what centrism does; and centrism does different kinds of things: some good, some bad, some inevitable, and some avoidable. Much in the spirit of Dr. House (the eponymous character in the TV show *House*) who excels in making "differential diagnoses," Said evaluates each centrist **text** or production circumstantially with reference to varying historical factors and conditions. He is not interested in producing a totalized, that is, an overall blanket criticism of centrism as an undifferentiated and homogeneous phenomenon.

Rather than deal with "centrism" as a philosophical predisposition, Said breaks centrism down into a variety of critical human practices and tendencies. For example, how does a reader deal with and understand literary works that are "centered" not in her own culture, but elsewhere? Is it possible to understand the meaning of an alien or "outside" culture from one's own point of view? If literature, by definition, is universal in scope, how should the reader and the critic negotiate this universality on the basis of their own national, ethnic, regional "centers?" The problem for Said is as simple as it is practical. When is centrism worthy of condemnation as in "ethnocentrism?" And when is "centrism" relatively benign and/or inescapable, as in "I can't help having been born and therefore finding myself centered in a certain time and place, and if that historical conditioning makes me 'centrist' with reference to my place of birth or origin, well then, I can't help it"? Surprisingly, in his lecture, "Freud and the non-European," Said defends, or we might say even exculpates, Sigmund Freud's Eurocentrism by arguing that Freud, given his time and place, could not but be Eurocentric. To demand of Freud that he not be Eurocentric would be literally pre-post-erous since Freud cannot be held accountable for not being aware of that of which he could not have been aware. In dire contrast, Said would hold Michel Foucault relentlessly accountable to his Eurocentrism since, by the time Foucault begins to function, huge movements of decolonization, in particular Algeria in relationship to France, are already in place: and so, Foucault cannot cushion himself with a historical alibi ("Michel Foucault as an Intellectual Imagination"; "An Ethics of Language"; and "Michel Foucault, 1927–1984").

And yet Said's position on centrism is deeply contradictory and ambivalent, for Said does maintain, even as he defends Freud's periodizable historical innocence or ignorance, that Freud was indeed well aware of the non-Western world and its immense heterogeneity. It is not clear if centrism is a historically individual form of awareness or an unavoidable structural principle of all perception, that is, since all perceiving has to begin some-where: a somewhere that acts as the center of that perception. It is also not clear if centrism can be avoided by way of appropriate protocols of auto-critique and self-reflexivity; or if centrism is the unavoidable horizon that shapes and structures all human perception. Said's elaboration of centrism becomes even more problematic when he propounds the thesis that it is pre-cisely because **Conrad** is uncompromisingly Eurocentric in his vision that he is able to generate a critique of Eurocentrism from within and thereby constitute himself as an inaugural point of reference for all **postcolonial** writers to come. When, for example, Said cites Conrad's "uncompromising Eurocentric vision" as the enabler of anti-centrist oppositionality, it is not clear if all centrisms in general beget or engender their own opposition, or if Conrad is a special instance of a centrism that anticipates its own critique. Indeed we may think it scandalous for Said to claim that it is precisely be-cause Conrad is uncompromising in his Eurocentric vision that he is able to generate antinomian readings of Eurocentrism.

To put it somewhat bluntly and practically, what is the difference be-tween (i) an unconscious centrist, (ii) a centrist by default, and (iii) a self-conscious centrist? Just substitute centrism with racism, and ask the same three questions. Once you are aware of your centrism, can you dis-lodge it, unlearn it, invest in it critically and deconstructively, rub centrism against the grain, and eventually find a way to be totally and utterly non- or a-centric? Said's vision, especially in the context of his positive readings of Conrad's practice of fictional craft, is one where centrism is acknowl-edged rigorously and put to use in such a way that it becomes its own counterpoint. Conrad's presentation of **narrative** is precious not because it transcends Eurocentrism and gets at the truth of Africa through empa-thy and political solidarity; but rather because it makes the center stutter, stammer, and come to terms with its own constitutive incoherence. There is a deep and vital connection between Said's deconstructive investment in centrism and his commitment to contrapuntal reading; for it is the center as common ground that sustains and accommodates the counterpoint as a structuring principle. In a manner that is analogous to Derridean prin-ciples of reading, Said too would cooperate in the project of extending the *longue durée* of centrism so as to enable, empower, and enfranchise critiques of centrism.

What if the center did not hold? Would mere anarchy be loosed upon the world? Is there no way out of the binary option of "center or else anarchy"? There must be some way to secure the reality of one world shared by all without the accompanying scourge of centrism. Perhaps there could be many centers and one world. Clearly Said is committed, despite feuds, quarrels, asymmetries, and abject inequalities, to the task of understanding and valorizing the world as one. But he needs to claim that the one world is the one world without falling prey to tautology. Of course the world is one experientially. Pain is universal, as is suffering, as is injustice, as are cruelty and oppression. I do not need to become you to understand your predicament and where you are coming from. And yet, there is a disquieting disconnect between such a oneness and the fragmented, compartmentalized ways in which we understand the world as Islamic, Christian, Hindu, Arabic, male, female, and so on. The challenge, as Said would have it, is how to be audacious enough to generalize from the very heart of our stultifying differences: differences that needlessly quarantine us within discrete and impermeable ghettos and enclaves and protectorates. Said's noble endeavor is to find a critical way to secure the world as one in our knowledge, in our epistemology. Would Said call himself a centrist in the name of one universal world sharable by all? Perhaps not: he would most likely turn to the notion of all our overlapping and intersecting histories which in their very differential deployment attest to the backdrop of a single common world. But he may want to hold on to the center for strategic reasons. As a perennially **oppositional critic** and **intellectual**, Said would want and require the dominance of centrism as the object of critical antagonism. The affirmation that comes after opposition may not require a center; but in Said's world, oppositionality and oppositional criticism is a perennial activity. There will always be centers; and the question is how to engage with them. The other interesting question to ask of Said is this: Is great literature, that is, literature that is capable of questioning itself and its will to truth, more capable of producing a real critique of centrism than, say, **theory**? I suspect that Said would be more hopeful on behalf of literature than of theory, for the simple reason that it is in literature, and not in theory, that "the existential tangles with the epistemological," to avail of Ranajit Guha's eloquent phrasing. To Said, the coming unstuck of Eurocentrism in Conrad's narrative is more real than, say, Heidegger's project of questioning the very history of the Western onto-theological tradition, or the attempt by a variety of poststructuralist theorists to deconstruct Eurocentric theory from within.

Conrad, Joseph   Edward Said just cannot keep away from Conrad: from his doctoral work (from which his book *Joseph Conrad and the Fiction of Autobiography* arose), all the way to the very end of his career, Said finds great critical use for and in Conrad's fiction. Unlike say, a Chinua Achebe who finds Conrad utterly irrelevant to **postcolonial** realities except as an initial enemy to be opposed and told off, Said even insists, as he does in "Freud and the non-European," that Conrad is the trailblazer for postcolonial writers to come – a perverse claim to make on behalf of a writer who, despite his famously avowed commitment to make the reader see, could see nothing but "the heart of darkness" in Africa. Is it because of his metropolitan ambivalence and his entrenched position as a professor and connoisseur of European literature that Said is compelled to see everlasting good in Conrad, one of the canonical figures of Western modernism? Or does he absolve Conrad of ethical and political guilt just because Conrad's artistry as a storyteller is nothing short of virtuosic? It is to these questions that we now turn.

Said makes a compelling case for Conrad in his essay, "Conrad: the Presentation of Narrative." It is in the context of Conrad that we can get a clear sense of what Said means by **worldliness** in literature. It is important to understand that worldliness is not the same thing as being political, or the same thing as didactic literature, or literature with a cause, or what Jean-Paul Sartre would call "literature *engagé*," the literature of commitment, or the content-loaded, manifesto-like writing that subsumes style under message. That is exactly why Said does not find it bothersome, or crippling for his critical purposes, that Conrad despite all his **virtuosity** remains Eurocentric and has nothing to say, empirically, conceptually, affectively, or cognitively, about African reality. He finds something else at work in Conrad's texts: and that is the work of language, that is, the work that language does in a Conrad novel. Far-fetched as it may sound, there is a significant connection between Martin Heidegger, the difficult and often mystifying German philosopher, who loves to hold forth about "the being of language" and "the language of being," and Said who is interested in the language of the world and the worlding of the world in the realm of language. What is common both to Heidegger and Said is an abiding concern for the intentionality that drives language. Language is a performance in the world; it is not just a system of communication and expression. In being the connoisseur of language, Said insists that language bear the burden of the world and its history in its very being. In other words, he is not an aesthete in the tradition of a Walter Pater or an Oscar Wilde, not an adherent of art for art's sake.

Said does not believe in the world as just given, or as an empirical fact, or as a self-evident and unmediated reality. The world has to be realized as the product of collective human, secular-historical labor. Literary work is very much a part of this labor, and literary work highlights language as the site where this labor takes place. It does not matter which way the literary work points ideologically – whether it is socialist, capitalist, feminist, **nationalist**, Euro- or Afro-centric; but what does and should matter is that literature declare itself self-consciously as of the world, in the world, deeply symptomatic of the world. It is Conrad's ongoing struggle with language in the name of the world that Said finds bracing and life-affirming.

Said begins his essay on Conrad thus: "Both in his fiction and in his autobiographical writing Conrad was trying to do something that his experience as a writer every where revealed to be impossible. This makes him interesting as the case of a writer whose working reality, his practical and even theoretical competence as a writer, was far in advance of what he was saying." He goes on to say that "Conrad's fate was to write fiction great for its presentation, not only for what it was representing" (*The World, the Text, and the Critic*, 90). This last sentence is of the utmost critical importance, for it is on the basis of this conviction and understanding that Said can forgive Conrad for not being able to represent, say, African reality. Conrad exonerates himself for making his presentation itself part of what he has to say. The doubts, the moral and political ambivalences, the happenstance and often aleatory nature of his composition, the vulnerability of the **narrative's** meaning and intention to narrative performance and hence the inability of the writing process to control its own development: all these and more such issues coexist with, complicate, and constitute Conrad's presentation of narrative, what Said terms "the interplay of antitheses." Existential, historical, biographical, and autobiographical complexities and problems compel Conrad into narrative; and here is the rub. Conrad's mastery of narrative, paradoxically and deconstructively if you will, reveals itself in its vulnerability to contingency and circumstances. The relationship of intention to what will eventually be meant is never stable or predictable in a Conrad story. The world is both intended and mis-intended, recognized and mis-recognized in the linguistic literary intention.

Another important feature in Conrad's narrative presentation that Said picks up on is orality. There is always an internal narrator or a teller who is telling the story, a story addressed to an internal audience; and there is an occasion for the oral transmission of the story. There is a dynamic and mutually transformative relationship between the oral happening and the formal **text**, both within the fictional narrative. It is the interaction between two or more elements that fascinates Said. Other examples of such mutual play are between absence and presence, where voice both highlights and compensates for physical absence; between the visual and the verbal, where the words are supposed to make you see and take you into a realm beyond words as though such a realm existed in and by itself whereas in lived actuality such a realm will not be allowed to transcend the mediation of language. Language functions in Conrad both as a promise to the beyond, a promise made in language, as well as a withdrawal or a negation of that very promise, in language again.

Said reads the play of the antithetical forces in Conrad's narratives with reference to a "center": the forces are centripetal or centrifugal. This is an important insight in the context of issues such Eurocentrism, Afrocentrism, logocentrism, and so on. The question of Conrad's Eurocentrism has been central to the political evaluation of Conrad's moral and political vision. How real is the center in his fiction? If Europe, because of its colonialist domination of the world, fantasizes itself as the center of the world, and if Europe is at the very heart of Conrad's fiction, what kind of Europe is it? Is it a Eurocentric Europe restored to its fantasy, or an eviscerated Europe, a Europe whose "present" center is rendered absent? Does Conrad, in Said's terms, stay within what is historically permissible to him, that is, the "truths" of colonialism, or does he stretch, or better still, allow himself to be stretched, beyond the constraints of actual history by the work of language? Even if he begins with the certitudes of the center and is compelled therefore to be centripetal in his narrative orientation, does he eventually generate sufficient centrifugal power and energy to radiate away from the center and visualize the center as an absent presence?

Said's answer is, Yes. For example, the celebrated modernist classic *Heart of Darkness*: it begins with the center, the putative so-called center in Europe. Is Europe really the center? Not really; but for the unfortunate and dehumanizing history of Colonialism, Europe would not have been the Center of anything. But history has happened, and once it has happened it is a *fait accompli*. Neither a European nor an African writer can begin their fiction as if colonialism had not happened and Europe not enthroned as the Center by way of Colonialist violence. As Said would argue in his book, ***Beginnings***, a work has intentionally to begin somewhere and that somewhere takes on the authority of a center, a center with a lower-case "c." But, Said never sacralizes the center or the beginning into the Beginning or the Center: it is all contingent. In the narrative to follow, the beginning can be deconstructed, quarreled with, turned against, rubbed against the grain. Thus, in *Heart of Darkness*, the story moves to Africa, the centrifugal move away from the center and yet needing the center (the very word centrifugal has the component "centri" in it). The story happens "there" in Africa, and the truth of the story turns into a lie, the lie that reaches the ear of the European Intended at the Center. This is the interactive play of presence and absence, the truth and the lie, the investment in and the disinvestment from the center that Said is talking about. The narrative lines attempt to get back to the Center as if the Center were there, in Conrad's first novel *Almayer's Folly* as in the *Heart of Darkness*, but it is only an endeavor that reveals the center as present in its absence and absent in its presence. What is most valuable to Said in Conrad's presentation of the narrative, and not just the re-presentative content within the fiction, is the fact that this quandary of reaching and not reaching, revealing and the revelation itself as a sound refutation and recantation of the revelation (the "horror" in the *Heart of Darkness*), these dilemmas and quandaries are posed rigorously and commented on orally, textually, in a variety of rhetorical contexts within the world of fiction. It is this presentation as performance that does the theoretical work (the same kind of claim that Said makes on behalf of Glenn Gould's virtuosity that is simultaneously performative and theoretical) that interrupts the **representation** and questions its truth claims. Any affirmation that takes place within the field of representation, the diegetic space of the happening of the story, is immediately subjected to severe negation.

What is significant about Conrad's narrative disposition is that it is about failure: a failure that produces rich knowledge and awareness. As Said puts it: "For what Conrad discovered was that the chasm between words saying and words meaning was widened, not lessened, by a talent for words written. To have chosen to write, then, is to have chosen in a particular way neither to say directly nor to mean exactly in the way he had hoped to say or to mean. No wonder that Conrad returned to this problematic concern repeatedly, a concern that his writing dramatized continuously and imaginatively" (*The World, the Text, and the Critic*, 91). Such meaningful failure is all the more compelling and ethically and politically progressive since the failure is of the center, that is, of the dominant discourse. It is the dominant discourse being deconstructed that is the ongoing motif of Conrad's fiction. Unlike postmodern fiction that resorts to something called meta-fiction to make its theoretical points, in the Conradian novel, "the existential tangles with the epistemological," and the presentation of the narrative provides an organic theoretical horizon for the representation going on within the story-telling space of the novel. In Said's terms, what transpires within the fictional space of Conrad's novels is both the promise of a world and the perennial withdrawal of such a world. The worlding of Conrad's world is constantly beset with performative failure or errancy: failure that in the very act of frustrating the author's pedagogical need for certitude enables critical insights that are more advanced than the certainties based on **centrism**. This is exactly why Said claims that Conrad was a writer "whose working reality was far in advance of what he was saying." It is Conrad's presentation of his own narrative that goes beyond the limitations of what the narrative can actually represent. Yet another way of saying this would be: it is Conrad's writerly openness that redeems him from merely re-presenting reality in the form of a predictable and fatuous tautology. To put it somewhat differently, in Conrad's fiction, thanks to Conrad's mode of presentation, reality unfolds as a syndrome, as a configuration of symptoms that necessitate critical diagnostic readings. Conrad's fictional mastery lies in fact in his ability to question his own mastery in the name of a reality that both stimulates and transcends his competence as a writer.

contrapuntal criticism   It would not be an exaggeration to say that "contrapuntal criticism" is to Edward Said what "difference" is to Jacques Derrida, or "discourse" to Michel Foucault. With the "contrapuntal" yoking together of Culture and Imperialism in his 1993 book, Said opens up a way of reading cultural **texts** that goes beyond the politics of blame and guilt ("The Music Itself: Glenn Gould's Contrapuntal Vision"). For after all, the title of his powerful 1993 book is *Culture and Imperialism,* and not "Culture or Imperialism." A gifted pianist himself and a profound student and connoisseur of Western classical music, Said borrows the term "counterpoint" from the formal vocabulary of Western classical music and deploys it with telling effect in the field of textual analysis: socio-political, cultural, and literary. Here is a convincing and persuasive example of the travel of a concept from one domain to another, with some real effects. Questions like "what is a text?" and "how should one read a text?" are not just elitist "super-structural" concerns with little bearing on reality and the world of historical circumstances. On the contrary, modes of analysis and criticism that emanate from a formal or academic context can and should be made to reverberate beyond their place of origin and illuminate the larger world of which they are an integral and organic part: that indeed is part of Said's ethic in his articulation of "contrapuntality." The other important concern of Said's is the making of meaning not unilaterally, but bi- and multi-laterally.

Let us take a brief look at the term "counterpoint" as it occurs in the context of Western music before we seek to understand Said's specific deployment of the term. In music, counterpoint is the combination of two or more melodic lines in a way that retains their independent contour and rhythm but brings them into a harmonic relationship. The term originates from the Latin *punctus contra punctus:* point against point. (I am reminded here of Aldous Huxley's intellectually garrulous and argumentative novel of ideas, *Point, Counter-Point.*) And again, this time in the words of John Rahn: "The internal structures that create each of the voices separately must contribute to the emergent structure of the polyphony, which in turn must reinforce and comment on the structure of the independent voices. The way that is accomplished, in detail is the counterpoint" (*Music Inside Out,* 177). Counterpoint is structured in relationality, which is to say that it is intentional not arbitrary, a structural elaboration and not a fortuitous or un-self-reflexive mode of expression. The relationship acknowledges and valorizes simultaneously both independence and interdependence. A double characterization of the same phenomenon raises interesting questions. If something is both independent and interdependent, which one is it really? Split within itself, in a way like Du Boisian double consciousness, how does counterpoint organize itself representationally? If it is two, analytically speaking, but one in its overall persuasion, how does it speak and what musical possibility does it "speak for"? Where is it truly itself: at the level of rhythm and contour where it is independent or at the level of harmony where it is interdependent? Both a performance and a **representation**, the counterpoint is a technique, a mode of meaning making that does not merely re-present a musical possibility that already exists. The possibility is the result of an invention, a particular form of musical imagining or elaboration that begets a particular kind of accountability and a particular kind of structured listening.

Most significantly, for Said, it is a matter of choice. Not all of Western classical compositions are marked by counterpoint, and it is not at all coincidental that Said should be excited by those works that have counterpoint as intrinsic to their form and performativity. The contrapuntal structure offers to Said a critical agon or forum where every point can be counter-pointed argumentatively, not with the intention of creating a schism but with the objective of realizing a shared, bi-laterally constructed totality. The polyphony and the interdependence on harmony are not factual givens; on the contrary, they are musical effects achieved through the application of a rigorous compositional principle known as counterpoint. A composer committed to counterpoint does not subscribe to the belief that harmony and counterpoint are absolutely separated from each other. She acknowledges the reality of two different calls, two different musical stimuli, the linear and the harmonic, and responds to both within the economy of the same musical text. It is not an "either/or" choice; nor is it an easy and fatuous accommodation of both principles. It is a structured form of mutual inclusion that necessitates a theoretical elaboration of antagonism before that very antagonism can be recuperated as an inclusive rationale of composition.

The counterpoint also initiates a complex relationship between composer and listener. The listener does not disable one of two wavelengths, the linearity or the counterpoint, as she is listening to the composition. In a way, the "other," the "counter" always haunts the same, the point, as its unavoidable *alter ego*. Both reciprocity of recognition and principled antagonism are co-intended equally in the concept of counterpoint. Recognition of and from one pole immediately activates the other pole as well. To really appreciate contrapuntal music, the listener has to listen to many goings-on all at the same time. Two modes of listening need to be exercised: modes that recognize each other as mutually vital even as each "does its own thing" within the structured totality. Recognition does not mean a bland and uncontested recognition, just as antagonism does not spell a breaking away from the opponent in implacable difference and irreconcilability. To put it in concrete terms, with respect to Said's work on behalf of the ongoing Palestinian struggle for national self-determination: there is a Palestinian viewpoint as well as an Israeli perspective. Real peace can only be the result of an honest, rigorous, and contrapuntal playing out of the two perspectives, that in their very antagonism require each other's recognition. The predicament of the two discrete histories can be resolved only through interdependence: an interdependence whose terms and criteria need to be worked out and elaborated with respect to the two overlapping histories.

What contrapuntal analysis does in the first place is to get rid of the sovereign text, that is, a text that speaks with just one voice and belongs to just one absolute perspective. The text cannot be anchored in a single meaning or seen as accountable to just one point of view or perspective that is indeed the correct and authentic perspective. The point-counterpoint structure opens up the text to a lively debate between opposing points of view that converge dialogically around the same text. There is antagonism conceived and stylized as dialogue, and there is antagonism understood as the function of dialogue. The counterpoint, in a fit of rage or indignation, does not secede from the text and inaugurate its own separatist regime. Both the point and the counterpoint work out and perform their antagonisms with respect to the same text. A Conrad novel may well be Eurocentric when viewed from a certain perspective, but this does not mean that the same text is not open to antagonistic and contrapuntal evaluation and judgment. Said understands that in a world that is structured in dominance, a world that is unevenly divided between East and West, the ex-colonizers and the ex-colonized, no history is entirely discrete or separate. Territories and experiences overlap, just as memories and experiences are shared but remembered differently by different peoples. For example, we could say that in the aftermath of decolonization, both Algeria and France are **postcolonial**, but in a different way, as are India and England, and so on.

Said is insistent that connections need to be made across discrepant experiences and that existent asymmetries need to be bridged and transcended in the name of a common and relational humanity in search of a universality to come. It is in this context that contrapuntal reading or analysis finds its mandate. When Said reads a text by Jane Austen or Charles Dickens or Albert Camus contrapuntally, the text is rendered accountable both as "culture" and as "imperialist" and "colonialist." Said's protocol is consistent with Walter Benjamin's famously moving diagnosis that "there is no document of civilization which is not at the same time a document of barbarism" ("Theses in the Philosophy of History," 256). His contrapuntal thesis also resonates in empathy with Salman Rushdie's declaration through one of his characters in *The Satanic Verses*: "What do the English know of their history? It happened overseas." Or, we could think of that poignant scene in Amitav Ghosh's *The Shadow Lines*, where Tridib and his English lover May Price view and understand the significance of the presence of the Victoria Memorial monument in the heart of Calcutta differently. Each perspective is postcolonial, but differently so: a point that Said makes eloquently in his 1986 essay in *Salmagundi*, "Intellectuals in a Post-colonial World," as he argues passionately for relational cooperation across and beyond the asymmetry, across and beyond the stultifying framework of blame on the one side and guilt on the other.

Contrapuntal analysis brings together the following principles: recognition, reciprocity, relationality, and antagonism. Contrapuntal analysis locates different actors, players, agents, perspectives, and readers of texts in all their difference within a common frame of reference: the same text as it enables, motivates, historicizes, and mobilizes more than one interpretation, more than one point of view, more than one will to truth. In the context of the contrapuntal imperative, a celebratory reading of all that is rich and precious and "cultural" in a Jane Austen novel is not allowed to be oblivious of the reality that this very rich culture of the Austen novel is structurally subtended by its constitutive involvement and complicity in the project of imperialism. Likewise, the contrapuntal ethic mandates that the metropolitan interpretation of the text cannot and dare not avoid an antagonistic confrontation with the "third world" interpretation of the same text. Both the point and the counterpoint are situated modally in the same world, and the purpose of contrapuntal analysis is to galvanize and set in motion a world-historical mode of accountability that will resist fragmentation, balkanization, and the narrow-mindedness of separatism and identity politics.

"Both common and discrepant": there lies the crux of the matter for Said, which is to say, not one or the other. The discrepant and the common are enjoined to influence and persuade each other. Discrepancy is recognized within the common, just as the common is identified as the backdrop of the discrepant. Said, in his own non-philosophical and non-theoretical way, is making a strong and significant claim about the very nature of history, our common human history. Not surprisingly, the operative concept here is "secular." The only credible, creditable, and accountable way to be historical is to be secular; and to be truly secular is to acknowledge and live up to the reality that no one history, whether it be American or Palestinian or African, can be thought of in isolation from other histories. To be secular is to be relationally historical, to be within one's own history as a function of negotiation with someone else's history, to negotiate with one's own history in response to the claims of the other's history. If this fundamental thesis of the relatedness of all histories to one another is true, then it is also equally true that this interrelationship highlights both commonality and discrepancy. To be truly secular is to forfeit the privileges of essentialism and/or nativism, as well as the false premise of doing one's own history within one's own protected enclave. To be rigorously secular is perennially to do battle against so-called civilizational antagonisms understood *à la* Samuel Huntington, to forever undo us–them divides, and to find ways of understanding your history in my terms and from my point of view and *vice versa*. Secular history takes place within multiple frames that are all vitally interconnected.

Here are a few questions that we could raise concerning Edward Said's contrapuntal ethic. Does contrapuntal criticism continue to privilege the location of the metropolis in spite of its strong invocation of formerly

colonized societies? If contrapuntality is relational in its mode of organization, how should the critic situate herself within the contrapuntal structure?
It is obvious that a contrapuntal way of making meaning is not the same
thing as canonical representation that is based on an easy and unproblem-
atic one-to-one correspondence between who is saying it and what is being
said. To be in a counterpoint is to be in both places at the same time. Or
is it a kind of uneasy and ambivalent shuttling between the metropolitan
and the other pole? If that is the case, can the counterpoint degenerate into
a posture of easy accommodation? How, for example, does the critic generate advocacy or partisanship from within the counterpoint? Is it possible
that contrapuntal criticism overvalues the importance of the intertwine-
ment and the overlapping of the two histories and in the process does not
do full justice to what is discrepant between the two histories? Given the
rich and long histories of the non-West, why does contrapuntal criticism
insist on honoring and acknowledging the colonial–imperial moment in
history as definitive and fundamental? Does contrapuntality, consciously or
unconsciously, endow a chronic *longue durée* to the double-bind of postcolonialism? What if the post-colony is keen on reading an end to the statute
of limitations imposed by the histories of Colonialism and Imperialism? It
could also be argued that in his benign ambassadorial intention to realize cooperation and solidarity between the metropolitan world and ex-colonized
societies, Said has significantly downplayed and neutralized some of the real
antagonisms and contradictions between the two worlds. It is conceivable
that postcolonial realities in India, Nigeria, and Kenya, and a host of other
locations, might want to emerge in directions that have nothing to do with
contrapuntal spaces. Finally, Said could be faulted for aestheticizing the
political a little too felicitously; for after all, antagonisms in real life and
the real world are not mere motifs susceptible to musical resolutions. The
post-colony might well find itself suffocated, domesticated, cosmetically
appeased, or negated within the spatiality of the counterpoint. An extreme
case in point is the manner in which Aijaz Ahmed, in my opinion, in his
polemically bristling book, *In Theory*, unfairly takes Edward Said to task
for his "metropolitan ambivalence." According to Ahmed, Said is just too
omnivorous, and wants it all: the pleasures of the West as well as the political
urgency of the non-West.

Culture and Imperialism   Edward Said, at the very beginning of his book,
The World, the Text, and the Critic, narrates a telling anecdote: that of an
official working in the US Department of Defense during the days of the

relentless bombings of Vietnam. This official is a friend of Said, and tells Said that the Secretary of Defense should not be misrecognized as a monster just because he has authorized the bloody bombings, for after all, he reads Durrell's *Alexandria Quartet*. The thesis is that someone capable of appreciating and valuing complex literature just could not be a "cold-blooded butcher." Two interesting inferences work here. One is that a cultured consumer of literature is automatically exempt from criminality and reprehensible political, governmental behavior. The other, not so obvious, inference is that the *Alexandria Quartet* as a resplendent literary work is innocent of all politics.

Another anecdote: here is something I often do, particularly in my undergraduate classes. I would ask my students the following question. How many of you love, and I confess that I do myself, the Beatles song, written by John Lennon, "Run for your life"? What about the line, "Catch you with another man, and that is the end of little girl"? Do you relate to the song exclusively as music? What about the words, and what about John Lennon and his famous anger and his insecurity with female sexuality? What about the relationship in general between a male rock music and the way it invokes women, girls, chicks (what about the Rolling Stones and inflatable female dolls, and the "dirty girl" in Pink Floyd's *The Wall*); what about Jim Morrison, the Doors and female sexuality? Would an awareness of these extra-textual factors influence your musical appreciation of the song? Would you, in the name of political correctness, stop enjoying a whole range of classic rock numbers once you become aware that they are all driven by a certain maleness, by testosterone superbly sublimated into rhythm, the angry snarl of the guitar? What, for example, about the famous epiphanic moments in *The Portrait of the Artist as a Young Man*: moments that are unthinkable except within a very specific male masturbatory psychodrama, a male gaze, and a worldview hatched by a certain religious mode of upbringing that makes it imperative for a burgeoning young man to think of women either as whores or as Madonnas?

Culture and Imperialism sums up with sustained brilliance Said's life-long endeavor to do justice to the complex and contradictory formation of that precious phenomenon called Culture: a phenomenon that we are taught, sometimes brainwashed, to value, revere, and learn from. The title of Said's book is *Culture and Imperialism*, and not "Culture or Imperialism." Following up, in his own way, on Walter Benjamin's insight about the inevitable co-implication of civilization and barbarism, Said writes an entire book that stakes its rationale in the "and" that inevitably connects Imperialism to Culture: without apologies for the appreciation of culture despite its embeddedness in Empire, without paranoia in the context of what seems an all-enveloping Imperialism. What is at work in this sense is a critical sensibility that is striving to transcend the paralyzing binary mode of blame on the one side and guilt on the other. The reason for Said's collocating both culture and imperialism within the same thought is pragmatic and strategic, and not just theoretical. Just as theorists such as Roland Barthes, Louis Althusser, Pierre Macherey, and Jacques Derrida had revolutionized the very meaning of the "text," and transformed the politics of "reading," Said in his *Culture and Imperialism* initiates a radically new and different practice of reading. What needs to be emphasized here is the fact that what Said is proposing is a "macro-political" as against a "micro-political" theory of reading. To put it differently, Said's literary readings do not stay within the **text**; instead, they recognize and address the larger macro-political world of Empire and Colony in the literary text. Said's uniqueness lies in his critical insistence that the world of the text and the world of Imperialism are flip sides of the same coin. The literary text is not synonymous with the text of Empire; but what is crucial is that the two texts, or the two worlds if you will, are ineluctably and symptomatically co-implicated. The "micro-political" refers to all the **professional** nuances and protocols of reading that professors of literature employ to squeeze and tease out the meanings of literary texts. The act of reading, in other words, connects the world of the text meaningfully and symptomatically with the goings-on in the real world. Readings are therefore neither innocent nor guilty without recourse. This is indeed a hugely consequential insight with profound and far-reaching implications for practitioners of Western literary criticism. Said himself is one such distinguished professional.

Let us look at it this way. Let us say you are a specialist in eighteenth-century and Victorian literature with a particular interest in the fiction of Jane Austen and Charles Dickens; or you are a specialist in late nineteenth- and twentieth-century literature with particular interest in the works of Baudelaire, Rimbaud, André Gide, Albert Camus, and Jean-Paul Sartre. If you are such a professional you will be bound to encounter in these texts repeated references to the Orient, to India, to Algeria, to Egypt, and so on. Are these references important or unimportant; primary or epiphenomenal; purely decorative details or basic structural components of the narrative form? Furthermore, if you are a literary scholar and not a political pamphleteer or propagandist, would you be justified in paying more than casual and cursory attention to characters who are floating between India and England or characters who go off to India at the end of the novel to run away from an insoluble domestic problem or anxiety? Here is how Said answers these questions and, in the process, opens up an unprecedented path for future generations of Western literary scholars and critics.

For starters, in *Culture and Imperialism* Said argues for the reality of a geopolitics where histories are both overlapping and contestable. Jane Austen's or Charles Dickens' England or London is as much modern as it is colonial, as much metropolitan as it is colonial. In the works of Austen, Dickens, and other authors, literature happens not in isolation from the politics of colonization and empire building. Indeed, the casual references to those far-off places are not so remote after all; without those references and those guilty colonial and imperialist connectivities, England and London cannot be what they are. Likewise, Albert Camus' ethically inflected theory of the absurd and his poignant invocations of alienation in the midst of Algerian landscapes and sunsets are inextricable from Camus' own experience as a French-Algerian brought into being by French Colonialism. Said thus makes it abundantly clear that the world within these literary texts could not even have been evoked or delineated except as a function and symptom of the macropolitics of Colonialism and Imperialism. In other words, these great literary master works are both culturally *and* imperially constituted. A student or a scholar of literature and culture would be ill advised not to pay attention to this constitutive ambivalence at the heart of these texts. Take the Imperialism away and Culture has no basis to stand on, while at the same time Culture creates its own patterns against and with the backdrop of Imperialism.

It is precisely by undertaking such a cognitive cartography of the co-territoriality of Culture and Imperialism that Said redefines literary scholarship and its accountability. In the wake of Said's pioneering work, it becomes mandatory for the Western humanist and the literary critic trained by Western **humanism** to consider and view Culture and Imperialism in the same frame. It will not do anymore, short of being laughed at for poor scholarship, for the literary scholar to continue to produce sanitized readings of literary texts, all the while disavowing the essential linkage between Culture and Imperialism in particular, between culture and politics in general. Not only are the two realms mutually implicated, but it is also true that the political is inscribed in the literary and the cultural text. Political criteria and concerns are mediated in and through literature and culture. It is the reading of the literary and the cultural as political, and the insight that the political is embodied and enriched contradictorily and ambivalently in the literary and cultural text that set Said apart from those other critics who "choose" when to be political and when not. Said disallows such a disingenuous choice. Said's example has been of great importance to the following generation of academic literary scholars seeking tenure in departments of English and comparative literature in the United States. Scholars who have been overtly political, polemical, or partisan in their methodological or interpretive orientation have always been in peril during times of tenure. They could easily be hounded out for being political in the wrong way, or for being political in the first place and in the process for having sullied the apolitical and trans-historical grandeur and serenity of Literature and Culture. But now, thanks to Said, we understand and legitimate the truth claims of literature and culture from a more complex and sophisticated perspective.

The singular empowering and transformative effect of Said, especially on scholars in departments of English and comparative literature in the 1970s and 1980s, was simply this. It had become possible, thanks to Edward Said, that they could aspire and attempt to be literary critics and be political in the same breath, in the same project. Thanks to the intricate and erudite ways in which Said had elaborated the relationship between the textual world and the world as text, the field of literature, as well as the critical study of literature, the world within the world, had been rendered macro-political. The pleasures of the text did not have to come in the way of the political just as the political could not negate the reality of the pleasures.

democratic criticism   It is in Said's late work, particularly in the first of his posthumous publications, *Humanism and Democratic Criticism,* that democracy begins to function as a significant term. It is not that the term did not have any interest for him earlier on, but that it was not a special component of Said's critical repertoire or vocabulary. When it does surface in this late work, it does so not in isolation but in a particular thematic and political relationship with two other important concepts: **humanism** and criticism. Perhaps it is not unimportant that it figures in an adjectival form, qualifying "criticism," a term that has an endless fascination for Said; not just criticism, but the fate of the humanities in general hangs in the balance.

For all practical purposes, for Said, democracy refers to an audience, a context, a public sphere for the free exchange, dissemination, and contestation of ideas, thoughts, and scholarship on a variety of issues. The opposite of democracy to Said would be the cult, the mysterious and arcane guild, esoteric professionalism, meritocracy, and the mystique of avant-gardism. Democracy is or should be all about the dismantling of inequalities among people, in particular inequalities in the opportunity to learn. Whether it is a concert hall, a lecture theater, or a drama auditorium, the performances in these sites, however challenging in form or content, should be meant for all, and not just for the initiated few. Democracies should of course foster, nurture, motivate, and incentivize **intellectuals**, but not as a special class or coterie that is in radical separation from the many.

A Said Dictionary, First Edition. R. Radhakrishnan.
© 2012 John Wiley & Sons, Ltd. Published 2012 by John Wiley & Sons, Ltd.

This point can be demonstrated by a simple example. Said would maintain that even if the text in question be T.S. Eliot's *The Waste Land*, the scholar-intellectual should be prepared to talk intelligibly about that mind-boggling modernist masterpiece to a general, lay audience that has no pretension to something called literary sensibility. The intellectual should not insist that the only site where she would hold forth about the poem is the classroom as a professor, or at a literature conference where she can unleash all her precious jargon and be instantly understood by her peers in the field. Said emphasizes that general intelligibility is all the more germane in the humanities that lie so close to lived life and its complexities. Literature and theories of literature are about life, its lived-ness, and therefore have the obligation to be intelligible to all. This is not to claim that subjects in the humanities are not complex or that specialized language is not necessary to illuminate the truths of literature and music and painting. The point is rather that, at a time when the humanities are already powerless and marginalized, it is the responsibility of the scholars and intellectuals in the field to make their domain and its strengths available to a large audience, otherwise known as the democratic public.

Said's complaint is that increasingly intellectuals in the humanities are refusing to and even becoming incapable of addressing the public sphere. It is as though in their capacity as connoisseurs they have nothing to say to the public. Their communication context is less than public. Said is not suggesting that democracy should just be one basic public sphere, and therefore that we should get rid of all mediations and all specialized contexts. All that he is asking for is that whatever transpires at the more advanced, the more specialized publics be intelligible at the democratic public sphere as well. Criticism is a second-order operation, and, autonomous as that order may be, it can only be relatively autonomous, that is, relative to something that is primary, namely, literature and its inherence in real life. To Said, it all comes down to language: its transparency/translucency/opacity. First of all, criticism cannot be its own hermetic justification. It is about something else; therefore it has an explanatory responsibility. It has to be both modal or methodological and representative of something objective, and real. In other words, criticism does not create its own object. What connects criticism to democracy is the crucial function of **representation**. Democracies that do not represent their peoples are not democracies. When they begin speaking gobbledygook that makes no sense to the people, that is when democracies cease being representative. When meaning splits from representation, it ceases to be meaning: that would be Said's thesis.

There is significant discussion of language in Said's *Humanism and Demo-cratic Criticism*. Language that mystifies, or is obscurantist in the name of expertise, is unethical and undemocratic: Said reiterates this over and over again. This kind of language is intended to keep the many away, even intim-idate them, make them feel inferior; and that cannot be democracy. Experts love to create smaller and more exclusive worlds where the many are not welcome: these worlds are insider worlds that fully intend to maintain rigid inside–outside distinctions. It is not coincidental that the front cover of his book, *Humanism and Democratic Criticism*, has the picture of a formidable book with ticket stub saying "Admit All" sticking out of the pages. Said, who spent most of his life in classrooms teaching students the beauties of literature, is of course aware that entry into the classroom is not automatic. He also makes sure that his students go out of the classroom more learned, more knowledgeable, better versed in the ways of literature and culture. The question is not about erudition, but the forms it takes. Knowledge is meant for transmissibility and not for monopolistic hoarding. In a democracy, where the people are the subject, knowledge in the final analysis is account-able to the public. It cannot be validated as a mystique. During times when the humanities and funding for the humanities is on the wane, and when, moreover, the tax-paying public has difficulty understanding the signifi-cance of the humanities, it would be ruinous and suicidal of academics in the humanities not to talk to the public at large. They need to make sense, and now is not the time to sound weird. Strategy apart, Said strongly be-lieves that there is no need to use outré or rebarbative language to sound profound; one can be profound and intelligible at the same time.

Said does take into consideration Judith Butler's caveat that what passes for democratic felicity and intelligibility may well be the seduction of pre-packaged style and formulaic banality. Easy style, commonsensical as it may sound, could well be its own kind of obfuscation. When democracy degenerates into inane formulae, empty shibboleth, or, worse still, becomes deceptive and untrustworthy in its very simplicity (as when simplicity is in fact the flip side of some form of dominance or of an oppressive status quo that refuses to be challenged or problematized), such articulations need to be defamiliarized by **theory**. This would be the preferred path of resolute theorists such as Judith Butler, Theodor Adorno, Paul de Man, Jacques Derrida, Louis Althusser, and Martin Heidegger, to name a few. While not in disagreement in principle with this attitude, Said would demur vehemently in practice and maintain that very often theory in the act of appointing itself as the agent of alienation exempts itself from its own forms of fallibility and arrogance. Proliferating its own non-simple, non-commonsensical vocabulary, theory begins to pretend as though alienation and defamiliarization were ends in themselves and therefore not accountable at the level of representative content. What is theory saying and to whom? That is the significant question for Said.

Clearly, Said is all in favor of improving the quality of democracy that has gone demotic, in the pejorative sense of the term. If the various projects of pushing democracy to its limits and beyond and transforming it towards horizons of deeper erudition could be broadly termed "the aristocratization of democracy" in the name of all, then Said is fully supportive of such an enterprise. But what he will not tolerate, as he will not in his appraisal of humanism, is the theoretical notion of a "break" from democracy in the name of democracy. Wall Street may have its own specialist pulls and imperatives, but at no point can Wall Street be allowed to honor its accountability in abeyance or repudiation of its accountability to Main Street. Democracy, to Said, is the idea of people in various pursuits at different levels of intensity, performing on a variety of registers of knowhow and intellectual and symbolic capital, seeking the meaning of life as amateurs, professionals, mavericks, and hybrids of one sort or another; and the important thing is that, despite the fact they inhabit their several small worlds, they are all in the same world in a state of ever-changing relationships. It is the common touch, in its differential tactility, that constitutes democracy for Said. To be touched by music, a poem, a nifty theoretical formulation is to be touched by life, its **worldliness** as it is realized by way of an ever-expanding orchestra of mediations: an orchestra, and this musical metaphor would appeal to Said, that never posits individuality and solo **virtuosity** against collective worldliness, or formal pyrotechnics against affect.

exile   To be an exile: who would want that? To be an exile is to be the alien, the outsider, the non-citizen, the other, the one who is locked out of all circuits of power, legitimacy, sovereignty. To be an exile is to live minimally, at a threshold that is no more than bare life; to non-belong to any community, collectivity, constituency. Moreover, there are exiles and exiles: a Henry James in England, a Salman Rushdie in London or New York, a refugee fleeing Nazi Germany, a member of a "boat people" escaping political persecution: there can be no equivalence among these vastly different states of exile. Some of these human conditions are abjectly historical and factual, and others metaphorical and intellectually symbolic without any attendant suffering or loss. Despite these stark discontinuities in the very meaning of the term "exile," in the world of culture and literature, in the world of **intellectuals**, there is nevertheless much romanticizing of the exilic state. Exile becomes a metaphoric and or an allegorical mode of existence; and in this mode exile becomes the ultimate trope of critical utopianism. Whereas exile as a real, material, historical condition is abject and impoverished, exile as imaginary perspective is nothing but rich with extraordinary and rare wisdom and insight. Said's use of this term is aptly double-conscious: on the one hand, there is the acute and agonizing awareness of Palestinian exile, the Palestinian lack of statehood; and on the other, the deliberate intellectual cultivation of exile as perspective: a perspective that soars above the limitations, the pettiness, and the provincialism of statehood, of national sovereignty, of all canonical modes of belonging. Said is certainly

A Said Dictionary, First Edition. R. Radhakrishnan.

part of a long-standing tradition of "the intellectual" who seeks exile as a desirable, even critical-utopian, condition of thought and thinking. Exile turns into an ideal *topos* that allows the intellectual to enjoy radical freedom from all manner of sovereign, ideological commitments and constraints. The intellectual's long-standing desire to be at home in the world by being nowhere and everywhere at the same time, to escape the prison-house of a single belonging, to valorize homelessness as the ultimate home and radical non-belonging as the only way to belong, finds its paradise in the notion or the idea of exile ("Reflections on Exile"; "Permission to Narrate").

Clearly, the same intellectuals who conceptualize exile as their fantasy location, very often are blessed with all the privileges and the *imprimatur* of national and sovereign belonging in their actual lives. The point is that they practice or perform exile as a perspective and a critical point of view to call into question, deconstruct, and problematize canonical and "identitarian" forms of belonging. Even though Edward Said was a diasporic Palestinian-American, he was very much an American who enjoyed, without any sense of guilt, high levels of eminence and visibility as professor–scholar–intellectual. He was not, strictly speaking, an exile. He perennially embodied and demonstrated in his work and sensibility a keen sense of the "elsewhere" even as he made a happy home in New York City. As he would describe eloquently in his memoir, *Out of Place*, his sense of always being "out of place" was as much theoretical and epistemological as it was political and existential. In other words, one could be an exile, literally speaking, as a result of forcible dislocation and dispossession (the example of Palestinians who became exiles with the establishment of the state of Israel in 1948: an event of celebration to one people that was an event of mourning for another); and one could practice or experience exile as a conscious disposition, critical deportment, ethico-political style or way of life, even as one was ensconced in the heartlands of hegemonic and sovereign identity.

The example that Said keeps coming back to again and again, in the context of the intellectual's secular, modernist condition of exile, is that of **Eric Auerbach** and his period of exile in Istanbul. In a manner that is reminiscent of Ralph Ellison's explosive *sotto voce* at the end of *Invisible Man*, "may be on some other wavelength I speak for you," Said endeavors to generalize and valorize the exilic point of view as a perspective that is richer, more fair and just, and more humane and complex than perspectives that are entrenched in any of the sovereign regimes or heartlands of identity. The condition of exile calls for a re-reading of the politics of "filiation" and enables an affiliative solidarity with the world that is more inclusive, more imaginative, more liberating than filial, natural, and umbilical modes of belonging. Said would argue that it was precisely because he was in exile that Auerbach was afforded a magnificently secular and critical perspective on Europe, his home: something that would have been unthinkable from within the heartland of his European home.

It is precisely by way of the alienation, by perspective, of his natural home, that Auerbach gains access to a deconstructive understanding, an understanding against the grain, of his own natal and native habitat. It is from such an exilic point of view that he is able to write richly and meaningfully about his home and its culture. The home or filial culture is both the same and not the same when it is submitted to the exilic perspective that combines belonging and solidarity with alienation and critique. Said is making the important argument that being part of a culture by virtue of birth is not the same as producing a conscious and intentional knowledge of that culture. It is quite simple: from the exilic point of view, one can see things, angles, and aspects that are foreclosed to a resident, citizen-sovereign point of view. What is to be emphasized here is that Said poses exile as perspective against essentialism or thoughtless insiderism. To have a perspective also means to be open to process: no perspective pre-knows what it is going to know by way of historical, secular process. Also, perspectives cannot be "homed" or domesticated by the native integrity of their subject matter. For example, to be American is not and should not be the same thing as being a bigoted card-carrying American incapable of critiquing America. One can be a critical and **oppositional** American fully capable of thinking un-American, non-American, even anti-American thoughts. On the contrary, essentialist notions of belonging rule out possibilities of radical dissent in the name of an unchanging, original identity.

No discussion of "exile" is complete without a corresponding and commensurate reference to **nationalism**, the nation state, and the rationale of citizenship. To be exiled in our own time and place automatically means being exiled from the privileges and the security of national belonging. The question, "Do you have a home?" translates effortlessly into, "Do you have a nationality?" The ideology of nationalism has been thoroughly naturalized to the extent that "nation" has become a synonym for "home." The political *imprimatur* of the nation as home has become the basic axiom of identity and belonging. Said's advocacy of the exilic condition is intended both as an affirmation of what exile has to offer as perspective, and as an uncompromising and rigorous critique of nationalism and its exclusionary identity politics. Said's strategic engagement with the *topos* of exile demonstrates time and again that if the "home" that humanity cherishes is nothing but "home as nation," then such a "home" is really not worth cherishing. When homes become nations, each home is pitted against another home for the simple reason that nationalism cannot survive without the underlying logic of Us and Them. In a world that is structured in dominance, in a world that has been formed by forces of Colonialism and Imperialism, homes are anything but natural, philosophical, or allegorical. The idea of "home" may well be, philosophically and theoretically speaking, coextensive with all humanity, but in the realpolitik of home as world, homes have been defined time and again as what one has and the other does not. The "other" by definition is *persona non grata* in an area where the "self" is at home as sovereign-citizen.

Said's intervention in the mutually constitutive politics of home and exile reminds us that the philosophic utopian vision of the "world as home" is betrayed, mis-recognized, and finally trashed by political regimes of home and home making. It is important to note that it is in its **contrapuntal**-antagonistic relationship to the politics of nationalism that exile assumes its critical valence. In other words, exile is not a state in itself or a utopian or allegorical resolution, like, say, the philosophical notion of *nirvana*, to the ills of historical existence. Said's objective – and whether he succeeds in this task is indeed debatable and has been debated for some time now – is double-inflected. Historically speaking, Said makes the all-important diagnosis that we all live within the "shadow lines" (Amitav Ghosh) of nationalism. In other words, despite all our powerful epistemological and theoretical critiques and recantations of nationalism, we all carry passports inscribed by the hegemony of the nation state. Despite our advocacy of globalization, and various forms of trans-nationalism, we all are still constituted by the ideological "hail" of nationalism. The lines of the nation state may well be lacking in substance, they may well be "shadowy," and yet they continue successfully to separate the Us from the Them. Said points out that there is an asynchronous or a disjunctive relationship between our theoretical refutation of nationalism and our continued reliance on the rationale of nationalism at the level of politics and political economy. To put it differently, we are forced, for pragmatic and time-honored reasons, to rely on the very concept that we have deconstructed and destabilized theoretically. If we take into account the ongoing plight of the Palestinian people, a people without a sovereign state, the situation becomes even more complex. How is it even "conscionable" to valorize exile as perspective when exile is the very political ill that has been plaguing the Palestinian people ever since the founding of the state of Israel in 1948? These are people who have had "exile" forced on them, and these are people – victims of victims, as Said phrases it eloquently in a number of his essays – who are looking to sovereign nationalization as an answer to their political homelessness. To valorize and celebrate homelessness and exile as critical-utopian perspectivism and at the same time defend the establishment of a Palestinian nation state: would that constitute a paradox, a contradiction? To put it in terms of the politics of exile, can exile even have a politics when the very realm of the political has been monopolized and signed for in the name of the nation state?

Said's point of departure in all of this is clearly the nation state, but that is all it is: a point of departure. The point of departure is clearly a form of historical demarcation, but no more. The point of departure has no definitive stranglehold over the narratives to come. Whatever the particular ideological features of the identity regime, whether it be in the name of the nation state or ethnicity or any other form of particularism, identity regimes are built on the principle of an Us and a Them. Some "other" has to be necessarily exiled so that "we as self" can enjoy the plenitude of "our own" sovereignty. To that extent, all critical thinking has to engage with "exile" in the form of what Jacques Derrida has described as "the double session." Exile as political lack or alienation has to be resisted, corrected, and rehabilitated, even as exile as point of view has to be cultivated rigorously in critical opposition to all identity regimes. Clearly, Said could be faulted here for intellectualizing the condition of exile prematurely, a little too pre-cociously. On whose behalf is Said valorizing the perspective of exile, and with whose permission? Is it also possible that behind Said's impassioned endorsement of the exilic condition, there lurks a romantic notion of the dissenting individual who excels in always being at superior odds with the people, with any form of enforced or formulaic collectivity. Said himself would hardly see this as a problem since he never was a spontaneous pop-ulist; in fact, in his world, the reality of the people requires representation of the intellectual, just as, reciprocally, the articulations of the intellectual need to be in an organic relationship with the people. For Said, the indi-vidual does not violate the legitimacy of the "we," just as the intellectual does not misrepresent the commonsensical knowledge of the laity. Under these conditions, exile functions as a critical-utopian potential that can be dreamed of by the intellectual in the name of the people. In other words, one can be a people and yet remain committed to the exilic perspective.

humanism   Every great scholar in the humanities is somehow implicated in that vast "-ism" called humanism, and Said is no exception. The great debates about humanism have focused on issues such as the following: Is humanism a **theory** or a practice? Is it a philosophically innocent concept or is it a political ideology? Is the "human" in humanism natural, or is it the fabrication of specific discursive regimes? Is humanism all good; or is it a mixture of good and bad? Is humanism in the ultimate analysis a celebration of anthropocentrism, or does it make room for something beyond the human? What is the connection between humanism and say, colonialism, imperialism, Afrocentrism, or Eurocentrism? Said's work, with its insistence on the human and on secular history, touches on most, if not all, of these fascinating and fraught aspects of humanism. As a human being (the "human" in the being), and as a gifted and brilliant scholar of the humanities (the "human" in a more specialized, scholarly, and textual setting), Said is probing the ways in which the human announces and makes its signature through cultural and literary **texts**. It has become a platitude to say that we in the humanities are students of humanistic thought. But what does that actually mean? Said's work is of great interest and use here. Whether he is interpreting Bach, or Yeats, or **Conrad**, or Jane Austen, he is always dealing not just with texts or their stylistic or aesthetic disposition, but also with the ways in which each text speaks for the human accountably, intentionally, and historically. To Said humanism is not a monolithic "-ism" that commands us as an oppressive and transcendent commandment.

A Said Dictionary, First Edition. R. Radhakrishnan.
© 2012 John Wiley & Sons, Ltd. Published 2012 by John Wiley & Sons, Ltd.

Instead humanism is both our horizon and the ongoing effect and function of what we as human beings do and achieve and establish through our culture and music and literature.

To a well-educated lay person, a term like "humanism" would sound quite transparent, innocent, good, and positive. At any rate, it would not sound so fraught and controversial as it does in the academic circle of the humanities. After all, humanism is cognate with such other terms as "human," "humane," and "humanitarian." How could humanism, then, denote or connote anything bad, evil, or politically and theoretically reprehensible? What is all the excitement about post-humanism and the denaturalization of the human into "the human"? Within the Western philosophical tradition (that is, not including Hindu or Arabic or Islamic humanisms), structuralism initiated the critical-theoretical assault on humanism and its safe and complacent anchorage in theology, metaphysics, or a phenomenology that privileges subjectivity and consciousness in the name of the human. There was the Barthesian celebration of the "death of the author," to be followed by Foucault's radical re-recognition of the author not as being or intending person but as "function," and Althusser's thorough calling into question the bad faith of a humanism that will not look at its own faults and biases critically, that is, a humanism that will not acknowledge the fact that it is an ideological construct and not just a form of natural piety or goodness. Even prior to the advent of structuralism as a putative rupture in the Western philosophical or metaphysical tradition, Martin Heidegger had penned his influential essay, "Letter on Humanism," in vigorous refutation of Sartrean existentialism that had reduced Being or *Dasein* to the merely human and its anthropocentric biases. By the time we come to full-fledged poststructuralism, the battle lines are clearly drawn between the "givens" of humanism and the contingencies of theory.

To add to all this complexity, there is also the question regarding the "occidental" origin of humanism and the travel of a Eurocentric humanism, by way of colonialism and colonial modernity, to Africa and Asia and the magnificent projects of decolonization taking place there. We have the plangent voice of a Frantz Fanon stretching his black body towards "a new humanism" powered by a radical politico-economic overhauling of the regime of Colonialism and its ugly Us–Them binarism. There are the old humanists, the new humanists, the anti-humanists, and the post-humanists. The critique of humanism is at least two-pronged: there is the structuralist demystification of Western humanism from within the West, and there is a world-historical showing up of humanism as nothing more than a repressive universalism that has paraded itself as colonialism, patriarchy, sexism, misogyny, heterosexual normativity, and so on. In other words, humanism has been recognized deconstructively as the *longue durée* that has authorized an entire range of repressive historical and political regimes in the name of a dominant **representation**. So, a decision has to be made. If the historical performance of humanism has been far from innocent, then, is it feasible and/or defensible to seek and separate and eventually cultivate and sustain a "good humanism," all the while avoiding and keeping at bay a "bad humanism"? Or would it be nobler and more valiant to totalize humanism and understand it symptomatically as an indivisible structure, and *ergo* abjure it absolutely in the name of the theoretically post-human? There is another trajectory to this ongoing controversy, one that does not engage Said's critical attention all that much, and that has to do with the very ontological measure of the human and its relationship to Nature, deep ecology, and planetary and non-human reality.

Humanism is a theme that pervaded Said's entire critical career, and with the posthumous publication of *Humanism and Democratic Criticism* Said makes it unequivocally clear as to where he stands in the debate on humanism. Said is indeed a humanist, but a self-reflexive humanist who believes that humanism can be rectified and transcended in the name of humanism itself. There is no need, as far as Said is concerned, to call for a total theoretical break from humanism. On the contrary, Said makes rich use of this polemical opportunity to settle scores with high theory. Said's pragmatic point of view is that humanism is nothing more than what it does and has done; and sure enough, the history of humanism has been far from meritorious or blemish-free. Rather than essentialize humanism or read it as a total structure that is condemned to repeat itself, Said understands humanism historically, that is, as a mix of the good, the bad, and the ugly. Said is not too far from echoing Hamlet's statement that "there is nothing either good or bad, but thinking makes it so." The important thing to notice here is that, within this understanding, thinking is vested with an authorial power and voice that is constitutive and agentive, rather than merely passive or symptomatic. Said's problem is not with the structuralist thesis that the human itself can only be a construct, for such a position is not all that different from Said's own notion of the "secular," a notion that will have nothing to do with essentialism that naturalizes the human and in the process quarantines it against contamination by genealogical or historical analysis, critique, and reflection.

Said's disillusionment with structuralism is quite specific, and not just generally theoretical. Taking sides with historians such as Hobsbawm and Anderson and cultural critics and theorists such as Raymond Williams and Stuart Hall, Said would argue that structuralism, in its endeavor to confer intelligibility on history, had thrown the baby out with the bath water. Structure, or structuralism, explains history away rather than explaining it in a historically contingent manner. The lines get drawn as History versus Theory/Structuralism. Structure, in Said's analysis, opts out of the circumstantiality of history and takes up a systemically omniscient stance *vis-à-vis* the goings-on of the world. The massive and monolithic temporality of structure occludes the multiple and eternally changing pulsations of lived life. Rather than take up its function as an instrument or as an analytic category, structure precipitates itself as its own ontology and takes the place of life itself. Whereas a radical high theorist such as Althusser argues with the utmost confidence that the "human as such" would have be demystified by theory, that is, the human is itself in the way and is therefore an obstacle to be dismantled as a necessary prolegomenon for a scientific production of knowledge, Said travels in exactly the opposite direction. To him, the very notion of theory demystifying life in the name of theoretical or scientific knowledge would smack of intellectual *hubris* and an unbridled professional arrogance. On a practical level, Said finds it annoying that high theorists, in the name of theory, do nothing at all to change or influence the world we live in. What they do instead is practice a politics of so-called purity, for fear of complicity with the real world and its contaminated state of affairs. Theorists take delight in enjoying their symptom of immobility and agentive paralysis, a state of affairs brought about by something called one's own inevitable and chronic structuredness. From Said's pragmatic perspective, the fact that the "human" is a construct does not result in the delegitimation of the human power and intention to act intentionally and agentively. Said would argue that the transcendent power that theory enjoys is neither natural nor empirical: it is a power created for theory by the theorists themselves for fear of entanglement in the **worldliness** of the world.

To Said humanism is a practice, a set of tools to be used, and not a philosophy. Said is utterly confident that human endeavor, commitment, and conviction can drive humanism in the right direction and in correction of its many errors and bad ways in history. He never overlooks or condones the fact that humanism has paraded itself in the forms of Eurocentrism, Colonial modernity, and so on. His contention is plain and simple: it is possible to practice a progressive and "good" humanism in the name of humanism itself, that is, without having to overhaul all of humanism through a radical theoretical critique. Said's impassioned advocacy of humanism against its bad self bears interesting resemblances with Fanon's agonized call for a new humanism and with Derridean deconstruction: and this is also a way of saying that the resemblances are limited. Fanon is a philosophical as well as a psychoanalytic thinker, who situates humanism in a double context: in history, as well as in metaphysical philosophical thought. Writing as he does from the heat and the heart of colonized agony, Fanon expresses a visceral hatred of European thought and pretense even as he avails of Hegel, Lacan, Freud, and Sartre. He is not as contrapuntally tolerant of the West as is Said. He is also more rigorous in pointing out that the humanism to come is inevitably compromised by its present historical predicament, namely, colonialism. There is no room or scope for transcendent posturing in Fanon in the name of humanism: the kind of benign posturing that takes place in E.M. Forster's *A Passage to India*. The political is too much with us and the truly human can only be realized as the function of a thorough political defeat of colonialism. The human has been besmirched and alienated from its true self by the history of colonialism and its vicious colonizer–colonized, master–slave divide. The true essence of the human, whether or not we use the term "essence" in an essentialist mode, has to be brought about by means of a radical, absolute, and uncompromising destruction of all structures of colonialism. This new humanism will be of a global and universal scale, and for Fanon, it will be spoken for by a postcolonial **nationalism** that will have connected with the peoples of Africa and Asia, the erstwhile colonized populations of the world. Clearly, Said does not entertain any such optimistic hopes on behalf of any kind of nationalism, not even the postcolonial kind.

Strange as it may sound, Said's belief in a critique of humanism in the name of humanism and his consequent non-belief in a theoretical break is quite similar to Derrida's famous declaration that there is no way to break out of the historical book known as logocentrism. One can at best, even as one is situated in it, turn the pages of that book in a certain way, indicating deconstructive dissent. Throughout his career, Derrida has remained scornful of "break theorists" and their lack of maturity. The difference between Derrida and Said is a matter of training as well as of academic temperament. The only tradition that Derrida works from is the Western metaphysical tradition, and any "politics" that can be attributed to Derrida can only be an offshoot, a by-product, or a corollary of his philosophical reading of Western philosophical texts. Said, on the other hand, despite his scholarly credentials in the domain of theory and philosophy, is not a philosophical thinker. It is interesting that in his book on humanism Said does indeed acknowledge the relevance as well as the rectitude of Martin Heidegger's symptomatic reading of humanism as a metaphysical statement of human essence (Heidegger is making his polemical claim in opposition to Jean-Paul Sartre's humanistic existentialism); and yet goes on with his political endorsement of humanistic practice. It is as though the Heideggerian critique does not matter, despite its rightness and relevance. Said just chooses to put philosophy in its place, refusing to grant philosophy anything more than a passing nod and a purely academic awareness.

Said's pragmatism makes us rethink what "theory" is all about. Is theory just another fancy name for what used to be called philosophy or philosophical thinking? If that is all it is, then it would seem perfectly reasonable to call its bluff and keep going ahead. Once the critic holds on to philosophy as a necessary and chronic burden or baggage, then philosophy is bound to haunt every human activity and endeavor with its superior mystification. To Said, a phenomenology controlled by philosophy, which is but another name for theory, is a phenomenology of mis-recognition. The world and the worlding of the world is happening elsewhere, and not within the precious cogitations of philosophy. It is in this spirit that Said chooses, rather than understanding individual choice itself as a predetermined linguistic or discursive condition, to think of humanism as a set of varied and contradictory human practices in secular history rather than as a lexical entry within the dictionary of philosophy. Said too, like Guha, the eminent South Asian subaltern historian, values that way of living and thinking, that temporality that eludes disciplinary determination. Guha, for example, bemoans the fact that "the existential and the epistemological do not tangle" any more within the aegis of discursive or disciplinary history; and that precisely is why Guha looks for the genuine pulsation of history not within the pronouncements of official and disciplinary historiography but elsewhere. Said's critical consciousness too locates and cherishes the "human" and its variable history neither in philosophical discourse nor in the dense and daunting jargon of professional specialization, but in that active, creative, and intentional realm between culture and system, between the world as text and the text as world.

intellectual, the   It is interesting that at a time when high **theory** and high theorists have retired the category of the intellectual as outmoded and even oppressive, Edward Said reclaims that category, and the sense of functional agency that goes with it, with great verve and a sense of urgency. High theory's opposition to the figure of the intellectual is covalent with its antagonism to the theme of **representation**. "Representation no longer exists," proclaimed Gilles Deleuze and Foucault in unison as they de-celebrated the intellectual, diagnosing her as part of the problem and not the solution. The intellectual, based on his putative superior awareness and erudition, presumes to speak for the people, and such a "speaking for" is invasive and coercive since the people in our time and age know how to speak for themselves and hardly require representation by the intellectual. The intellectual, from this point of view, appears as a presumptuous and elitist form of so-called universal consciousness that arrogates to itself the function of speaking for the populace, the so-called ordinary people. There are two interrelated issues here: one, the representation of "collectivity" by an individual; and the representation of "lay" or "commonsensical" intelligence by intellectual expertise or specialization.

High theory's critique of "representation" is staged on both registers; and, what is more, theory seeks to undermine the epistemological claims of representation. In other words, high theory advances the thesis that the procedure or the apparatus known as representation is incapable of delivering the goods. Truth or knowledge is no longer captive to the regime of

A Said Dictionary, First Edition. R. Radhakrishnan.
© 2012 John Wiley & Sons, Ltd. Published 2012 by John Wiley & Sons, Ltd.

representation: that is, truth or knowledge cannot be "spoken for" in the good old humanist fashion. For the most part, high theory dwells in the realms of post-representation, where the role of the intellectual has shrunk to one of **professional** expertise. The intellectual is no longer "organic" to society, in Antonio Gramsci's sense of the term; instead we now have, *à la* Michel Foucault, the category of the specific intellectual whose contributions to society and the world at large are specific to her location. The specific intellectual is not organic, that is, she does not represent, by way of organic politico-ideological connectedness, any society; nor is she a public intellectual capable of broadcasting messages to the world at large from her specific professional location. The specific intellectual is an expert, professional producer of knowledge, a micro-practitioner of methodology whose concerns have nothing to do with large, macro-political issues such as freedom, justice, equality, decolonization, emancipation, and so on. The specific intellectual, by very definition and professional disposition, cannot be aligned with the public, the populace at large. While Antonio Gramsci famously declared that while all human beings are intellectuals, some of us become professional intellectuals by virtue of our special aptitudes and training, and in doing so still remain in a relationship of organic representation to our populist constituency, Foucault and Deleuze are happy to de-link professionalism from worldly practice.

It is precisely in this context that Edward Said makes his important **humanist** intervention. Like Marx who believed that there do exist people who are in need of representation, like Du Bois who articulated his thesis of the intellectual as "the talented tenth," and of course Gramsci who endorsed the intellectual as a leader of the people not because he wanted to perpetuate the leader–led divide, the same Gramsci who envisions the intellectual as the "permanent persuader," Said reinvigorates the category of the intellectual against the seductions of a mercenary professionalism. A mercenary professional is one who just does her job. Rather than profess a value, a point of view, a certain way of being and acting in the world, that is, rather than "profess" in the strong moral and political sense of the term, the professional degenerates into a mere practitioner, *sans* value, *sans* commitment, *sans* **worldliness**. Said insists, contrary to those high theorists influenced by poststructuralism, that the intellectual ought to represent and stand for certain values and positions and choices, and in the process occupy a public position.

It is not a coincidence that Said's 1993 BBC Reith lectures were entitled "Representations of the Intellectual." The intellectual has the obligation to speak for and speak to the world. Said's agenda for the intellectual is quite simple: use knowledge in the name of the world rather than use knowledge as an excuse for not dealing with the world. Said's position here reminds us of the famous lines in *Hamlet*: "There are more things in heaven and earth, Horatio, / Than are dreamt of in your philosophy." Said does not ever, in the name of transparency or simplicity, deny the fact that the intellectual needs to build models and systems of thought and interpretation to make sense of the world. His point is that the professional intellectual is too often prone to misrecognize the model for the world, the system for the living reality. It is in the name of the world and its worldliness that professional intellectualism should be practiced and not the other way around. It may well be that in rendering the world or reality readable and intelligible, the intellectual is textualizing or making a **text** of the world, but that is no reason to proclaim, *à la* Jacques Derrida, that "there is nothing outside the text." The text cannot be its own auto-telic (a phrase used by none other than T.S. Eliot) object; nor should the reader, the democratic citizen, buy into the mystical belief that the text is all that there is, and that the world is no more and no less than a reality effect or textual function brought into being by the erudition and the scholarly prowess of the professional intellectual. Said shrewdly reads a complicitous relationship between the so-called "linguistic turn" and the hegemonic ascendancy of the professional intellectual in the humanities. The literary critic may have a relationship to language that is more specialized and nuanced than that of the lay reader, but this does not mean that to the critic language has become a world of its own and has taken the place of reality itself. What should matter, both to the lay and the expert reader, are the ways in which the world or reality is mediated by the text. Indeed, it is quite likely and even desirable that the expert reader may, by virtue of training and erudition, know more about this formal process of mediation than the non-expert reader who could be satisfied with the mere "what" or the paraphrasable content of the communication. But this business of "knowing more," or knowing in a more complex way, according to Said, should not justify the maintenance of an elite class or a secret guild that does not see itself as accountable to the public at large.

In his formulation of the intellectual, Said imbues the expert with a pedagogical dimension. The expert is also a teacher who is deeply committed to sharing and disseminating her precious insights with the public at large in a language that is readable by all. In a democracy where "the all," and not just "the few," matter, the intellectual, despite her professional credentials and baggage, has the obligation to remain public and communicate her finer understanding of phenomena to the world at large. It is in the name of the world at large that even the meticulous nuances of specialized scholarship are validated and endorsed. In representing the meaning of the text, the intellectual is also representing that meaning to the people, and envisioning herself as a representative.

The finer point that Said is making here is that there are always worldly connections, based on politics, ideas, values, ideology, power, privilege, and so on, between the world of the text and the world at large. These organic connections are forgotten or they are occluded when specialist knowledge begins to certify and credential itself exclusively within the classroom or the laboratory. In this entire polemic, Said is at great pains not to let the world of letters and scholarship off the hook in the name of the beautiful and immaculate ivory tower. As he demonstrates in his famous analysis of the example of the Beethoven-loving State Department official who had ordered the bombing of a small and powerless "enemy country," the world of literary value cannot be used to exculpate horrors and injustice in real life. Literature is neither an alibi for real life, nor a device of ideal purity that launders away our implication in the good and bad of real life. The mandate of the intellectual, Said would argue, is to live in that dynamic and volatile continuum that connects culture/literature to the world. It is up to the intellectual, then, to demonstrate the worldliness of the realm of culture and literature. The intellectual is in an intense and accountable relationship of representation, of "speaking for," with the world: a role that is further enhanced and intensified by her relationship to the world of the text. It is only appropriate that one of Said's most influential books has the title *The World, the Text, and the Critic*. For Said, the two terms "intellectual" and "critic" are almost synonymous and mutually exchangeable.

Said signifies the word "public" in the term "public intellectual" two ways: the intellectual in her capacity as intellectual should have something worthwhile and valuable to say about issues that are public and macro-political (thinkers and philosophers like Noam Chomsky, Howard Zinn, bell hooks, Du Bois, Cornel West, Arundhati Roy, Jean-Paul Sartre, and Bertrand Russell come to mind), and secondly, she should be addressing the public at large in a language that is not hermetic, esoteric, and calculated to alienate the "many." The intellectual herself should function, perform, advocate, and hold forth as a "representative" voice and advance and offer to the public at large "representations" of truth. Every now and then, *a fortiori*, Said would make a loaded reference to the title of Julien Benda's work on intellectuals and intellectuality, *La trahisons des clercs*, to point up the theme of loyalty and treason, solidarity and critique, disinterested and Olympian objectivity, and rigorous and scrupulous partisanship. A number of questions arise. Who, then, is an intellectual? Where and to whom does she belong? Is the intellectual a loner and a soloist or a team player? Is the intellectual a protagonistic or an antagonistic (**oppositional**) figure? In the name of what value or *a priori* principle does the intellectual speak? What does the term "truth" mean to the intellectual, and when the intellectual speaks the truth, who is the interlocutor? To whom is the truth addressed? ("Intellectuals in the Post-Colonial World"; "Representing the Colonized").

Edward Said's classic coordination of the intellectual opens up the "**between**" between Culture and System. Operating much in the Socratic mode of the intellectual as a responsible gadfly who will refuse the seductive comforts of dogma and orthodoxy, of received truths and mystical illuminations on the one hand, and the complacent security of formulaic knowledges, pre-packaged answers, shabby quick-fixes, and ideologically foregone resolutions on the other, the Saidian intellectual is a critical-utopian individual consciousness that seeks to find a home in critical homelessness, that is, to realize the critique as a form of solidarity and historicize solidarity as a form of critical belonging. One of Said's mottos was: no solidarity before critique. To belong in an obediently filiative manner to one's given or "born" constituency, or to practice in a docile and exemplary manner the methodology that one has learned professionally, is not a hallmark of excellence in Said's grade book. To question the natural pieties and rectitudes of filiation in the name of an oppositional-secular **affiliation**, and to practice critical consciousness outside the box of professionalism: that would earn high marks from Said. In Said's world, the intellectual as critic is a "maverick" figure, if we can even use that term positively after Sarah Palin's grotesque misappropriation of it: maverick, but not a rebel without a cause. In Said's lexicon, the intellectual as individual can and ought to share a cause with the populace at large, but such an organic sharing does not result in an undifferentiated or a natural and un-self-reflexive belonging with the group. The "I" certainly has no density without the "We," and at the same time the "We" is not a form of an *a priori* given that automatically possesses or subsumes the "I." Said is as keen to protect the individual from forms of authoritarian collectivization as he is to indemnify the intellectual against spontaneous, natal, and nativist forms of truth and knowledge.

Recalling to mind the Greek notion of *parrhesia*, written about by Michel Foucault, Said implicates the public intellectual in the project of uttering uncomfortable and unpalatable truths against Power, against dominance, against hegemony, against regnant regimes, whatever their nature or pedigree. The Saidian public intellectual is hamstrung by multiple complicities: the state, corporations, capital, professional guilds, and the like. There is a great temptation to play it easy, play it safe, go with the grain, and not challenge the orthodoxies of state, culture, identity, religion, and so on. An American intellectual is constrained, by the orthodoxy of **nationalism**, to come up with nothing but American truths. A Marxist will stay within Marxist parameters. A so-called "free world" intellectual is so brainwashed by capitalism that he does not even recognize capitalism as an ideology. A Hindu will be seeking Hindu truths and a Muslim will be committed to the pursuit of Islamic truths. Truths become fiercely identitarian, narrow, provincial, parochial, jingoist, bigoted, xenophobic, and so on. The pursuit of knowledge and truth turns into tame forms of acquiescence in the status quo, and the intellectual turns into an apologist for business as usual, or turns into a paranoid practitioner of his petty truth.

In the final analysis, for Said, the public intellectual is also the oppositional intellectual who refuses to come home to any final truth. Servant of no regime, puppet of no orthodoxy, the predictable practitioner of no "-ism" or methodology, the official supporter of no ideology or faith, the proponent of no manifesto that is anchored in its own inviolable positivity, the intellectual is the "permanent persuader" (Gramsci) who is not afraid to resist all and every form of seduction by Power in all its myriad manifestations: political, corporate, institutional, national, religious, and sacred.

linguicity   This is a rare example of a word coined by Said. Linguicity has to do with the intrinsic property of language. What is language and what does it do? What is the relationship of human beings to language? Is there an essence to language, or is language no more and no less than what it does? Who or what makes a language do something? Said is particularly interested in elaborating the relationship between intentionality and language. Can intentionality be conceived of something pre-linguistic, or is intentionality nothing but a linguistic effect? Said's formulation of 'linguicity" is a critical response to what he sees as the linguistic excesses of structuralism and poststructuralism. Thanks to Ferdinand de Saussure and the work of the structuralists, the "linguistic turn," both in the human sciences and the humanities, had been made axiomatic. From then on, language was to be seen not just as a reflection or as a mediation of reality, but as constitutive of reality. Not only was language the signifier of meaning and reality, but now the "signified" or the "referent" itself was brought within the semantic as well as formal jurisdiction of language. Literally, there is and there can be "nothing outside the **text**," whereby textuality, or the condition of being characterizable as a text, is the chief guarantor of meaning and meaningworthiness. After the radical linguistic turn, which could be read critically as the inflation of language or as a total usurpation of meaning by linguistic formalism, nothing would ever be the same again. Reality itself had to be validated as a text, that is, as a linguistic construct. If, prior to the linguistic turn, language could be dealt with and maintained in its place as

A Said Dictionary, First Edition. R. Radhakrishnan.

© 2012 John Wiley & Sons, Ltd. Published 2012 by John Wiley & Sons, Ltd.

mere instrumentality, now, after the "turn," language had become, in one *coup*, both ontological and epistemological, both reality and the knowledge of such a reality. In other words, language was both its own "being" and "knowing." A particularly radical example of the structuralist preemption of conventional meaning is that much-cited linguistic analysis of a Baudelaire poem by Lévi-Strauss and Jacobsen where they relentlessly break down the language of the poem into its syntactic, phonemic, phonetic, phonological, graphemic, and constituent parts without once raising the question of the "meaning" of the poem. Archibald MacLeish would say in his own way that a poem does not mean, but is, with the same intention of upping the ante on behalf of form or structure as against simple or paraphrasable meaning. Meaning in its conventional sense had almost become an uninteresting by-product of the performance of language ("Abecedarium Culturae"; "The Totalitarianism of Mind"; "What Is Beyond Formalism?").

To put it somewhat provocatively, language had de-naturalized the Real into a mere construct. It was around this time that the vogue began of using the famous quotation mark sign around even the most self-evident and commonsensical terms such as "life," "reality," "experience," "the self," "meaning," and so on, to suggest that all the pious and innocent "realities" that we had believed in as primordial, natural, and un- or pre-constructed were indeed no more than constructs, linguistic effects. (A hilarious deployment of this behavior takes place in a scene from the highly popular American sitcom *Friends* where Joey, the least literate of the six central characters, in a disastrous endeavor to display his erudition, begins to bracket innocuous everyday words like "and" and "or.") By this time, Roland Barthes, in solidarity with Alain Robbe-Grillet of the *nouveau roman*, had proved that "the heart of the matter was dead," and made the alarming diagnosis of "the death of the author." Michel Foucault would write his anti- or post-humanist essay, "What is an Author?" Both Barthes and Foucault, each in his own way, would contend that the realities that we assume as natural are in fact functions and constructs of impersonal and trans-personal systems and structures. To be an author is to perform the function of an author within a circulatory system of production, reception, exchange, and distribution. The older notion of the author as someone who wields language powerfully and unilaterally is replaced by a different worldview where the author is no more than the description of certain functions and tasks.

The critical target of the structuralist enterprise was phenomenology; and the indirect object of ridicule was a novel like Jean-Paul Sartre's *Nausea* where Roquentin, the protagonist, experiences violent nausea precisely during those moments and conjunctures when words fail to connect with things in a meaningful way. The structuralist response to Roquentin was: What an idiot, to be looking for that kind of a union between words and things! Did he not know that language is just a convention? The structuralist is happy with the thought that there is no essential connection between reality and language. All we have is the convention known as language, and there is nothing beyond or outside language. The author may well have an intention, but this very intention is intelligible only as an effect of language, and not as an external force or energy that drives and commands language.

In one of his brilliant early essays, "Abecedarium Culturae" (reproduced as one of the chapters of his book, *Beginnings: Intention and Method*), Said makes his position about language and "linguicity" very clear ("Criticism Between Culture and System," in *The World, the Text and the Critic*; "Roads Taken and Not Taken"). As a lover and aesthete of language, Said has no problem with the thesis that language is constitutive, and not merely reflective, of reality. What bothers him, however, are the social implications and consequences of such a theory. Said contends that structuralism and poststructuralism push "linguacentricity" too far and in the process mute or neutralize the socio-historical dimensions of the linguistic constitution of reality. (Said would be quite approving, for example, of Bakhtin, Medvedev, and Voloshinov who share the Saussurean view of the linguistic turn but develop it differently towards a socially dialectic theory of language.) Said is happy to be functioning and thinking like a language-centric theorist, but Said is keen to take language elsewhere than to the predictable poststructuralist terminus of text and textuality. We can perceive Said reading structuralism and poststructuralism diagnostically, against the grain. Even as he acknowledges the gains made by structuralism in the business of producing knowledge and patterns of intelligibility, Said refuses to be an obedient card-carrying structuralist. He is not an all-or-nothing proponent of structuralism. There are aspects of structuralism that he is for, and there are other aspects that he is against. It is a hallmark of Said's critical intelligence that in all his dealings with philosophies, schools of thought, doctrines, and well-established "-isms," that he reserves for himself the right to be selective and eclectic. He sees no virtue or advantage in accepting or rejecting "-isms" *tout court*.

It is fascinating to watch Said attempt to hoist structuralism with its own petard: his claim is that in the name of demystifying earlier forms of essentialism and **centrism**, structuralism has perpetrated its own particular form of centricity. In assuming that reality has nowhere to go but to language for its meaning, structuralism has ended up, to use the fashionable and yet useful jargon, totalizing itself and its claim on reality. In other words, in pretending to be transparent to itself, structuralism fails to notice that it has given birth, consciously or unconsciously, advertently or inadvertently, to its own indisputable essence or form of authority, that is, "linguicity." Linguicity is structuralism's own political and ideological unconscious. Said has no issue with the structuralist procedure of textualizing reality so that reality may be rendered readable; the problem is with the structuralist overstatement (hypostasis, if you will, a transformation by virtue of which a form of knowing is essentialized and deified as the very object of knowledge) of a form of practice, that is, reading, as a theory of reality in and by itself. Linguicity turns structuralism into a totalitarian system that admits of no outsides, no alternatives to the transparency of structure. Said's use of the adjective "totalitarian" is far from dramatic, for he literally means that the system turns repressive and rules out options and possibilities that are not "always already" part of the structure. Structuralist readings become exercises in the status quo, and structure hardens into a form of *a priori* against which no intentional or agential meaning can be launched, or even conceived. Structure becomes a prison-house and human intentions languish in servitude to the authority of structure ("The Problem of Textuality").

First and foremost, Said is at pains to establish how "linguicity" functions as a form of ideological mystification. Linguicity officially sanctions a certain blindness whereby the structuralist is allowed to overlook certain pre-existing realities. The structuralist is permitted to believe in the rectitude of structure even if that structure misreads a world that antedates the temporality of structure. Reductive in its operational will, structure is content to stay in a realm where it is assumed that there exists a harmonious and reliable "mirror relationship" between structure and its object, as though "there exists a prior existence of clarity and exchange." Myths become crucial analytic categories in the structuralist endeavor to read "the real" into "the intelligible." Innocent as it may sound, such a venture is indeed ideologically virulent. In direct complicity with anthropology, with its binary emphasis on Us and Them, Self and Other, the native and the researcher, structuralism imposes its meaning on reality unilaterally, much in the mode of a colonizing master. What Said is focusing critically on is the tendency of structuralism to reduce reality into ahistorical binary structures. In this respect, Said has a lot in common with critics and historians such as Raymond Williams, E.P. Thompson, Richard Hoggart, Perry Anderson, and others in Britain who had argued strongly for the poverty of structuralism, and indicted structuralism for blithely throwing out the baby with the bath water, for having explained history away in the name of elucidating history.

In the final analysis, what bothers Said about linguicity is the fact that it renders structure a *fait accompli*. Structure is a done deal; it is always already there as its own cause and explanation, always fully formed and always there, but never available for analysis as a contingent historical process prone as much to failure and incompletion as to success and completion. Structuralist-Marxism, certainly, deals precisely with these issues: ideology and structure, structure and the unconscious, diagnostic and symptomatic readings of structure (Louis Althusser and Pierre Macherey), but Said is not persuaded by Althusser and his followers who, in his reading, continue to be ahistorical in their addiction to structure. It is also true that linguistic analysis makes distinctions between synchronic (a slice of time at a given moment) and diachronic (the study of a phenomenon over a period of time) modes of analysis; and between language as *la langue* (as a system of rules and regulations) and *la parole* (language as used by actual speakers with variations such as accent, dialects, idiolects, and so on). And yet, Said's contention would be that the linguistic model, despite variations, still functions not in the name of worldly reality, but with reference to its own internal coherence.

Said also draws our attention to the difference between a benign politics of transcription and an active politics of translation. Translation involves individual choices, recognitions and misrecognitions, the going awry of as well as the reliable rendition of intentions and intentionality. According to the transcription model, all that the structuralist reader does is innocently to transcribe, without any friction or complication, reality into intelligibility. It is equally significant that he associates structuralism with the rhetoric of justification whereby structure is assumed to be equal and equivalent with reality, whereas in fact and in history reality is far from equitable or just, and is on the contrary structured in dominance. Structure becomes the be all and the end all, the *summum bonum* of all that is, as though what is not covered by structure is not part of reality. Historical traces, contested and contradictory memories, unequal and asymmetrical struggles, complicatedly overlapping and intersecting narratives are flattened out in the name of the universality as well the universal intelligibility of structure and its essential "lingua-centricity."

narrative This is a crucial category for Said, who preferred to work almost exclusively with the novel form. Narratives, from Said's perspective, are nothing if not secular. They are of this world and partake of the condition of human historicity. It is not a coincidence that a worldly critic like Said puts so much emphasis on narrative both as a process of worlding and meaning making and as a general trope for the human condition. Narratives as contingent and vulnerable performances produce meaning as a function of the act of story telling. Each narrative creates its subject as it goes along, circumstantially, and in response to the many other narratives that occupy the same field. The commitment to narrative is also a commitment to the plurality as well as the interconnectedness of many narratives. When different narratives come together in acknowledgment of their mutual connectivity, and this coming together could be harmonious or antagonistic, symmetrical or asymmetrical, even or uneven, possibilities emerge towards the imagining of a new and a more inclusive and a more egalitarian world based on a genuinely negotiated multilateralism. Narrative is not guaranteed any kind of teleological resolution. In many ways it is the direct and exact opposite of the immaculate conception or of the concept of incarnation. Identities, entities, and subjects are constituted in, by, and through narration. There is no *a priori* subject (divine, providential, messianic, metaphysical, or trans-historical) that steers the narrative from a position of mastery.

A Said Dictionary, First Edition. R. Radhakrishnan.
© 2012 John Wiley & Sons, Ltd. Published 2012 by John Wiley & Sons, Ltd.

In a similar fashion, the lessons to be learned from the narrative are the function of the narrative process. In other words, the narrative is not the mere instrumentalization of lessons or imperatives that are already available as concepts, essences, warrants, or guarantees. Narrative plays a genealogical function. Just as he demonstrates in the context of "**beginnings**," here too Said points out that any narrative could have been otherwise. He does not deny the fact that narratives make strong truth claims, but these claims are contingent and not necessary. Narrative is a heuristic, a learning device that is not committed to an originary truth or a sacred *denouement*. It is in the realm of contingency and fallibility and in the realm of performative vulnerability and waywardness, rather than in the zone of pedagogical incorrigibility, that narrative makes and unmakes itself. Its authority is immanent and not transcendent.

Said loves to make distinctions between narratives that are self-conscious and frame themselves as narratives and those that do not. Said is interested in the errancy of narrative and its ability to capture and thematize this errancy rather than in narratives that refuse self-staging since they are too secure and complacent in their vaunted correctness: hence his everlasting interest in **Conrad** and Conrad's narrative strategies. Unlike Chinua Achebe who has no difficulty in arraigning Conrad of unequivocal Eurocentrism, Said cherishes the ambivalence and loss of certitude in Conrad's narratives. The narrating persona of Marlow is of unending critical interest to Said. Conrad may well be Eurocentric to start with; but what matters even more to Said is the fact that this centrism is perennially problematized and destabilized by narrative recursiveness. It is as though the primary solidarity of the narrative to its worldview, say, Eurocentrism, is submitted to a thorough internal critique. Thus Conrad, whose ethic is to make the reader "see," ends up with a vision of horror and darkness. This lesson of failure itself is the result of historical production. It is through critical self-staging that the narrative learns from its failure. Eurocentrism is both posited and rendered ineffective as a narrative strategy. This meta-aspect of narrative performs the function of critical **theory**. Of equal importance to Said is the notion of framing or presentation, a technique that prevents the truth from coinciding with itself. Said insists that narratives and narrations have a double content: the narrative is both a representation of some real or "exterior" content, but it is also about its own self-presentation. From Said's point of view, a narrative that is merely a representation of reality is methodologically, ideologically, and aesthetically suspect for the simple reason that such a narrative would be based on arrogance: a complacent assumption that the truth of reality would be automatically captured within its representational space. This would indeed be a dominant narrative that sees no scope for error or failure. To put it in parlance that would have been particularly palatable to Said, the world would have already "worlded" in mute accordance with the parameters of the narrative: no antagonisms, no contrapuntal resistance, no chance of loss of meaning, no possibility of a productive *mésalliance* between narrative as representation and narrative as self-presentation. An Indian presumes that the Indian story is the world's story, as does the American, the Frenchman, and so on, each on her own behalf.

In many ways, Said's position would seem to resemble certain salient motifs in postmodernism and poststructuralism: meta-fiction in postmodernism, and the category of "purloined meaning" memorably exemplified by Jacques Lacan in his seminar on Edgar Allan Poe's short story, "The Purloined Letter." But a lot more is at stake for Said than the mere subtleties of language or a fictional mold. For one thing, in Said's terms, narratives are in the world, and whether they are misdirected or not, whether they are successfully oriented or not, they enable the construction of specific worlds and worldviews. The meta-level **virtuosity** functions not like a rebel without a cause, but with real consequences. Unlike as in radical poststructuralist theory, errancy in the narrative does not empty the narrative of its ideological and historical consequences. To be misled by language has contrapuntal consequences. Errancy does not abrogate meaning or render it entirely indeterminate. Every narrative is open to correction by some other narrative, in the absence of absolute Truth.

How do narratives constitute themselves, and in response to what? In his strongly appreciative reading of the presentation of narrative in Conrad, Said makes two important claims. In Conrad's fiction, narrative is the locus where planned events and chance happen together. Rather than secure the narrative in its own safe worldview, Conrad's fiction dramatizes the antagonistic tension between the story's ethico-political and epistemological claims and the conditions of telling of the story. The effect is that narrative in Conrad remains simultaneously strong and vulnerable, structured as well as open to aleatory misdirection. Said's thesis is that the more virtuosic the writer, the less capable he is of securing his intention from mishaps and untoward departures and arrivals. The second reality is that in Conrad's fiction, narrative emanates from a speaking voice which in turn assumes or presumes an audience, a set of interlocutors, a community, that is, a world of sorts. The narrative performs two important functions: (i) it honors the individual voice, its accents, inflections, emphases, and investments, even as it posits that voice in relationship to a larger communal, socio-political, and historical context, and (ii) it functions both experientially/existentially and formally, which is to say that the speaking voice in its spontaneous and imaginative expressiveness is also a constructed and stylized performance. Narrative is realized by Said as that perennially negotiable site where the individual and the community, the I and the We, a "solidary" belonging to the community and the critique of the community, can be articulated together in an ongoing relationship of commitment and interrogation. Also, Said's formulation avoids a pernicious form of either/or: that the narrative has to be either pure voice or pure formal system. Narrative, in Said's reading, functions not as unmediated pure agency, but as agency that works it expressively and contingently through the rigor of system and structure. Structure/system does not preempt agency and intentionality in its own name, just as agency and intentionality do not instrumentalize and dominate structure unilaterally. Said in a way could be seen here to conform to what Michel Foucault, in his magisterial work *The Order of Things*, termed "the constituting-constituted" relationship between language and the human subject.

It is important for Said that narrative remain intensely worldly, but not acquiescently or incorrigibly worldly. To Said, "**worldliness**" is not a form of rectitude, political-aesthetic or otherwise, but instead it is a form of an ongoing creative relationality. Secular, human narratives constantly weave an unpredictable relationship between themselves and the world to which they belong. Narratives, to begin with, could well be Eurocentric, Afrocentric, Sinocentric, andro- or gyno-centric; but this does not mean that narratives carry the burden of their provenance as an unshakeable ideological straitjacket. In other words, narratives are not filially bound to where they come from. Quite to the contrary, secular narratives, unlike manifestations of essence or providential or exceptionalist or messianic narratives, begin with received histories, but only to re-read them, read them against the grain, and question their authority through internal critique, or in response to the truth claims of other and often antagonistic historical narratives. Said is always alive to the possibilities of counterpoint within one's narrative. The truths of history, then, are never self-evident; they are indeed the function of several narrative performances, not all of which are in agreement with one another's "givens." Truths as imaginative insights are constantly produced *between* histories, and not as properties of certain histories with prior sanctions and privileges. Narrative has the obligation to question received wisdom, even when the wisdom would seem to emanate from one's own people, nation, party, or theoretical creed.

To appreciate the importance of Said's insight, we only need to think of the violent ways in which nations and classes and ethnicities and identities enslave narrative production in their official names and prevent possibilities of antagonistic narration: such as "my country, right or wrong," "my people, right or wrong," "my gender, right or wrong," "my class, right or wrong," "my culture, right or wrong," and so on. Equally precious is Said's critical understanding that narratives, in the name of all humanity, are never single: by definition multiple, heterogeneous, and intransigent, narratives intersect and overlap in predictable and unpredictable ways. If, in a sense, all humanity is one and yet its very putative oneness is a function of myriad contradictory narratives, then the real problem is this: how can I talk about my history in your terms, and furthermore, how can I historicize myself in a manner that is not inimical to you? In a world-historical situation where, to quote from the always eloquent Salman Rushdie, "different realities have leaked into one another," how can narrative as a vital human function avoid the disastrous Samuel Huntingtonian vision of several "us-ses and thems" divided by chronic and non-negotiable civilizational differences? The spaces where narratives perform are neither "insider" nor "outsider" spaces. The spatiality of narratives forever confounds the differences between "intra-" and "inter," and promotes translations and conversions between insides and outsides, between intra-communal and inter-communal valences.

Finally, Said never takes narrative for granted. One of Said's moving phrases, in the context of the Palestinian people, is the phrase "permission to narrate." Some people are allowed the privilege of narration, and others are stifled even though they have legitimate and marvelous stories to tell. One of Edward Said's most poignant projects is the book he wrote in collaboration with the French photographer Jean Mohr, *After the Last Sky*: a book made up of narrative by Said and photographs by Jean Mohr that demonstrates, embodies, and instantiates the daily lives of hundreds of thousands of Palestinians under Israeli occupation. These are people who have not been allowed to document, chronicle, and narrativize their quotidian lives into public and national reality; and what this book achieves is a double articulation. These lives constitute a narrative in and by themselves, and indeed they do not need to do anything more to prove that they exist. And yet, since their lives are not heard as narratives by the state of Israel and by the international community at large, they do not exist as hegemonic narratives. Somewhere between presence and absence, between their real presence to themselves and their absence to the international community of hegemonic nations and nation states, these, like the subaltern voice, speak and do not speak. It is with the intention of liberating them from that limbo, and making them legitimate subjects of multilateral global recognition, that Said defends the Palestinian right to speak for itself, represent itself into existence. Narratives are perspectival embodiments, and perspectivism by definition does not foreclose dissent or critique. Said is not even vaguely suggesting that Palestinian narratives, just because they are Palestinian, constitute Palestinian truth. Quite to the contrary, the onus is on the narrative to produce its truth as simultaneously intellectual and populist. As is well known, Edward Said was as unsparing in his critique of the PLO and of Yasser Arafat as he was of **Zionism** and the Israeli state. In the final analysis, narratives are committed to the temporal and historical nature of reality. If from a commonsensical point of view, reality just seems to "be," as a done deal and a *fait accompli*, independent of the narrative will to meaning, Said's analysis demystifies such a worldview and points out that all realities are constituted by narratives ("Permission to Narrate").

nationalism   So, in the final balancing act, was Edward Said a nationalist who believed in the value of nationalism? Or was he a strategic nationalist in the special context of Palestine? He made no bones about his partisanship on behalf of the Palestinian state to come, he was a diasporic member of the Palestinian National Council; he has delivered innumerable lectures and composed thousands of words in support of the establishment of a Palestinian state ("Chomsky and the Question of Palestine"; "The Palestine Question and the American Context"). But he was also a deep cosmopolitan, someone in love with the notion of **exile**, of radical intellectual nonbelonging, who had nothing positive to say, intellectually, philosophically, or theoretically, about nationalism. Is his cosmopolitanism post-nationalist, trans-nationalist, or anti-nationalist? How is it possible for Said to function both as an indefatigable critic of nationalism (not unlike other thinkers such as Immanuel Wallerstein, Etienne Balibar, Rabindranath Tagore, and others) and as a selective supporter of nationalism in the name of the Palestinian people and their cause? Was he a hypocrite, an inconsistent thinker incapable of finding a moment of stillness, of equilibrium between the epistemology of nationalism and the politics of nationalism? Unlike postmodernists, globalists, trans-nationalists, post-nationalists, and diasporic detractors of nationalism, Said did not fear using the term "nationalism" over and over again in his work. He did not have to run away from the term to express his disillusionment with it; and at the same time he was not captive to it just because he used it all the time. It could be argued that much like Martin Heidegger or like Jacques Derrida, Said used the word "nationalism" *sous rature* (under erasure) to indicate a double attitude to the valences of the term. (Both Heidegger and Derrida use this strategy to express the following predicament. The older term is not useable any more, and yet, there is no need to create a new term or word ("neologism"). The better way is to use the older word and immediately cross it out so that both the word and its crossing out are seen together. The quarrel with the past is registered as a radical quarrel while at the same time the historical trace of the quarrel is maintained rather than obliterated. This strategy is similar to that of the "counter-memory" in Foucault. An amusing example of this is the house numbering rationale followed in certain parts of Chennai, India, where the same house will have both the old number and the new number as part of its address. Old No. 75, New No. 14 would be a typical address in certain neighborhoods in Chennai. The important thing to note is that this economy of recognizing places works much like a palimpsest that displays trace after trace of inscription and superscription without losing any of the traces of the scripts.)

What is indeed moving and persuasive about Said's stance *vis-à-vis* nationalism is the fact he is unafraid to be symptomatic. In other words, rather than pretend that he has a well-synchronized, unified, and monovalent theory of nationalism, he positions himself and his thought in the most glaring fissure of our times: the fissure called nationalism. Nationalism is too much with us even as nationalism has been shown up over and over again for its poverty, its hate-filled provincialism, its lack of tenability as a concept in the history of ideas. Rather than pose as a theoretical trans-nationalist in the context of the all too real nationalisms on the ground, rather than accept nationalism as a necessary evil and abandon other communitarian imaginings, Said locates his limited advocacy of Palestinian nationalism within a broader, shall we say, universal refutation of nationalist ideology and thought.

Historical and theoretical considerations intersect, albeit not harmoniously, in Said's meditations on the history, the nature, and the future of nationalism. Said is an astutely pragmatic thinker in whose thought the critical-utopian impulses of theoretical vision and the constraints of historical circumstance interrogate each other relentlessly. Said cannot pretend, in theory, that nationalism does not exist or that it is possible for a people, the Palestinian people, the only ones with a history and a reality but no state, to become historically hegemonic without also acquiring sovereign national statehood. Nationalism is all we have, even though the very thing that we have is indefensible theoretically speaking, objectionable for a variety of reasons, and historically tainted and culpable in all sorts of ways.

Without national belonging, without a passport, without citizenship and the privileges it entails, a people cannot be a people; and a person cannot be a person. Home and nation have been transfixed in forced reciprocity, and the very idea of home or being at home in the world without the armature of the nation state has been rendered utterly insubstantial. It is quite simple: you do not have a nationality, you do not have a legitimate home. The philosophical/metaphysical/ethical/spiritual/ontological idea of home requires political embodiment and shape, and the only political home of our times is the nation. In such a world-historical situation, the only way to deal honestly with the nation state is by way of a carefully cultivated critical ambivalence. The hegemony of the nationalism needs to be deconstructed from within: there are no pure theoretical breaks from the regime of nationalism.

As he acknowledges both the necessity and the fatal flaws of nationalism, Said submits nationalism not to a so-called universal gaze, but a decolonized, that is, **postcolonial** gaze. Rather than tamely capitulate to the disingenuous thesis that nationalism, along with colonial modernity, is a necessary stage on the way to the political production of Universal Reason through developmentalism, Said understands nationalism as a phenomenon that, in a world inherited from Colonialism and Imperialism, problematically connects the West with the Rest. It is customary to make a definitive distinction between colonizing nationalisms and decolonizing nationalisms. Nationalism in the colonized world is made up of two phases: the antagonistic or revolutionary phase when the colonized decolonize themselves by way of nationalism, and the protagonistic phase after decolonization, when the newly born postcolonial nation is expected to connect with its own people. What works as a revolutionary principle does not automatically work in the postcolonial context. The morning after independence often turns into the mourning after (a powerful example of this situation in postcolonial fiction is Ngugi wa Thiong'o's *A Grain of Wheat*), and the revolution turns into a counter-revolution for lack of clear principles of populist organization. Who are we now that we are decolonized? Have we automatically become a nation by virtue of having decolonized ourselves? What does it mean to be a nation on our own terms, without lapsing into the calamity of what Partha Chatterjee has memorably termed "derivative discourse," and how do we ratify ourselves? A thorny issue that Said completely overlooks, but one that haunts a number of postcolonial thinkers, is that the very term "nation" is not indigenous to the many cultures and peoples of Africa and Asia. Rabindranath Tagore would go so far as to say that "nation" is not a word in any of the Indian languages. Said's concern is slightly different, but equally valid. Nationalism turns into a form of uncritical smug insiderism: now that the colonizer has been thrown out we are okay, secure in our "essential" identities. Nationalism turns anti-secular and degenerates into nativism. Rather than inaugurate the transformative politics of **representation**, the nascent nation state becomes prey to identity politics. In a variety of third world contexts, a self-sanctioning nationalism takes an atavistic turn (a possibility of which Frantz Fanon is deeply apprehensive) and morphs into visceral tribalism. Either that, or nationalism is hijacked by fundamentalism and we end up with Islamic nationalisms and Hindu nationalisms ("Nationalism, Human Rights, and Interpretation").

The opposite of nationalism to Said is not globalization or ethnicity or trans-nationalism, but secularism. This is by no means a self-evident antagonism. So let us see how Said understands it. What Said is focusing on is not the mere descriptive dimension of words like nation, nationalism, and the people, but the normativity that lurks underneath the seemingly innocuous descriptions. Why is there such guilt-free ethnic cleansing? How does someone suddenly become the other, the scapegoat who has to be sacrificed, so that "we" may ratify ourselves as a tribal nation? The problem is not with collectivity as such, but rather with how collectivities are valorized and legitimated. What is the principle involved here that binds a people as a people? Is this normative principle an *a priori* and how did it become an *a priori*? Are the principles that are involved in people-production historical or trans-historical? The target of Said's critique here is religion and the fundamentalisms spawned by religion, its non-secular, other-wordly dynamic. It is unfortunate that Said does not devote much energy to discussing the relevance of religion to collective as well as individual existence. It seems to be a major flaw that Said does not develop a continuum where religion and the secular can stage their performances together toward the development of what we may term "universal rationality." It is also unfortunate that unlike, say, William Connolly, Charles Taylor, Talal Asad, Ashis Nandy, Partha Chatterjee, and Rustom Bharucha, Said does not submit secularism to a sustained geopolitical critique, particularly from the point of view of non-Western societies. The same Said who co-thinks **culture and imperialism**, colonialism and modernity, remains incapable of co-thinking secularism and colonialism. To Said secularism is above reproach, universally speaking. As a result, he omits to provide a genealogical account of how Western secularism was made available as a superior remedy to the stark, unregenerate communal ills of Asian and African societies, cultures, and symbolic systems. Can there be a Hindu or an Islamic secularism? Is it really the case that what we call secularism should indeed be marked as Judeo-Christian secularism (this would be close to William Connolly's thesis)? Can one be a secular fundamentalist or a secular fanatic? Is there not the need, as Bruce Robbins would have it, to "secularize secularism," rather than take it for granted that secularism is somehow born, or is naturally secular? These questions do not ever figure within Said's problematic. Secularism presides benignly over all of Said's projects in the form of an unassailable first principle.

But these reservations do not invalidate Said's reading of the politics of secularism against that of nationalism. The brunt of Said's critique of nationalism is that nationalism generates a vicious divisive identity politics. Nationalism turns into a kind of new religion. Just as we would talk about Jews and Gentiles, Believers and Infidels, Christians and non-Christians, Hindus and non-Hindus, Muslims and non-Muslims, we now talk about nationals and non-nationals. The nation exacts of the human subject a sovereign, indivisible, non-contradictory allegiance; and sure enough, nations are pitted against one another in the name of nationalism, and blood has to be shed in the name of one's nation. As Etienne Balibar would argue, at this point nationalism begins to collaborate with racism as it looks to consolidate the One national subject at the expense of difference, multiplicity, and heterogeneity. The national begins to function as a vicious and punitive gatekeeper that suppresses sub-national revolts based on minority status, gender, class, and sexuality, and at the same time functions as a threshold for the take-off towards the trans-national, the global, the cosmopolitan, and the planetary. Obsessed with the *pluribus unum* mandate, nationalism invalidates forms of **between-ness**, hybridity, and liminal, dual, multiple, and borderly states of being. Most significantly, and here Said's version of secularism works particularly well, the nation state establishes itself both as means and ends, idealizes itself as the ultimate template of collective identity, and closes down borders with normative zeal. Nationalism and its identity politics arrest the flow of history when histories become plural, diasporic, trans-national, and disseminative. Unlike secular temporality that invites history perennially to question, reroute, and transform itself in the name of histories to come, the historicity of nationalism assumes a menacing teleological, and, dare we say, dystopic finality.

How does Palestinian nationalism fit into all this? Is it an inevitable nationalism in the sense that if the Palestinians do not become a nation, they will forever be aliens and nobodies in what is their own legitimate home: a home that has been taken away from them by the violent establishment of the Israeli state? Is Palestine a special case that is fated not to repeat the errors of what Said calls "invidious" nationalism? Is nationalism the appropriate vehicle or vessel for the fulfillment of Palestinian political destiny? Palestinian nationalism has a difficult double duty to perform: it has to provide a legitimate national home to a homeless and stateless people, and at the same function as what Said calls "vanguard nationalism." So, what does he mean by vanguard nationalism? The poignant irony here is that those very people who will be late and long beleaguered entrants to the mixed history of nationalism have to bear the burden of leading the way towards a better and humane nationalism. Said reemphasizes the point that "we are not a religious movement" when referring to Palestinian nationalism. Unlike **Zionism** that was instrumental in the founding of the state of Israel and the consequent un-homing of Palestinians, Palestinian nationalism is secular through and through and completely disaffiliated with any myth of trans-historical origin. It is a historical nationalism that does not resort to myths of primordiality or chosen destiny to validate its political claims. Said also takes care to differentiate the Palestinian from a whole range of religious fundamentalist nationalisms in the Middle East. Fundamentalisms, unlike secularism that believes in shared histories between different peoples, cultures, and nations, are based on notions of purity that separate people from people: a separation based not on history and empirical detail, but based exclusively in the hateful will to separate, segregate, and divide people. Whereas a secular solidarity motivated by **affiliation** seeks to build a community based on shared and negotiable differences, fundamentalist nationhood deploys spurious notions of origin, forever discrediting refugees, exiles, immigrants, and basically any group that is not identified as part of the original providential covenant between a mythical people and their mythical god/s.

Said offers himself and the world a choice: a future where the World, rife with separatism, is divided into rigid and non-porous identities, hermetic civilizational monads, each glorying in its rabid discreteness from other identities, nation states for ever going at each other in a competitive zero-sum winner-take-all game; or a World characterized by overlapping and contested territories, overlapping and contested concerns, forms of reciprocity that acknowledge the mixed-up-ness of all histories, a non-paranoid World that is unafraid of the other for the simple reason that the other is always within and the self always off-center in response to its constitution elsewhere. His choice, of course, is the latter, a vision that will not allow our one World to be balkanized into separate militarized castles with moats, drawbridges, and fiercely patrolled borders.

oppositional criticism/consciousness Could Edward Said have been anything but an oppositional critic? Is it possible to think of Said as the Minister of Education in a Palestinian state, or as appointed head of a national cultural organization in the United States, or as president, provost, dean, or even chair of a department at Columbia University, or any other university? It is indeed ironic that Said consented to be the President of the Modern Language association for a year; for indeed, in general, it is difficult to think of his presence in titular, representative, or institutionally binding terms. All of these roles seem so anomalous: they are all so *not* Edward Said. Clearly, Edward Said belongs to a long and rich tradition of **intellectuals** both in the West and the rest of the world who have functioned as Socratic gadflies to **speak truth to power** and keep the world and the rulers of the world honest. It could even be claimed that the very term "oppositional critic" is a tautology, for surely a critic is by definition a "nay sayer" rather than an "aye sayer," someone who, in the name of the perennial revolution or in the name of a critical utopianism, will do battle with any status quo, even of the good, progressive, and desirable kind, simply because it is not good enough. Whether it is a Michel Foucault who dreams of an eternal unrest in the name of the will to knowledge, or a Jacques Derrida forever dedicated to the non-arrival and the perennial postponement of differe(a)nce, or a Noam Chomsky and his brand of political anarchism, or even Marx who dreams of the final and ultimate withering away of the State, the critic has always valorized an oppositional consciousness that will not be suborned

A Said Dictionary, First Edition. R. Radhakrishnan.
© 2012 John Wiley & Sons, Ltd. Published 2012 by John Wiley & Sons, Ltd.

or seduced by patronage, or bought and sold to the highest bidder. To this ongoing tradition of radical critical non-belonging, Edward Said adds his own resonance as he understands and unpacks the cultural politics of op-positionality with reference to his own time and place. Said's brand of being oppositional is both macro-political, that is, in terms of culture, identity, and filiative belonging, and micro-political, that is, with reference to system, methodology, and modes of **professional** practice.

And indeed, as he explains it in one of his most powerful and persuasive essays, "Criticism Between Culture and System" (in *The World, the Text, and the Critic*), oppositional criticism is best realized in the vulnerable but rich and creative spaces of the "between." Said's oppositionality is two-pronged: against notions of cultural purity that insist that solidarity precede critique, and against systems of thought, such as poststructuralism, postmodernism, new historicism, Lacanian psychoanalysis, Marxism, deconstruction, and so on, that turn into "wall to wall discourses" with the result that professional fetishism takes the place of reality. In the first instance, the critic is con-strained to toe a certain filial line, whereas in the second instance, the critic turns into a card-carrying practitioner of a particular **theory** or "-ism," and as such, is more interested in exemplifying a certain methodology and wearing a professional or systemic badge rather than in connecting with the world "outside," the world of changing historical circumstances. The two pitfalls that Said would like to avoid at all cost are: an uncritical iden-tity politics, and a smug and self-sanctioning professionalism. In contrast with one of his distinguished colleagues at Columbia University, Gayatri Chakravorty Spivak, who believes in modal thinking and in the impor-tance of wearing labels such as Marxist, feminist, subaltern, and so on, Said would employ critical consciousness "amateurishly" against the professional imperative.

It is in the name of the world, indeed the ongoing worlding of the world, that Said breaks ranks both with identity politics and the politics of so-called pure theory. Epistemologically and theoretically speaking, Said seems to have realized quite profoundly that "there are more things in heaven and earth than can be dreamt of through any one philosophy," and that the multi-perspectival "becoming" of the world cannot and ought not to be reduced to identity wars, fundamentalist civilizational feuds, and es-sentialist wrangles. It could be said that with *Orientalism*, Said had found his project, and from that point onward, it was the project that would decide which theories Said might use and how, and not the other way around. In a sense, once Said finds his project, his criticism turns maverick, eclectic, and opportunistic; he is simply not interested any more in being identified and recognized as poststructuralist, Foucauldian, and so on. It is against uncritical notions of "belonging" that Said's oppositional criticism is aimed, and belonging could be ontological, epistemological, political, cultural, theoretical, methodological, professional. How to articulate, within the same consciousness, the need for solidarity with the urgency for criticism; or better still, how to realize solidarity as a perennial function of criticism and how to historicize criticism by perennially providing it with an object, that is, solidarity: that would not be an inaccurate summing up of Said's agenda. For example, it is quite well known that Said, member in exile of the Palestinian National Council and an avid supporter of the Palestinian national cause, was also the Said who developed into an uncompromising critic of Yasser Arafat and his politics of sycophancy, cronyism, and corruption. Like Chinua Achebe who fearlessly criticized every despotic postcolonial Nigerian regime but in solidarity with Nigeria and the people of Nigeria, Said too is unafraid to direct criticism at the very cause that enables solidarity in the first place.

The question that comes up is this. Why does Said choose the term critical/oppositional consciousness and not the category of the "critique" that would seem to serve his purpose quite well? In fact, with the publication of *The World, the Text, and the Critic*, Edward Said had fallen foul of the entire poststructuralist theory camp that accused him of the crime of recidivism: of having fallen back into good old **humanism** after his meritorious and brilliant use of high theory in a book such as *Beginnings*. As a matter of fact, it is a matter of much pride and excitement to a whole generation of younger scholars such as myself, Donald Pease, Susan Jeffords, Robert Young, Steven Mailloux, Aram Veeser, David Lloyd and others were actually "there" when one of the first critical confrontations took place between the "recidivist Said" and the theory establishment. This took place at the 1982 Summer Session of the School of Criticism and Theory at Northwestern University, where Said offered his colloquium on "Secular Criticism." This presentation was full of positive and celebratory references to Matthew Arnold, **Eric Auerbach**, and other literary theorists and historians who were part of the pre-theory school of Old Humanism. No less a less theorist than Paul de Man, who too was part of the core faculty that summer at the SCT, took Said to task for having abandoned the more complex theoretical modes of resistance in favor of easy but flawed humanist options, all in the name of political efficacy. Said responded quite heatedly to De Man's criticism with his own trenchant critique of high theory and its steadfast abstinence from history for fear of complicity in matters real, worldly, and circumstantial.

In his return to old-fashioned humanism by way of oppositional critical consciousness, Said is showcasing his concern and solicitude (i) for the individual and individual creativity as against the depersonalized discourse or system that renders all notions of change futile or theoretically impossible, and (ii) for a historical and phenomenological conception of intentionality and human agency as against the purely linguistic, and to Said, hermetic, critique that leaves no agential room for human intentionality. From this point onwards to the end of his life, and particularly in his posthumously published work, *Humanism and Democratic Criticism*, Said would hotly contest high theory's claims of epistemological "breaks" from history, that is, post-humanism. Happy to locate his oppositional consciousness within the *longue durée* of humanism with all its contingent continuities and discontinuities, its meritorious as well as reprehensible track record, Said states over and over again that theory's superior claim to its oppositional valence is spurious, empirically and historically hollow and unverifiable. From Said's point of view, systemic or discursive critique either persuades humanity that all hope is naive or futile and that the only viable option for the human subject is to understand its chronic "subjection" to discourse and therefore do no more than enjoy its own symptomatic condition with no cure or agential transformation in sight, or quarantines itself within its own immaculate temporality that is, to use the popular jargon, "always already" one step ahead of history and its vulgar rhythms and flows. Rather than fetishize oppositionality as its own constituency, Said asks the disconcerting question that the child asks of the emperor's new clothes: opposition to what? To put it in popular theoretical parlance, Said is asking for a real "transitive" oppositional consciousness, refusing in the process to be satisfied by an "intransitive" oppositional stance that often has nothing to be oppositional about. To put it rather bluntly, Said's direct and candid question to Foucault, Derrida, Lacan, and the rest is: What are you for, and what are you against? In other words, Said is asking for the worldly coordinates of theory.

Whereas to the high theorists, the famous "linguistic turn," after Ferdinand de Saussure, enables the most uncompromising and rigorous forms of self-reflexivity and of critique, to Said, the linguistic turn stands for the arrogant and narcissistic inflation of language and the consequent etiolation of **worldliness** by theory, and the evisceration of reality by language. In a situation of theoretical totalization, all opposition turns into intra-mural play with no real consequence. Theory's highest and purest claim to radicality is that it has brought about the critical realization that everything real is a function or a construct; and this includes "the individual," "reality," and "the human." Said's response, and let us keep in mind that Said himself is a passionate connoisseur of language as style, form, and performance, is: so what? The real may after all only be a construct and a production, rather than something natural. But such an understanding of the real and of reality does not in any way render human practice and human action unreal or illusive. In other words, there is a way to reconcile the reality of human action and praxis with an epistemology that reveals our foundations to be contingent and our reality to be no more and no less than a construct. When it comes to demonstrating oppositional worldly politics, there is no doubt whatever that Said's record is stellar and visible for all to behold and appreciate or criticize. Unlike the high theorists who can all be identified comfortably and exclusively within the national rubric as French, German, or Italian, Said's macropolitical identity is split, fractured, richly ambivalent, double-conscious, and superbly intransigent to proper assimilation.

It is indeed true that Said's project does have much in common, in principle, with Derrida's eternally differing and different deconstruction, with Deleuze and Guattari's nomadology and rhizomatics, and Foucauldian self-destabilization in the name of the will to knowledge; but the big difference is that in Said's case it is the political and the historical that validate theory and epistemology, and not the other way around. In a sense, with his confident and unapologetic use of the term "consciousness," Said is indeed returning to phenomenology and the politics thereof. The difference between a mere critique and criticism based on critical consciousness, for Said, is all the difference between a mechanical–linguistic–discursive procedure driven by a system of thought and a worldly intervention capable of originality, re-sourcefulness, and a keen eye for alternatives. Critical consciousness allows Said room both to be oppositional (and oppositional in many different directions at the same time), and to be a maverick in his strategic, opportunistic, but non-exemplary use of theory, theorists, and theoretical models. Like Raymond Williams, Said's objective in his return to critical individual oppositional consciousness is to enable and galvanize "resources of hope," a strong Raymond Williams phrase and the title of one of his many books, instead of being paralyzed by something called structure, system, or discourse (so-called *la langue*) or of being always-already foretold, preempted, and anticipated predictably by the rationale of the system. While Said has no problem in consenting to the constructedness of the human individual (that to him would be *de rigueur* on the basis of his secular epistemology), he does indeed object strenuously to the grand thesis of constructedness if that entails the surrendering of intentionality and agency to the discursive imperative.

Said does not hesitate to use postmodern spatial terms such as "the nodal point" in the context of individual consciousness; and here is Said's difference from postmodern orthodoxy. To Said, there is an intentional point to being located at the nodal point. Locatedness or situatedness, and here Said takes us back to Jean-Paul Sartre's notion of "situations," enlivens historical awareness. To put it differently, the nodal point is neither post-historical nor totally constitutive of history, but rather a sensitive or fraught situation that opens up the individual consciousness to its own historicity. The nodal networks of postmodern construction and organization do not, for Said, constitute a mysterious or deterministic matrix where individuality is utterly defeated and neutralized. In resorting to the individual, Said is also making sure that collectivity, the we, or species being (to use Marx's term), is not imposed from above in a doctrinaire fashion to quell individual resistance to solidarity. To Said, an active awareness of the collective context is not the same thing as capitulating to the collective context as though that context were more real, more politically valid or desirable than the individual context. It is important to understand that in Said's critical world, collectivity and non-belonging are not mutually contra-indicated; on the contrary, the two terms constitute each other in an ongoing process of recognitions and re-recognitions. We can also observe how critical consciousness helps Said avoid the trap of the never-ending theory–practice dilemma. The work or the performance of oppositional critical consciousness has nothing to do with the practical application of a theory that is first understood conceptually and generally. Even more: with the return of critical consciousness, Said finds his own voice in response to his own situatedness as a distinguished Palestinian-in-exile American professor of Western culture and literature.

Said's retrieval of individual consciousness also heralds a phenomenolog-ical return to "perspectivism" and all the creativity that goes with perspecti-val play and work. Perspectives, in phenomenology, are both given and are the starting points for fresh creation and original deviation and exploration. Perspectives are not intended as repetitions of some preexisting totality or objectivity. As argued magnificently by Sartre and Merleau-Ponty, with per-spective comes historical awareness and historical action. The critic becomes an actor again: he is no longer a correct functionary whose function is no more than the professional maintenance and repetition of a dogma. Circum-stance and distinction take the place of conformity and belonging; and here

Said targets both macro-political and micro-political belonging. To Said, to belong, as though "belonging" is what existence should be all about, is not a desirable state of affairs, whether the belonging is to Arab or male or American identity, or to a professional school of thought called poststructuralism, or deconstruction, or Marxism. Likewise, the blind and repetitive practice of home and homeliness is abhorrent to Said. The mandate of oppositional critical consciousness is to be eternally vigilant and suspicious of such seductive formulations as "one's home," and "one's people." What critical consciousness is committed to is the practice of "distance": distance from home, orthodoxy, filiation, from culture and system. Said is quite happy to use an old-fashioned literary trope, that is, "irony," to characterize his stance. To him, the language of literature and of humanism is preferable to that of theory. But what is important to keep in mind is the fact that Said is consciously returning to this terminology *after* his immersion in theory. My point is that the return is polemical and not naive: after Said's return to the literary culture of humanism, neither theory nor humanism can afford to be complacent, and remain the same and carry on business as usual. His choice in a way speaks to us all and exhorts each one of us to make her own situated choice, rather than succumb to system or methodology in utter passivity.

Orient/Oriental/Orientalism   It is obvious that Edward Said did not coin any of these terms: these usages have existed for a very long time without any critical fanfare or polemical notoriety. But with the publication in 1978 of Edward Said's academic bestseller, *Orientalism*, these terms have taken on a controversial public visibility. Not just that, that one book has been credited with having launched an entire new academic formation known as **postcoloniality** or postcolonial **theory**. It was as though this one book had engineered a paradigm shift. Suddenly, terms like Third World Studies, Commonwealth Literature, Anglophone and Francophone literature and literary criticism had lost their *caché*. All the momentum as well as all the theoretical prestige was with the term postcolonial studies and postcoloniality. The axis as well as the alignment had shifted somehow with the publication of *Orientalism*. But at the same time, there was the uneasy feeling that postcoloniality was predominantly (a) a metropolitan phenomenon, and (b) an academic formation fuelled not by political urgency but by Western or Eurocentric high theory. There would be strong criticisms that to be talking about postcoloniality when realities were in fact still neocolonial was nothing short of a theoretical misrecognition of how

the world actually looked and felt. However controversial and contradictory the reception of the book may have been, *Orientalism* was reviewed,
re-reviewed, and debated endlessly in a variety of forums, and Edward Said
became, if not a household name, a well-known global public **intellectual**.
The book achieved rare distinction within academia and at the same time it
attracted lively attention from the literate world of readers out in the world:
readers with no academic affiliation whatsoever. Thanks to the emergence
of the book, there have been vigorous, even acrimonious, contestations
about the relationship between partisanship and scholarship, literature and
politics, East and West, Islam and Christianity, Colonialism and Modernity,
and so on. There must have been something unique about the conjunctural
positioning of the book that immediately made it the object of multiple
attention and evaluation. So, what was so uniquely influential about the
contents of the book; and how did one book simultaneously address a range
of issues without losing focus?

It would be useful to begin with a brief analysis of the two epigraphs
that Said uses to begin his book. The first, from Karl Marx's *The Eighteenth
Brumaire of Louis Bonaparte* goes thus: "They cannot represent themselves,
they must be represented." The second epigraph is from Benjamin Disraeli's
Tancred, "The East is a career." The first quotation focuses squarely on the
all-important issue of **representation**. Is representation, to put it crudely
and bluntly, a benevolent practice or an oppressive performance? When the
Orientalist speaks for the Orient, is s/he doing the Orientals a favor since
they cannot represent themselves; or is he violating their right to speak for
themselves? Moreover, who decides and on what basis that "they" are too
dumb or illiterate to be capable of representing themselves and producing
their own knowledge about themselves and their history? Was the Orientalist
scholar invited by the Orientals themselves to come, visit and study the
Orient with the objective of educating the Orientals about their own reality:
a reality they inhabit and constitute without any idea why or how? And
this is where the second epigraph comes in. When the East is named and
identified as a career, automatically the Orientalist scholar or "knower"
from the Occident/West is anointed and certified as the **professional** with a
destined career in the East. It is hardly a coincidence that the fiction of the
Brontë sisters or Jane Austen ends with a character taking off to the Orient
to take up a career and further her future and financial security. In other
words, the area known as Arabic, Maghreb, India, and so on, is renamed as
the "Orient" with reference to the West/Occident ("Narrative, Geography,
and Interpretation"; "American Intellectuals and the Middle East").

What is taking place here is literally a forced "orientation" of those areas with reference to the authority of the professional West. In being oriented, these geopolitical areas are being recognized and identified as East of and as East to the omniscient gaze of the professional West. It is in the name of the professional gaze of the Orientalist that the Orient becomes the Orient, and in becoming the Orient it also becomes that reality that is dependent on representation from without. Here is how the formation works. It is *not* the case that there is a region called the Orient that dictates the need for a field called Orientalism and an expert called the Orientalist. It is the other way around. It begins with a particular kind of desire for knowledge called Orientalism; and it is this desire that constructs an entire field called Orientalism that remains an unresisting captive of this desire. This foregoing formulation is Said's original contribution in his groundbreaking work *Orientalism*.

What exactly was Said arguing: that there is no place called the Orient? Was he contending that Orientalism as a body of knowledge was chronically flawed? If so, were the flaws ideological, methodological, formal? Where was he himself speaking from? Was his discourse occidental, oriental, neither, somewhere in between? Was he an insider or an outsider? Was he maintaining that the "orient" had been mystified and misrecognized by Orientalism? If that is the case, is there then a real "middle east," a real Orient; and who would be the best spokesperson of the Oriental Real? If he was seeking to demystify and correct the errors of Orientalist scholarship, he must surely have access to some correct version of the Orient. Is there such a correct version and where does one find it? Was Said making a distinction between an inherent reality that is open only to insiders in some numinous and unmediated way, and mere "representations" that are bound to misread reality? And in any case, who is an outsider and who is an insider? Is an Arab, just by virtue of the historical and empirical fact that she is an Arab, more privy to Arab reality and Arab truth than a non-Arab? Could the Arab too not get it wrong about her reality, reliant as she is on representations?

Given Said's secular perspective, he could not be arguing that "insiders" possessed the truth about their condition in some essential, trans-historical, trans-representational way. Furthermore, what was the putative object or subject of Said's *Orientalism*? What was it about and how did the work, methodologically, produce its object? On the one hand there were area studies scholars and Middle Eastern Study pundits who claimed that Said was not one of them. His book was not purportedly about their world, for Said was not one of them, either filiatively or affiliatively. He was no native who belonged. Said was of the West, trained by Western **humanism** and Western theory and literary criticism; and indeed, the entire book could be read as no more and no less than an application of Foucauldian discourse theory to Orientalism. If all that Said was doing was to deploy Western high theory to call the bluff of Orientalism, how then is his intervention all that different from those projects of deconstruction that were still mired within the hegemony of Eurocentric thought? *Orientalism* places its author neither here nor there, neither squarely in the Occident nor definitively and normatively within the Orient. Methodologically indebted to the West but a solicitous partisan and defender of the East against Occidental misrecognition and stereotyping, Said and his *Orientalism* occupy an in-between position that cannot be parsed properly within the grammar of representation.

So, what exactly was Said's thesis in *Orientalism*, and why did it become an academic best seller? Why is it lauded as that one book that inaugurated something called postcolonial studies? For one thing, it was an academic book, written by an already distinguished literary critic, well trained in the lore of Western humanism, on a topic that commanded both specialist and popular attention. The term "oriental" had come to stay in mainstream language, and it had become customary, even natural and spontaneous, to refer to a whole range of peoples from China, the Koreas, Japan, Philippines, Indonesia, and Malaysia as "orientals." Not just that, lay wisdom had no problem in dividing the world up into the West and the East, and there was always that famous and axiomatic line from Rudyard Kipling about the East being East and the West being West, with little possibility of a meaningful meeting between the two. How could one forget the haunting and doomed ending of E.M. Forster's *A Passage to India* where the very sky and the earth and the stomping horses mandate that there can be no true friendship between an occidental and an oriental? The crux of the matter is that stereotypes had usurped the place of knowledge and successfully occupied the popular imagination. To this day, just say the word "Arab" or "Palestinian," and instantly conjured up are certain stereotypical images of the terrorist, the anarchist, the anti-Christ, the ruthless Islamic fundamentalist, the lazy and/or sensual native who resists progress, secularism, and democratic enlightenment. Contemporary TV and film scripts teem with characters whose psychological interiority, whose ontological profile so to speak, is drawn from a ready-made lexicon of oriental stereotypes. Said's book educates the general reader and the general public and tells them how these stereotypes work and how they have been produced systematically by the discourse known as Orientalism.

The book had a dramatic reception: overwhelmingly positive as well as scathingly critical. First, we turn to the criticisms. There were those theorists who felt that Said had hoisted himself with his own petard: that he had unwittingly reproduced the very binary dispensation of East–West, of Self–Other that he was seeking to deconstruct, and that he had not sufficiently problematized, or thought through the contradictions of his own subject position. Moreover, in his polemical zeal to critique stereotypical misrepresentations, overgeneralizations, and essentialist misrecognitions, had Said not inadvertently repeated the very vicious fallacy that he had set out to combat: the fallacy of essentialist characterization and totalization? Had he not unwittingly created a monolithic West/Occident utterly lacking in internal differentiations and heterogeneity? True, Said does make distinctions between French Colonialism and British Colonialism; and yet, terms like "the Enlightenment" and "the West" remain unproblematized and undifferentiated in Said's discourse. Had Said, in his mode of political partisanship with the Orient, overlooked his critical accountability to the West?

More than anything, Said's work compels us to look at a piece of scholarly work simultaneously both in terms of knowledge and in terms of power and the power effect. Foucault's ground-breaking insight had been that knowledge does not humanize power in the name of some transcendent "good," but rather that knowledge itself is an effect of power, and that power as a constitutive force behind knowledge is indeed ubiquitous. Discourses of knowledge are neither disinterested nor invested in a Truth that is beyond the hazardous play of power; on the contrary, truth, or truths in the plural are strategic regions or spaces that are coordinated into existence by the will to power. Following up on the lead provided by Friedrich Nietzsche, Foucault articulates and theorizes the inescapable Power–Knowledge nexus. If humanism believes in the possibility of **speaking truth to power** in the name of something essentially human, Foucault discredits the humanist project with the counter-claim that humanism as a body of knowledge itself is not only ideologically partisan but also the product of a certain will to power.

The Foucauldian problematic, as Said inherits it in his *Orientalism*, is this: if all discourses of knowledge, whether they emanate from insiders and outsiders, are constituted by the will to power, then, how does one distinguish between good power and bad power? To make it more specific, is it even possible to make anything, any area, any subject matter the object of knowledge without at the same time making it the object of power, of professional power? If the "real" of any place or culture such as "the Orient" can only be accessed through representations in discourse, and if discourses are not independent of the will to power, is there any room left where distinctions can be made between those knowledges that dominate, enslave, and control, and those that are non-coercive, liberating, and decolonizing? To bring back Disraeli into the conversation, what would the difference be if an Easterner, rather than a Westerner, produced knowledge about the East? Could that production also not be construed as a careerist move? Could that perspective be somehow trusted intrinsically to carry the charge of truth more honestly, more objectively and reliably on the one hand, and more subjectively and existentially on the other, than that of the intrusive and invasive Occidental? The important question that Said poses here is this: Is there room for the privilege of "insiderism" in the production of scholarly knowledge? Is someone an insider by virtue of birth and nativity, that is, filiatively, or by virtue of their dedication, commitment, and rigor to a body of scholarship through the process of **affiliation**? Furthermore, if there is nothing called a totally objective and disinterested production of knowledge, how does one adjudicate between one interested version and another? To put it differently, all we have are representations; and if each representation is valid and legitimate for its own reasons of interest, what objective criteria are available to help us choose one representation over another?

It is indeed ironic that immediately after the eventful publication of *Orientalism*, Said was approached by the US State Department with a request: "Could you please help us in understanding the Oriental psyche?" I distinctly remember Said narrating, with palpable anger and anguish, this incident to his students at the 1982 summer session of the School of Criticism and Theory, held at Northwestern University. His point was that the request from the US State Department had begged the question of what *Orientalism* was all about, and indeed, he was being set up as the native informant for purposes of anthropological domination and control. In a way, this anecdote ironically sums up the significance of the publication of *Orientalism*. For starters, there is the theme of recognition, and of course, mis-recognition. The book had something to say to everybody, which also meant that in being accessible and interesting to everybody, it was radically vulnerable to perspectival misunderstanding. Secondly, a book of academic erudition, precisely because it was a scholarly work, became embroiled in worldly controversy and debate. When was the last time, and when indeed will be the next time, when the publication of a tome by a learned university professor initiates passionate, even acrimonious debate in the world at large about geopolitics, the nature of reality and its representation, and relationships among the several cultures and civilizations that constitute our contemporary human situation? When was the last time when one and the same book was identified and recognized as disciplinary, inter-disciplinary, trans-disciplinary, and non-disciplinary, regional as well as global, Western *and* non-Western, and of specialist *and* lay interest?

With the publication of *Orientalism*, Said is literally born as a public intellectual nationally, sub-nationally, and internationally. What is indeed fascinating is the fact that the themes and the issues that make up the book are of great interest both to the scholar and the citizen at large. Bias, value, representation, relationships within and between different peoples, Self and Other, East and West, foreign policy and domestic policy, the relationship of the scholarly world to the world of politics and power: who is not both interested and vitally implicated in the thinking through of these issues in their daily lives? And suddenly, there appeared a book that dealt with scholarly passion with precisely this terrain: a terrain that needed to be understood self-consciously as a terrain rather than experienced just as a field of practice. Such a book was *Orientalism* that in its very appeal to the scholar and the non-scholar alike opened up academia to worldly passion and interest and rendered the "real world" vulnerable to scholarly cultivation and practice.

philology   Philology is defined by *Webster's Dictionary* as "the study of literature and disciplines relevant to literature and language as used in literature," and "the study of human speech especially as the vehicle of literature and as a field of study that sheds light on cultural history; also related to historical and comparative linguistics." If that is philology, can Edward Said be far behind? It is quite obvious how philology becomes the site where Said can initiate and achieve his agenda on multiple fronts: culture, language, literary language, history, cultural history, comparative studies. At a time when it was fashionable to be on the theory bandwagon, Said turned to philology, that ancient and classic formation so much indebted to European **humanism** and humanistic studies.

   Said's emphasis is on the world, the linguistic and literary **text**, and the critic. Said's focus, as an individual and a critic, is the world and its worlding in certain sites and locations. What better point of entry than philology, which elegantly and with complexity braids together history and language both in its quotidian and literary dimension? With philology, Said can touch base with language as communication, language as formal construct, language as a mediation of reality, language as a vehicle, embodiment, a symptom of culture; and finally, since language is not any *one* language but language in general, Said has the scope to study language in its intra-linguistic, inter-linguistic, and comparatist aspects. Unlike the poststructuralist aesthetes and theorists of language who are happy to concede to the linguistic turn in the name of a hermetic textuality, Said seeks in

A Said Dictionary, First Edition. R. Radhakrishnan.
© 2012 John Wiley & Sons, Ltd. Published 2012 by John Wiley & Sons, Ltd.

philology a lively connection between word and world. In philology Said addresses the world in all its multiple mediatedness.

In his essay, "Islam, Philology, and French Culture: Renan and Messignon" (in *The World, the Text, and the Critic*), Said makes some of his most astute comments about philology as a way of critically knowing the world. It is typical of Said's critical intelligence that in this essay he instrumentalizes philology not as an end in itself but as a connective and as a relational mode of analysis that situates Islam and French culture within the same frame; and within the same frame Said makes telling distinctions between the methods of Renan and those of Messignon, each of whom in his way recuperates the flaws and fallacies of **Orientalism**; in other words, their philological accounts miss the point of Islam. In his appreciative understanding of philology as a discipline, just as he does with other terms, he gives "philology" his own spin and makes it part of his vocabulary. As he does so, he also makes a connection between old-fashioned philology and the New Philology that takes substantively into account the narratives and documents produced by the colonized populations in their own languages and symbolic structures. It is obvious that Said is interested in philology for its relational orientation, even more so if the relationship is of the asymmetrical kind as between West and East, between the colonizer and the colonized, between Judeo-Christianity and Islam.

To begin with, Said associates philology as a method and a discipline with the secular mindset. Philology marks the moment if not of the death of religion, at least of the superannuation of religion as an analytic or interpretive framework. With philology gone is the kind of transcendence that we associate with religious or sacral studies. What philology is concerned with is a certain linguistic immanence (I am thinking here of what Foucault has to say about "words and things" in his magisterial work, *The Order of Things*, and in particular his theoretical elaboration of what he calls "the analytic of finitude" in the context of the implosion of reality into language) whereby the world becomes more historical and empirical, rather than the embodiment of an idea or the fulfillment of a pre-given sacred teleology. Philology, in England and France, plays a pivotal role in understanding the other, that is, Islam. Philology, Said observes, is cast in the classical anthropological mold wherein the dominant Self produces knowledge about the Other. To say anthropological is also to say the colonialist model of knowledge that makes a point of wanting to know the Other, but only to say, after the knowing happens, that the Other is inferior, or antique, or incapable of fitting into the progressive era of Reason: in other words, through the operation of knowledge to deny co-evalness to the Other.

As he makes definitive distinctions between British philology and French philology, Said ends up characterizing each of the two philological methods both intra-historically and inter-historically. Said proves the point that there is a deep constitutive connection between the way British and French philological disciplines understand themselves within their national culture and the manner in which they seek to understand Islam as the Other. (This is a line of scholarly investigation that Gauri Viswanathan, Edward Said's student and a leading postcolonial theorist, has pursued with distinction in works such as *The Masks of Conquest* and *Outside the Fold.*) According to him the English disciplinary model remains tied, umbilically as it were, to the religious, Judeo-Christian philosophic model and its non-acceptance of the rupture caused by the emergence of language as its own phenomenon; whereas the French model develops as an institutional disciplinary model, professional to the core.

Said identifies both Renan and Massignon as comparatists, and goes on to evaluate how each of them uses philology as a differential strategy to understand the alterity, the otherness, of Islam. Philology becomes a masterful player in the world-historical construction of the Self–Other problematic. It becomes the task of philology to establish, with the help of linguistic sources, the time in which different histories play out their drama. "The philologist's job," Said writes, "must be to connect that postlapsarian moment just after language's birth with the present, then to show how the dense web of relationships between language users is a secular reality from which the future will emerge" ("Islam, Philology, and French Culture," 279). It is no doubt the case that philology in the hands of Renan and Massignon still remains captive to the fallacies of Orientalism. It is indeed the philological nature of their work that helps Said to determine that "Renan's epistemological attitude toward Islam, therefore, is one of divestiture and judgment, Massignon's of sympathetic assumption and rapprochement" ("Islam, Philology, and French Culture," 282). Both of them are willing to accept that Islam can be a legitimate object of study; and both of them fall a prey to the assumption that their scholarship will get rid of all obstacles with the result that Islam will be seen as the object of their representation. In Said's adjudication, "Renan is the philologist as judge," whereas Massignon figures as "the philologist as guest, as spiritual traveler extraordinary" ("Islam, Philology, and French Culture," 288). Trapped as they are within the regime of Orientalism, they come well short of the philologist's task, that of affirming a coeval and secular reality based on the interactions among multiple language users, and on that multi-lateral, multi-linguistic basis capable of generating a historically accountable future. As Said puts it with great clarity, "One scholar understands the religion in secular terms but missed what in Islam still gives its adherents genuine nourishment. The other sees in it religious terms but largely ignores the secular differences that exist within the variegated Islamic world. In both instances, then, Orientalism perceives and is blinded by what it perceives" ("Islam, Philology, and French Culture," 276).

Just as Said will not jettison humanism *tout court* just because it has had a bad record, but will instead correct and improve and rethink humanism in the name of humanism, here too, Said refuses to throw the baby out with the bath water. Rather than trust an arid theory based on an ahistorical textualism, Said holds on to philology on the assumption that it does not have to be captive to Orientalist premises or anthropological imperatives. Why this belief? Because philology is language at its best: both itself and a documentation of culture, both literary and the historical pulsation of history, both language as artistic expression and the vehicle of life. Most significantly it is a dense mesh of relationality, for to be a philologist is not to be marooned within one language, but to study the interrelationship among languages and to undertake other cultures in a spirit of reciprocity and shared languages, to build an egalitarian comparatism into the very heart of the humanities. Furthermore, a philologist cannot but be uncompromisingly secular: a scholar who will not resort to the lie of primordial origins, or seek trans-historical truths all the while flouting the historical truths of and in language. Language becomes that worldly site where different histories may be seen, experienced, and understood as they act out the human condition in a related, contested, and overlapping way. In philology Said finds satisfaction as a human being, a literary scholar, a humanist critic, and a comparative student of the humanities and the human condition in all its differential but common reality.

postcoloniality   Every student of world literature now knows: no Edward Said, no postcoloniality. To be more precise: no *Orientalism*, no postcoloniality. Before postcoloniality there had been formations such as Third World, Commonwealth, Anglophone, Francophone. Then came postcoloniality. Many critics felt that this was a hoax, no more than old wine in a new bottle. The feeling in some quarters was that this new "post" was the result of a metropolitan academic conspiracy hatched by diasporic intellectuals from the Third World who just felt like coining the term "postcoloniality" in alignment with poststructuralism, postmodernism, and so on. There were other critics who felt that it was unconscionable and theoretically glib to speak of postcoloniality when times were still neocolonial. Devout Marxist critics were firmly persuaded that the formation called postcoloniality, with its strong connection to metropolitan high theory, had been emptied of any kind of political content and resistance. So, what really happened or did not happen with the publication of Said's *Orientalism* in 1978? Had Said redefined the nature and scope of the study of Third World literature? Had *Orientalism* got at the truth of decolonization and beyond in an utterly unprecedented way? Had Said re-imagined the geopolitical cartography of postcoloniality? Had the theoretical/epistemological location now been generalized beyond the literal latitudes and longitudes of Africa and Asia? Had *Orientalism* gone farther than any other Third World discourse in taking on the West not just politically, but in calling its epistemological bluff? Or was it simply that it was irresistible to watch someone hoist, with excruciating brilliance and passion, the West with his own petard? Had the project of "dismantling the master's house with the master's own tools" become more salient than building up "the Third World" on its own terms and criteria? To some it seemed as if with Said's advent, the Third World had been de-regionalized and made an equal partner in all the elite theoretical conversations; whereas to others with the immense popularity of Said's work and the emergence of postcoloniality, too much had been conceded to the metropolitan location. The detractors of postcoloniality felt that the conversation, the location, and the themes of what had been the Third World had changed disastrously, and once again, the non-West had been held hostage to the prowess of Western thought. And finally, whatever regional specificity and political clout the Third World might have had had been surrendered to the alien currency of Eurocentric theory. In short, postcoloniality had come to mean what Said has called in **Culture and Imperialism** the "**voyage in**," which is to say, the impact Third World **intellectuals** have on the metropolitan center ("Intellectuals in the Post-Colonial World"; "Third World Intellectuals and Metropolitan Culture").

The second problem is the characteristic postcolonial problem of what Partha Chatterjee has resoundingly diagnosed as "derivativeness." In Said's account, the East, and the post-colony in general, remains dependent on Western modes of scholarship for its liberation and self-expression. Besides, there was difficulty in establishing the nature of Said's constituency. Is he speaking for the East, the non-West, the Palestinian, the postcolonial citizen? Who is his audience: the East, the West, or both, and if both, is that not a baleful contradiction? To add to all this, Said's location is in the heart of the metropolitan West, and his "assigned subject position," as Foucault would have it, is that of a scholar deeply entrenched in Western modernity and its tradition of high culture and literature and literary criticism. Both locationally and subject positionally, Said is chronically compromised. He can neither be a spokesperson for the Orient since he is not of it; nor can he produce an "authentic" version of the Orient since his methodology is alien, occidental. Perhaps he could be given the benefit of doubt when it comes to his ability to talk back with rebellious panache to the discourse of European Enlightenment and European high **theory**; but that is a different matter, a different agenda. It is not the same thing as affirming the Third World in the mode of a protagonist. The upshot of it all is the diagnostic finding that Said cannot be entrusted, encumbered as he is by what Aijaz Ahmad calls his "metropolitan ambivalence," with the task of speaking for the non-West; at best he could be its advocate in a Western forum.

This raises the all-important question of the location, both epistemic and geographic, of this thing called postcoloniality. The most unfavorable and virulent criticism of postcoloniality was that thanks to Edward Said it had become the delectable professional haven of diasporic intellectuals from the Third World who could now have the best of both worlds: they could symbolically flaunt their solidarity with Africa and Asia, carry on nevertheless with their dalliance with Eurocentric high theory (Derrida, Foucault, Lacan, Althusser, and so on), problematize all forms of political and cultural **representation** in the name of a radical theoretical *jouissance* that is always-already post-national, diasporic, and even post-political. There are two interconnected issues here. The first has to do with the dominance of the "post," or what has been called the theoretical condition of "post-ality." How do we know that the post- is even real: just because Jean-Francois Lyotard has claimed that humanity is now in a postmodern epistemological condition? Let alone the fact that there are scholars who claim that the postmodern is still only modern: why should we assume that there is or should be something called postcoloniality, just because there is poststructuralism, just because there is postmodernism? Is the creation of the post-, the so-called "after," no more than a theoretical fabrication, a fabrication that belies Third World realities that are in fact, and in history, still neocolonial? As Anthony Appiah's influential essay asks, "is the post- in the postmodernism" the same as "the post- in postcolonial"? From the point of view of the political critics of postcoloniality, the fashionable category of the "post" acts as a floating signifier creating seeming similarities where indeed there are none. From this point of view, postcoloniality's use of European high theory is a form of professional self-indulgence; in other words, there is no organic connection or solidarity between the theory and the socio-political and cultural formations of the ex-colonized lands of Africa and Asia.

The second interconnected theme is that of representation. Whom does postcoloniality represent or speak for? It would appear that under the aegis of postcoloniality, **nationalism**, that canonical citadel of the Third World's decolonized political autonomy and integrity, had been discredited. In its place had been installed a battery of terms such as **exile**, the diaspora, the non-resident, and the figure of the intellectual over and above the organic claims of nationalism. The problem here was twofold, according to critics of postcoloniality. First, postcoloniality had taken away any kind of geographic and locational specificity from the Third World. Postcoloniality was every-where, including New York, London, and Paris. Second, postcoloniality had become the pet project of diasporic intellectuals with a Third World ori-gin, who had become high and mighty wielders of high Eurocentric theory. What used to be Third World and Anglo- and Francophone Studies had now been tamed into a cultural intellectual sensibility whose intimate inter-locutor was the academic West. Not only had postcoloniality been weaned away from projects of political and populist resistance to neocolonialism and the dominance of the first world, but also it had become a kind of *carte blanche* for intellectuals to pursue their own epistemological agendas. It was in this spirit that influential critics such as Arif Dirlik would claim that postcoloniality lacked any kind of definitional clarity or integrity.

One thing is clear, however: Said did not intend postcoloniality to be the privileged preserve of any one group or people or constituency, and I refer here in particular to the influential essay that he wrote for *Salmagundi*, "Intellectuals in a postcolonial world." It also has to be conceded, as the very title of the *Salmagundi* essay makes instantly clear, that the question of the intellectual has a driving force in all of Said's writings. Is postcoloniality the tenor and the question of the intellectual the vehicle, or is it the other way around? A number of questions arise. Is the world postcolonial? If that is the case, is postcoloniality a burden that is distributed evenly across the entire world? To be even more specific, after the powerful global event of decolonization, are both India and England, are both Algeria and France postcolonial? Who can claim postcoloniality as their rightful motif or histor-ical baggage? And Said's response is nothing short of brilliant: of course both India and England, Algeria and France ought to be postcolonial, with great consequences to all parties concerned. There is no gainsaying the historical reality that because of two centuries or more of the history of colonialism, histories have been coercively yoked together. This is not to deny that India and England were subjects of their own respective histories prior to the on-slaught of colonialism. But what Said brings into this geopolitical context is the crucial notion of asymmetry. The two countries are related to each other, but each country remembers the history of colonialism differently. The two memories are asymmetrical in their relationship to each other. This, incidentally, is a situation that the South African novelist Nadine Gordimer explores trenchantly time and again, particularly in *Burger's Daughter*. For her the question is, how does the time of post-apartheid assign asymmetrically different but related positions to the white and black populations? Even closer in spirit to Said's way of historicizing postcoloniality is that vibrant moment in Amitav Ghosh's novel, *The Shadow Lines*, when Tridib, the Bengali intellectual, and May Price, his English lover, meet in Calcutta and the venue is the monumental building, the Victoria Memorial. This stately yet ugly building that has become an indivisible part of the quotidian goings-on of life in Calcutta affects the two characters differently. May Price is horrified and is filled with feelings of uncontrollable shame when she sees this ugly symbol of English colonialism direct traffic right in the heart of Calcutta. She feels physically ill at ease, and she is close to retching. Tridib, on the other hand, is quite calm. Not only is he used to it, but he is utterly confident that the Victoria Memorial is not even British any more, for the folks of Calcutta through an act of creative signification have made it their own. He even tells May Price, "It is our ruin."

Is too much being conceded here in the name of a warm and fuzzy and oceanic **humanism**? Said's main intention in invoking asymmetry is not to fetishize it, or to build asymmetry as a pious border or wall between the two memories, the two "discrepant experiences," as Said puts it in *Culture and Imperialism*. His urgent motivation is to exhort the Indian and the British, the Algerian and the French to go rigorously and accountably beyond the ugly and punishing "politics of blame and guilt." The invocation of the asymmetry within the binary structure of recognition is also an impassioned invitation towards, shall we say, a new humanism, a new global human secular community that is both prepared to look back and face the past unflinchingly and at the same time envision a collective move forward based on the revisionism. Said would in fact be deeply committed to the task of realizing postcoloniality as a worldwide, universal value. This does not necessarily come in the way of India or Nigeria or Algeria coming up with its own preferred blueprint of their postcoloniality. And indeed, there will and should be differences among national, governmental, institutional, sovereign instantiations of postcoloniality. But the postcolonial human condition will have to reflect worldwide, albeit differentially, what we, all the peoples of the world, have learned from and after (post-) the ignoble and reprehensible legacy of colonialism. Not averse at all to the specificity of the human condition, whether it be postcolonial, postmodern, Egyptian or Palestinian or Chinese, Said's fundamental anxiety is that specificity may ossify into a form of non-negotiable difference, into mutually exclusive identity claims that reject the very idea of a common ground in the name of their own specific political correctness. We only need to think of one of his very last ventures, his collaborative project with the musician and music conductor Daniel Barenboim (*Parallels and Paradoxes*, a project that sought to bring together Palestinian and Israeli composers and musicians in the name of music), to get a sense of what he meant by our postcolonial human condition: a condition when generalizations need to be made courageously precisely during those conjunctures when generalizations seem thoroughly non-feasible.

professionalism   Edward Said, throughout his career, was involved in a number of intense debates with several of his colleagues, notably Stanley Fish, Cathy Gallagher, Richard Rorty, Walter Benn Michaels, Bruce Robbins, and Gerald Graff, about the nature and meaning of the terms "professional" and "professionalism." Who are the professionals, and what do they do and what do they know? How do they connect through their performance their knowledge with their practice? In the name of what principle or value do they perform? Who is the antonym of the professional: the amateur, the generalist, the committed activist, or the lay person? Is a professional a mercenary whose primary ethic is to do a job well in relation to the re-muneration as specified in the contract? Said's main thesis in this debate is that thanks to excessive specialization and heedless exponential profession-alization, professionals have stopped professing anything at all. To profess, in the strong ethico-political sense of the term, is to acknowledge and le-gitimate a "value" and to observe that value through one's practice: as in, I profess Gandhi-ism, or feminist-socialism. To profess something is to be self-reflexively normative. Professing is also a matter of ideological perspec-tivism, which is to say that, in professing something, the professor as well as the professional makes a choice, takes sides, makes a commitment to a point of view, and to a particular worldview, belief, or value system. In other words, professionalism is the practice of neither quietism nor neutrality. It is not for that matter a form of acquiescence to the status quo in the name of one's job that is intended to make no waves, ruffle no feathers. And the professional is not just someone who just does something in response to a command, a contract, a salary, without ever questioning the nature of her job and what it is all about. (I am thinking here of the famously stoic but naively vulnerable butler Mr. Stevens in Kazuo Ishiguro's memorable fiction, *Remains of the Day*, who literally follows the dumb logic of "Theirs but to reason why, / Theirs but to do and die.")

And here is a valence that should strike home after Bernie Madoff (and what he made off with) and all the unconscionable shenanigans of Wall Street and the stock market. What is the connection between Wall Street and Main Street? What does Wall Street know in secret that will eventually maim and devastate Main Street? Are Wall Street professionals mere mercenaries who can do what they want in the name of professional speculation and risk taking, citing in the process jargon and mumbo-jumbo, all the while thumbing their noses at Main Street? If indeed Wall Street bankers and financiers are knowledge-professionals, in whose name are they organizing and deploying their knowledge?

At a time when terms like "professionalism" and "professionalization" seem to have earned much capital as positive terminology, Said turns tables on the terms, and calls their bluff. Said's main point is that professionalism comes in the way of **worldliness**, and that professionals, in their mono-maniacal and self-serving loyalty to their profession, have brainwashed themselves into the delusion that the world is no more and no less than the blip they see in their technical frames and methodological windows. For such professionals, the world implodes into their frames. We must keep in mind, however, that Said himself was a distinguished professional who observed and practiced his professional *dharma* with extreme care and rigor. The problem is not with professionalism *per se*, but rather with particular usages and cultivations of the term. An anecdote perhaps will clarify Said's take on the issue. In the summer of 1982, I was part of a group mostly made up of doctoral students on the verge of completing their dissertations, and a few young assistant professors who had just begun their academic careers, who were Said's students at the summer session of the School for Criticism and Theory, at Northwestern University. At an informal meeting with him, we were exploring possibilities of how best to make a difference in the world, not just do our jobs. We were all committed to changing the world, not to be seduced by "business as usual," to offer real resistance to dominance and hegemony, to **speak truth to power** fearlessly and without compromise. One student was interested perhaps in abandoning academia and becoming a lawyer so that she could take up one *pro bono* case after another, in search of a better, more just world. Said's question to us as a group was: It is admirable to want to change the world, but in what capacity? One of us responded: as a professor of literature. Said's instant response was, "In that case, get tenure." Surely, such an answer could not have emanated from someone who either disdained professionalism or subscribed to the belief that worldliness and commitment to professionalism are mutually exclusive or incommensurable ("Response to Stanley Fish").

Said's thesis is that no one in the name of realpolitik can become part of worldliness without mediation or **representation**. Moreover, reality is not more real in one location than another. Reality is equally real in a classroom, a court of law, the corporate conference room, the doctor's office, the assembly line, the agricultural farm. It would be nothing short of romanticism or perhaps even exoticism to abandon one profession in the fantastic belief that some other profession is intrinsically more real and political, or naturally less complicit or not complicit at all with the dominant or hegemonic world order. Worldliness requires a base, a location, a subject position: worldly as a doctor, a lawyer, a mechanic, a professor of comparative literature, an actor, a car mechanic. The strategy is not to shake off the mediation "as a whatever" in the name of the Real, but rather, to learn to work, practice, and instrumentalize the profession in ways that connect with the world. Just as he would argue in the politics of the **text** and its relationship to the world as context, here too Said's contention is that the relationship between the profession and the world is porous, and that the professional site should be realized as relatively autonomous. The understanding produced in the professional site should be understood in larger terms with reference to the larger world of which the professional topos is a part.

Said's position here could be compared to that of Fredric Jameson's understanding of the term "totality." At a time when "totality" had become a tainted word, suggestive immediately of "totalization," authoritarianism, Fascism, and abuse of the part or the fragment by totality, Jameson as a postmodern Marxist kept insisting that just because in our postmodern times the totality is not immediately sensible, perceptible, and intelligible does not automatically mean that we are rid of totality or that totality does not exist any more. If anything, there is all the more reason for the human subject as producer, consumer, and a seemingly impersonal global nodal point in a vast and ever-ramifying network to insist on wanting to know what her connection is with a totality that is un-sutured, un-hinged, or paradoxically present as absent. Similarly, when we are lost in the world of specialization and professional calculations, we make our peace with the small cubicle where do we our work, with that jargon or argot or specialized discourse that sustains our work, and are indeed quite happy not to know what is happening in other cubicles or how all the different locations of work connect to create a total scene. The stereotypical definition of a specialist as someone who knows more and more about less and less comes to mind. Also relevant are concepts such as "author function" that reduce human ingenuity and creativity into mere functionalism. Said would certainly approve of Ralph Waldo Emerson's plangent complaint that "man thinking" had degenerated or ossified into "the thinker" or "the philosopher." Said's challenge to the professional who is cocooned and immured in his practice is the following set of questions. Why do you do what you do? Whom do you work for? Whom does your employer work for? Who or what is behind the corporation or the institution that you work for? If the answer is "the state," or "capital," then, what about the behavior of the state and capital, and are you in agreement with the behavior and the tendencies of the state and of capital? Is your working for them the result of principled and ideological consent, or are you just doing your job, in blissful oblivion and abeyance of these larger ideological, ethical, and macro-political questions? The chances are that most of us will not have an answer either because we have not thought about them, or because we think of these questions as irrelevant in the context of our professional competence. Even if the questions exercise moral and political authority on us, in our capacity as professionals we will not negotiate with them. Our work continues as always despite the troublesome nature of the questions. It is as though there are two worlds that are in a non-relationship: the world where we work and the world where these questions matter and cause more than a ripple.

The point that Said wants to drive home is that professionalism is not a matter of choiceless obedience, of irresistible interpellation by one's job. The space of the job and of the profession can be occupied and exercised with a difference. It is not all a *fait accompli* whereby the nature of the job has always already preempted the worldly creativity and inventiveness of the professional, the job holder. The professional site can be occupied, and its subject position deployed against the grain, against authority, self-reflexively: all in the name not of the professional work ethic but of worldliness. Working autocritically and deconstructively from within the cartography of the profession, the critical professional can open up an "outside," a "without," a constitutive *hors-texte* in whose name the profession can be held accountable. One need only think of the ongoing squabbles between Wall Street and Main Street to appreciate the importance of Said's critique. There is always choice as there is intentionality and there is agency. To be a true worldly professional is to be able to wield and assume responsibility in a double move: in the name of the world by way of one's job. The world is not to be reduced to a professional imperative; it is one's profession that should rise to the challenge as well as the opportunity offered by the world. To conclude with reference to the Benjamin Disraeli epigraph in *Orientalism*, "The East is a career," Said responds in thunder, "No, absolutely not: the world is not a career." And why would he respond thus? It is simply because, to Said, the world should not be a mere career, but a source of profound political responsibility.

representation   A number of years ago, was a lively conference cospon-
sored by Princeton University and Rutgers University, New Brunswick on the
twin themes of Reality and Representation. Out of this conference emerged
two vibrant one of which proclaimed, "Get Real," and the other opined, "No
Reality without Representation." It is possible to imagine Edward Said nod-
ding "Yes" to both pronouncements and taking his place between the two
to indicate (i) that getting real is a good thing to do in so far as it encourages
proactive action taking, intervention through choice and agency, and the
active dynamic avoidance of lethargy or quietism in the hope that somehow
reality will happen by default, and (ii) that getting real as a visceral manifesto
cannot take the place of the rigorous and painstaking labor of representation
as though "getting real" were some magical mantra that would somehow
numinously connect with the Real in abeyance of the realms of representation and mediation. The only legitimate way to get real, for Said, is by way of
representation and its secular history. Representation, the world, the **text**,
critical consciousness, and the **intellectual**: this conjuncture pretty much
sums up what Edward Said is all about ("Representing the Colonized").

   At a time when "representation" was going out of theoretical fashion
and to be "post-representational" constituted the cutting-edge of theoretical being and consciousness, Said returns to representation, against the
grain of trendy theory, and re-charges it with old and necessary values. In a
way, Said's retrieval of representation could be positioned alongside Gayatri
Chakravorty Spivak's famous defense of representation in her powerful essay, "Can the Subaltern Speak?" where she takes Gilles Deleuze and Michel

A Said Dictionary, First Edition. R. Radhakrishnan.
© 2012 John Wiley & Sons, Ltd. Published 2012 by John Wiley & Sons, Ltd.

Foucault to task for prematurely announcing the death of representation in the name of high **theory**. Speaking very much in the tradition of Karl Marx who wrote in *The Eighteenth Brumaire of Louis Bonaparte*, "They cannot represent themselves; they must be represented," and of Antonio Gramsci who insisted that representation is valid and necessary in an uneven world, Spivak points out that in their theoretical haste Deleuze and Foucault had ended up conflating two different semantic or thematic strains of "representation": one philosophical, and the other political. Her basic quarrel with them is that in effecting this conflation they had privileged philosophy/theory and erased the political or took the political for granted in the name of the former.

Said, in typical style, and unlike Spivak who is very much in the theory game, undertakes his advocacy of representation in a non-reactive mode. He is really not interested in the task of rescuing representation from attacks by theory. Too much rides for him, and too much positive is at stake for Said in representation and the politics of representation: so much indeed, that he is not bothered by theory's *tout court* demolition of representation. It is because Said positions representation in a different field of forces and influences than the one favored by "high theory," that he draws for it and from it a different set of valences and possibilities. First and foremost, to Said representation is a relentless opponent of any form of "presence" that is sedimented and rendered sacred as "essence," "natural," "primordial," "self-evident," and "trans-historical." In other words, unlike as in the deconstructive philosophic tradition that loves to play on the hyphen that both separates and connects re-presentation to presence, Said would have nothing to do with any sort of putative presence. In Said's thoroughly secular-historical world, not only is there no essence to begin with, but also, there is no essence that is the product or function of existence. All we have is representation and its worldly, all too worldly, human, all too human effects and consequences ("Opponents, Audiences, Constituencies, and Community").

It is important to note here that there is a definitive strategic-modal difference between Said's critique of essentialism and the philosophic critique of essentialism evident in the works of Heidegger, Derrida, Lacan, Althusser, and Foucault. The latter thinkers are truly deconstructive in their approach, that is, they seek to destroy the master's house with the master's tools, to use Audre Lorde's locution. Said, on the other hand, breaks rank with the theory afforded by the philosophical tradition, and goes ahead with his practical project of realizing history through representation. To Said, representations are symptomatic of knowledges that cannot be disinterested, knowledges that are enmeshed, in their putative objectivity, in power and relations of power. The questions that Said is interested in asking again and again are these: How does any self know itself or produce itself as knowledge? When it comes to the production of knowledge, how are distinctions to be made between knowledges that coerce and dominate and those that are based on reciprocity, recognition, and dialog? Clearly, Said has learned deeply from Foucault that the truth of knowledge cannot be separated from the power of knowledge. It is time to recall here one of the issues that haunted *Orientalism*. What exactly was Said saying about the truth of the Orient? Was there a truth to be discovered faithfully? If Said was on the one hand finding fault with Orientalist representations without at the same time producing a correct reading himself, what exactly was he saying?

Said's position all along has been that there is no truth that is already there awaiting correct discovery by the seeker. Said does not subscribe to an adequation model of truth. If there is no truth that is already there to correct and guide the seeker of knowledge, how does one choose and adjudicate among different representations, each of which is differently motivated, differently interested, and differently perspectival? Here is Said's crucial contribution. Representations are worldly, historical, secular performances that cannot pre-know their own truth. In other words, representations do not function as teacherly interventions that are already backed by the right answers. There is no pre-knowledge of whatever kind or provenance. Furthermore, representations as point of view commitments do not admit of facile insider–outsider distinctions. Just because I am an Arab I am not in proximal touch with the truth of Arab reality. I have to produce my reality and my knowledge of my reality through an act of representing myself; that is, I have to alienate myself from myself in the very act of representing myself. "I am my self, ergo, I know myself" is a manifesto of arrogant ignorance that is abhorrent to Said. Insiderism leads to uncritical nativism and holy essentialism: positions that were anathema to Said.

There is even more at stake here. Whereas canonical defenders of the politics of representation are content to say that representation of the self by the self is the most legitimate form of knowledge and leave it at that, Said complicates the matter further by insisting that representation is by definition bi-lateral. The "other" and other histories are already involved and implicated in the self's representation of itself. Any valid act of self-representation must be located not just within one's own history but in a relational space where one's own history is already in a constitutive relationship with someone else's history. Said makes an all-important distinction between the right every point of view has to narrate its own story, and the right of that point of view to tell its own story as though it were its own private and inviolable story where "others" have played no part and have no part to play. The self–other dynamic is crucial to Said. Recognition by the other is crucial for the legitimation of the self's representation of itself. To put it somewhat simply: I have every right to represent myself any way I want; and yet, to the extent that I am not able to elicit a response of recognition from you, my self-representation is ethically and politically flawed.

Said's representational bilateralism is strongly fuelled by the Palestine–Israel situation. It is impossible to talk of Palestinian history without reference to Israeli history and the history of **Zionism**. Both antagonists as partners towards a potential peace based on a two-state solution, an emerging Palestine and an already dominant Israeli state, find themselves enacting the self–other dialectic in all its philosophical as well as historical complexity. Palestine's self-representation requires Israeli recognition just as much as Israeli self-representation is in dire need of Palestinian recognition. **Contrapuntal** representation is what Said is after. It is within the larger and more inclusive rationale of the counterpoint that even the so-called axiomatic politics of representation finds its true worldly, secular-historical meaning and realizes its full potential. What is impressive in this context is that the same Said who makes a strategic distinction between "who is saying it" and "what is being said," refuses to monumentalize this distinction as though it were a natural principle that divides human beings and their interests. Said earns full credit for his impressive follow through with the politics of representation ("Zionism from the Standpoint of Its Victims").

Having identified representation as irreducibly interested and perspectival – in other words, an Arab has a right to narrate her own story rather than be forced to listen to someone else's version of her own story – Said goes on to make the even more significant claim that the Arab's version is also a version, and not the truth itself. "What is being said" is thus both dependent and independent of "who is saying it." Though it would seem initially, that in the act of safeguarding the right of the Arab to produce her own narrative, Said is being a protectionist in total and unconditional support of the Arab point of view and its representational truth claims, in reality Said is achieving a very different politics altogether. He is in fact weaning "truth" away from the stranglehold of identity politics towards an open field of representation and representational politics where in the final analysis "what is being said" matters more than the mere cosmetic or epidermal rectitude of "who is saying it." Just as he would maintain against all odds that generalizations need to be made just when they seem least viable or plausible, Said opens up representational truths to the broader and more inclusive realm of generalizability. The objective is not to create secret and impermeable connections between truth as esoteric and the position of the privileged truth seeker as an "insider," but indeed, quite the opposite. "Speaking for" is meant to be practiced inclusively in the name of the All: as demonstrated by the cover motif of his posthumously published book, *Humanism and Democratic Criticism*, with the ticket stub saying "Admit All" sticking out of the pages of a voluminous, closed book.

It is interesting to see how Edward Said's pragmatic delineation of representation, despite or perhaps because of its disregard of the philosophical thesis of the Self and the Other, achieves a significant breakthrough. Whereas philosophical proponents of the theme of Alterity, the Other with the big O, seem paralyzed and debilitated chronically by their own symptoms (an ongoing scenario where the Other is posited both as real and as inaccessible to the Self, or as real exclusively as a function of its fundamental inaccessibility to the Self), Said steps beyond the glorified realm of the symptom towards something that resembles a cure. Here, in short, is the asymmetry between Said's plan of action and the agenda of high theory. High theory incriminates representation *tout court*, announces the death of representation, untroubled by the fact that in reality we all live in a world where representation is well, alive and kicking. High theory revels in its pure utopianism, celebrating its disjunction from the ways of the world, whereas Said, who could be called a "critical utopianist," stays within the realm of representation to examine, explore, and straighten out its kinks, flaws, and fault lines so as to fine tune it and enable it to do its job better. To Said, abandoning the grammar of representation is to abandon the world and its all too historical ways. He holds on to representation just as he holds on to **humanism** critically. In his pragmatic defense both of humanism and representation, Said does not look for a theoretical break as a precondition for any real change on the ground. His firm belief and conviction is that whatever has gone wrong in the realm of representation can be fixed through a different and rectified practice of representation just as humanism can be mended in the name of a better and improved humanism that has learned from its past mistakes, all without a post-humanist theoretical revolution.

As he had already made it abundantly clear in the context of *Orientalism* and the discussions that followed, representations had to be dialogically structured and intended with the "other" historically and eloquently present in the representation. There was nothing intrinsically wrong in positioning the "Orient" as a theme of conversation between East and West: the important caveat is that both East and West had to be active and articulate interlocutors in the conversation. The East cannot be a silent and repressed accomplice while Western expertise holds forth "about" the Orient. Moreover, different interests can be differentiated on the basis of their intention: is the intention to colonize, dominate, and control the object of analysis, or is the intention something akin to an open, permeable, and non-coercive production of knowledge with emancipatory consequences and potential for both parties? That makes all the difference; and that is all the difference that is needed. To put it somewhat simply, to Said "representation is what representation does," and therefore, theory's epistemological discrediting of representation remains merely theoretical.

There is another significant difference between Said's attitude to representation and high theory's dismissal of representation, and that difference has to do with the sub-theme of the intellectual. Why does Said hold on so passionately to the theme of the intellectual when intellectuals such as Foucault and Deleuze, with whom Said has so much in common otherwise, make the unwavering diagnosis that intellectuals who perpetuate the dire offense of "representing the people" are the problem not the answer, the malady and not the cure? To put an allegorical spin on this theme, is representation the tenor and the intellectual the vehicle; or is it the other way round? Could Said be deemed an elitist because he defends the role of the intellectual in an overall populist-democratic context where the people have come into their own, can speak for themselves, and have no need for intellectual spokespersonship? We may want to ask Said where he stands when it comes to (i) the individual–collectivity relationship, and (ii) the intellectual–people connection. Said, in this context, has much in common with the great Italian Marxist thinker–Communist organizer–cultural theorist–intellectual Antonio Gramsci, the powerful African-American thinker–philosopher–sociologist–activist intellectual W.E.B. Du Bois, and, from Martinique, the charismatic and explosive theorist of postcolonial humanism, Frantz Fanon. What is common to all of these activist intellectuals is their belief in the politics of representation and the binding solidarity between the "I" and the "We," between the masses and the intellectuals. Gramsci would argue that there can be an organic alignment between the interests of the people and those of the intellectual; Du Bois would entrust the "talented tenth," that is, the black intellectual class, to speak for black populism; and Fanon would insist on the urgent need for decolonized African nations to produce critical postcolonial intellectuals who would be of the people in vision and perspective. The problem for them, as it is for Said, is not to get rid of the very category of the intellectual as outdated, redundant, and untrustworthy (this would be the diagnosis offered by Michel Foucault), but rather to create through genuine transformation the right kind of connection and bonding between the people at large and the class known as "the intellectuals." In other words, it is possible to distinguish historically between legitimate and illegitimate intellectuals.

And yet, Said's role as an intellectual should not be conflated with Gramsci or Fanon or Du Bois. Said is not a class man or a "race" man or a national consciousness man. His intellectual work does not have the canonical or the orthodox backing of a category such as class or a formation such as a populist national consciousness or double consciousness. He does not, in the classical sense of the term, speak for or speak from any underlying category. Nor does he as an individual "I" derive his eloquence from "his people" in a spirit of populism. Said is first and foremost a critical, **oppositional** individual who resists any kind of collectivization, any kind of subsumption to a species being. Said comes at the whole problem, by way of Julien Benda and his delineation of the "treason of intellectuals," intellectuals who had turned into apologistic clerks of orthodoxy and the status quo. Quite in the tradition of the Socratic intellectual as an ever rigorous and vigilantly oppositional gadfly, Said commits the intellectual as individual to the world of history, of circumstances, a world structured by power, ideology, uneven flows of privilege, cultural capital, and so on. It is by way of representation that Said demystifies the traditional intellectual and his ivory tower. Said's bottom line is this: not even an intellectual's esoteric high-flying pure research and scholarship is free of the taint of representation. It is representation that binds even the high-minded intellectual, whether she likes it or not, to the world of history. Her productions are, despite their hermetic scholarly intra-mural orientation, representations of the world, at the very least, by default.

There is no question that Said is a supreme "individualist" who does not believe in an easy belonging with the people. As a matter of fact, people or populist phenomenology as a thing in itself or as a force of history hardly figures in Said's thinking. He is unapologetically an individual-centric and intellectual-centric thinker who is keen to avoid, from the individual's perspective, the fallacy of solipsism/narcissism/subjectivism; and from the intellectual standpoint, to avoid the error of hermeticism and the practice of

scholarship as an esoteric "wall to wall" discursive **virtuosity**. It is representation that comes to Said's rescue. It is representation that restores the world
and **worldliness** to Edward Said, the individual and Said, the academic critic.
Unlike Marx, or Gramsci, or a Bakhtin, or even a Raymond Williams, who
are by very definition species-being- or community- or collectivity-centric
thinkers, Said just assumes the centrality of the individual as well as of the
intellectual. He is really not interested in a genealogical or a philosophically
diagnostic understanding (the etiology) of the categories known as "the
individual" and "the intellectual." Said has a pragmatic definition of each
concept, that is, anything is what it does, and he is content to stay and
perform within the space opened up by that definition.

It must be said, in the context of the politics of representation, that
Said is intensely a "for the people man," and not a people-man: hence
the insistence on representation. Said will defend intellectuality, its subtle
nuances, hard-fought complexities, irresolvable contradictions; but what
he will not defend is an intellectuality that refuses to be worldly in the name
of its own expertise and specialist autonomy. In much the same way, Said
is a resolute and uncompromising individual, like Ralph Ellison and James
Baldwin, who will not prioritize some self-evident and transparent notion
of collectivity or community over the individual and the individual's right
not to belong or belong in an exilic or oppositional mode. But here, too,
Said would remind us that in the very act of "speaking" is also "speaking
for": in other words, representation is built into every articulation as the
necessary precondition for its meaning. Perhaps we might even stretch the
analogy further and say that Said's advocacy of representational meaning as
ubiquitous and always "given" in its worldliness is a lot like Maurice Merleau-
Ponty's phenomenological insistence that we are condemned to meaning;
that is, there is no getting away from the omnipresence of meaning. In Said's
context, it would be the omnipresence of representation.

It is not coincidental that the theme of one of Said's series of lectures is
Representations of the Intellectual. The title does an effective double take: on
the one hand, the articulations of the intellectual understood and valorized
as representations of the world, and on the other, the meaningful representation of the very concept of "the intellectual." On the one hand, worldliness
or reality is presented as the function of representation of the intellectual;
and on the other, the figure of the intellectual is denied any kind of conceptual or epistemological autonomy, and is in fact rendered susceptible
to an act of representation from without, which is to say, the intellectual
cannot get away with a self-image that avoids or sidesteps the danger of

being represented by the world. It is this dyadic reciprocity between "representation" and "intellectuality" that in the ultimate analysis rescues the Saidian intellectual from the trap of elitism. If the criticism is that Said is a high culture intellectual rather than a popular culture intellectual, then, that is quite all right. His contemporaries never expected him to comment on the Beatles, or the blues, or jazz, or rap. He had no problem with that; he would have no problem acknowledging that intellectuality could and should have multiple bases. His important message to us is that no amount or no kind of scholarly, academic, or professional work, however profound or rarefied, can pretend to be non- or post-representational. Theory would be the overall name for such a pretentious and disingenuous claim.

secular criticism   It is interesting that the adjective "secular" is a lot more operative in Said's critical vocabulary than the noun form "secularism." Said would hold forth on secular politics, secular interpretation, secular analysis, and secular criticism, all of which are vital to his critical performance. Unlike some of his distinguished contemporaries such as Ashis Nandy, Dipesh Chakrabarty, Partha Chatterjee, Talal Asad, Rustom Bharucha, Charles Taylor, William Connolly, and others who take on secularism substantively and frontally in terms of its relationship to religion, spirituality, metaphysics, and questions of faith, Said is satisfied to avow every now and then his disinterest in religion, metaphysics, and faith, and then go on to identify himself as secular through and through. He is really not interested in submitting secularism to a thorough genealogical scrutiny, or evaluating the epistemological claims of secularism in relation to other forms of knowledge, or detecting hidden ideological forms of complicity between church and state and the sublation, in secularism, of certain aspects and dimensions of Judeo-Christian axiology, or producing a symptomatic reading of how secularism was introduced to the non-West at a certain historical juncture, as part and parcel of the template of colonial modernity, or of differentiating between secularism as a political platform and secularism as epistemology, and finally, raising a controversial question such as, "Is it possible to be a secular fundamentalist?" Not being a philosopher or a philosophic thinker, time and again, as in his critical engagement with humanism, Said strategically sidesteps a comprehensive conceptual or theoretical engagement with secularism, and instead deploys the term "secular" opportunistically, and it

A Said Dictionary, First Edition. R. Radhakrishnan.
© 2012 John Wiley & Sons, Ltd. Published 2012 by John Wiley & Sons, Ltd.

might be said, persuasively, to cover a limited range of issues that constitute his problematic.

With this preface, let us see how Said defines and describes the secular mindset. Secular, to Said, is synonymous with "historical," in so far as history is made for humanity by humanity without any recourse to providence, hidden origins, sacred, mysterious covenants with prophecies, and other trans-historical essences masquerading in the name of chosen peoples, **narratives**, and destinies. In a secular world that is nothing but historical, there can be no room for an identity politics based on divine guarantees that are not historically real or verifiable. Moreover, in a secular world, different histories of different peoples and groups and cultures have to negotiate with one another coevally in full acknowledgment of the "historical" reality of their mutual imbrications, overlaps, and contestations. In other words, no participant is allowed to pull the rank of primordiality to trump over the merely historical claims of other peoples, or pretend to be acting in sacred alignment with messianic or providential temporalities ("Secular Criticism").

Well before the publication of his essay, "Secular Criticism," we can see Said passionately espousing the secular attitude by way of his abiding appreciation of **Giambattista Vico's** *The New Science*. What makes Said's idiosyncratic use of secularism uniquely trenchant is the fact that he pits secularism against the kind of feral, separatist, and jingoistic and "blood and guts" identity politics that **nationalism** often fosters. To put it somewhat reductively, two contesting secular parties are more capable of coming to an amicable solution that does not violate either party than two warring contestants one of whom is a Christian and the other a Muslim, or one of whom is a Hindu and the other a Muslim. It is not that secularism does not have its own deeply held convictions or that it does not prosecute its own truth claims resolutely and with ideological vehemence and conviction; what marks the difference is the manner in which the secular imagination validates and legitimates its truth claims.

In the name of what does secularism legitimate its perspective? It is clearly not in the name of God, or Allah, or Rama, or Zion, or a divinely decreed right of a chosen people to return to a primordial home, or in the name of an identity that absolutely precedes the historical subject, or in the name of an ideal possibility, or essence, or an immaculate architectonics of origin as prophetic fulfillment. It is in the name of history as an active and human process that secular thinking makes its truth claims. These truth claims are not absolute or irrefragable. These truths are not the vindications of primordial assumptions about any one identity, be it Hindu, Muslim, or anything else. Unlike identity politics, which, in Said's reading, stems from a trans-historical and/or primordial conviction, a conviction that will not submit itself to historical verification or correction, secular politics is based on the politics of **representation** that does not pre-know its object. Fraught questions such as "Who is a Jew?" "Who is an Arab?" "Who is a woman?" "Who is an American?" can be resolved either with holy and pious references to myths of origins that dictate who anyone is or can be, or by way of a secular politics of representation that aligns "identity" with the actual processes of history. Within the secular world of historical representation, "presence" is what representation does or achieves. Unlike identity politics that fixes who one is once and for all, and often quarantines the question of who one is from the problematic question of who the other is, the politics of representation does not lay down an immutable relationship between "who is speaking" and "what is being said," and, moreover, insists that the historical claims of any one group or collective identity be read relationally in terms of the claims of another group.

To put it somewhat starkly, there can be no Israeli identity without reference to a Palestinian identity, and the right of Jews to return to their homeland cannot be honored primordially with reference to a mythic home and mythic diaspora. The Jewish right to return has to represent itself along-side the Palestinian right to return to a Palestine: a Palestine that was lost to the Palestinians as a result of the Balfour Declaration and the violent creation of an independent Israel. The day of rejoicing for Israelis was a day of plangent mourning for Palestinians who, as Said memorably argued in one of his essays, had become the abject victims of people who themselves had been victims of the Holocaust. Secular thinking demands that different representational paradigms work themselves out, in a world of shared and overlapping histories, not in separatist isolation but in contestatory, con-trapuntal, and cooperative alignment with other histories: in other words, no mystification of historical reality by any one or group in the name of spurious trans-historical claims of authenticity, origination, and so on.

Said's secular thinking is intended in opposition (i) to religious modes of analysis that often tend to become other-worldly and mythical in their denial of lived histories, and (ii) against ossified forms of nationalisms that have turned into un-self-reflexive and chauvinistic and/or xenophobic cele-brations of nativism and so-called autochthony. What makes Said's critical trajectory unique is that he invokes the secular against the national (a point well made in Amir Mufti's recent essay, "Secular Criticism"), rather than trot out the by now well-worn thesis that nationalism is the political armature for the epistemology of secularism. Like others – for example, Immanuel Wallerstein and Etienne Balibar – Said lays bare the ethico-political as well as epistemological bankruptcy of nationalism as a mode of imagined communal belonging. Unlike his theoretically facile European counterparts, Said has to cast an ambivalent eye on the politics of nationalism; for he cannot be unmindful of the Palestinian people without a national home, or dismissive of the meritorious record of a whole range of decolonizing nationalisms in Africa and Asia. Said's polemical point is that once nationalism comes out of its phase of decolonization and attempts to historicize itself in its own protagonistic terms, it flounders, it fails. Based on a virulent rationale of an Us and a Them, nationalisms produce minorities all over the world, and are easily hijacked by exclusionary identitarian movements, informed and fuelled by nostalgic visions of a golden past that never existed. Nationalisms create homes for one set of people narrowly defined so that some "other" people may experience these very homes as their spaces of **exile**. As a result we have Hindu and Islamic and Celtic and Anglo-Saxon nationalisms that thrive on the notion of the excluded "other." The nation becomes for Said, as it does for Rabindranath Tagore, a virulent and punitive home that builds walls and fences around itself and, consequently, the home turns into an antagonist of the world. Paradoxically, the home becomes a militarized zone whose sole purpose is to keep the world "out."

The term "secular" functions for Said as the name for a state of being that by definition is nameless, or cannot have a name. The "secular," in many ways, for Said, is a near synonym for the "homeless" and the "exilic," and as such remains a critical-utopian form of longing for a state of being that is at best literary or theoretical. We live in a world divided into nation states even as we ruefully acknowledge the insufficiency of nation states to speak for our trans-national, post-national, planetary, and diasporic realities and experiences. In Said's work, the "secular" works consistently as a perspectival energy or force or will or intention that refuses to accommodate itself within what Amitav Ghosh has eloquently termed the "shadow lines" of nationalism. There is an intimate critical-utopian connection between the "exilic" and the "secular" in Said's work, where "exile" represents a theoretical living out of what hegemonic and dominant realities preclude or negate. We see adumbrations of this in his essay on secular criticism: an essay where the term "secular" is never really described or defined, but is always gestured towards obliquely as an ever-receding horizon that is not reducible to a specific nameable landscape. In this essay, "secular" is articulated with critical consciousness that in turn is understood and valorized as "**opposi-tional**" in perspective. As Said begins this essay, he mentions four kinds of criticism (practical criticism, academic literary history, literary appreciation and interpretation, and finally **theory** as it comes from Europe) that have been practiced so far in the history of Western literature. He identifies the essays that constitute the entire volume *The World, the Text, the Critic* as belonging to one or other of the four forms, and goes on to anticipate an emerging worldly and critical enterprise that "can only be practiced outside and beyond the consensus ruling the art today in the four accepted forms I mentioned earlier" (p. 5).

The secular stands for a different way of taking up critical accountability for the worlding of the world, that is, the worlding of the world as a readable, historical **text**. The secular stance is also a perspectival stance: the taking up of a position that is forever "**between**," where "between-ness" connotes freedom from different kinds of exactions, orthodoxies, and predictable pieties, and formulaic rituals. As he works his rhetoric between the given-ness of filiation and the openness of **affiliation** that may choose to endorse, revise, or oppose filiation, Said openly idealizes the "exilic" point of view as the most worldly of positions. It is precisely from the dispossessed and alienated point of view of exile that the known world may be perennially de-familiarized and re-understood in truly generous, non-dogmatic, inclusive, and transformative ways. It is no coincidence that **Eric Auerbach** is the hero in this chapter: the Auerbach who writes his monumental work *Mimesis* not from a location of profound accommodation, but from a position of exile from the culture that he so loves and of which he is a part. A truly secular consciousness negates the very notion of home and homeliness and in the process makes the whole world a home. To be at home in the world is to acquire the ability to denaturalize every home from the point of view of exile and of critical non-belonging. It is only when home is nailed down to notions of filial, proper, and orthodox belonging that the home begins to resemble a prison. In Said's critical double vision, home and exile are forever articulated together in a differential relationship where "home" is real only to the extent that it becomes the object for the critical/exilic point of view, and "exile" is real only to the extent that it exists as a perennial perspective from which home can forever be destabilized and rendered un-natural. Simultaneously political and epistemological, the exilic point of view captures both the reality of a philosophic vision as well as the dire on-the-ground realities of Palestinian dispossession and the Palestinian exilic longing for a national home. The secular sensibility needs a home not as substance, essence, point of arrival and/or departure, as an anchor or a stable haven for the final landing of identity, but as a problematic subject as well as object for the operations of critical thought and critical consciousness. To be secular is to realize a radical "out-of place-ness" not as a historical given but as the product and function of critical consciousness. If every document of civilization is also a document of barbarism, and if every home in history has exiled some carefully chosen "other," then the only viable attitude to home is that of critical ambivalence. Homes that exact uncritical solidarity and preempt critique and criticism in the name of natural or filial belonging are to be avoided and rejected with summary conviction and integrity.

Distance from home: that is the crucial phrase. If home is to be realized as a world for all human beings, then it automatically follows that "home," in its narrow, identitarian, provincial, jingoistic, and xenophobic sense, has to be thoroughly deconstructed and rendered unfit for accommodation. Said's take on home here resembles a certain strain of poststructuralism and deconstruction that I described in one of my early essays ("Ethnic Identity and Poststructuralist Differance") as the project of practicing on the one hand a certain strategic "identity politics" while at the same time engaging in the deconstruction of "identity as such," that is, of Identity with a capital "I." What also comes to mind here is Gloria Anzaldua's ambivalent as well as counter-mnemonic invocation of "home." The rich and intense debates between Mohandas Gandhi and Rabindranath Tagore, between the Mahatma and the Poet, in the context of India's freedom struggle, also raised the all-important question of *Visva Bharathi*, of India as the World, and the World as India. Neither Tagore nor Gandhi, despite the heat of the moment of decolonization, was a "nationalist." To Gandhi, nationality was a term quite alien to the Indian ethos as well as epistemology, and Tagore, who excoriated nationalism as a petty worldview, had in mind a vision of a de-territorialized India that would be diasporized the world over.

In short, the "secular" is an agile and restless critical performance that avoids the pitfalls of orthodox identity on the one hand and the dangers and the seductions of systemic, and therefore formulaic and inflexible, forms of thinking, on the other. Said's use of the term "secular" does a lot more than merely reiterate the canonical theme of "separation of Religion and State." It does something more, something that is not necessarily intended in the orig-inal semantics of the term. Said's genius lies in the manner in which he uses the term to advance the cause of what we might term "the historical practice of human history," that is, a practice that totally disallows the sacralization of one's own history in the name of providence, chosen-ness of a people, exceptionalism, assumptions of essence, nativism, primordiality, and so on. Said's intervention is even deeper and more imaginative than that. Under the compelling and binding rubric of "secular," he remaps the very meaning of what it means to be historical. For Said, to be historical means to be touched by several histories all at the same time. An American, for example, in the name of practicing or remaining true to her history, cannot quarantine or hijack American history from its connectedness and imbrication with other histories. To be historical is to be both intra-historical and inter-historical in the same pulse and in the same breath. "Discrepant and overlapping" are the terms that Said uses again and again with normative zeal to drive home the point that we all live in the same world that is sutured together differentially within a binding overlap. To live just by one's own histori-cal imperative sundered from other histories is a counter-empirical lie, for the simple and demonstrable reason that there is no such phenomenon as "one's own history" that is an island unto itself. It is the overlap that makes history secular and historical, but the overlap is not a benign overlap. It is indeed a discrepant overlap characterized by unevenness and asymmetry. In short, for Said, the world is a secularly historical theater where history can be enacted symptomatically and multi-laterally, a stage where history and its inequalities can be identified, dealt with, and transformed from a point of view that has room and place for everyone and not just some chosen or dominant perspective that arrogates to itself the privilege of acting on behalf of all other histories. In short, it is in the name of the secular that Said calls for the generalization of human historicity on the very basis of the discrepant overlap. "Secular" is to Said what "class" is to Marx. Each term in its own way endeavors to create trans-local and shareable solidarities across seemingly impassable differences and incommensurabilities.

speaking truth to power   (or, the production of non-coercive truth) Here is a theme that is common and dear to both Edward Said and Michel Fou-cault, though they go about their tasks on different lines. **Oppositionality** is a wavelength that Said lives and dies and swears by, unswervingly and unconditionally. Whether it be system or culture or nationality or the cor-rectness of a political movement, Said can always be heard in the voice of a critical consciousness that succeeds in voicing opposition from within the very heart of solidarity. It is well known how much Said's work as a critical partisan of the Palestinian national cause was censored by the PLO under the control of Yasser Arafat. Said spoke several unpleasant truths, and produced truth against the grain of every possible doctrinal orthodoxy. He did practice *parrhesia* pretty much all through his life after the publication of *Orientalism* in 1978. He was condemned, vilified, described as the "professor of terror," and received regular death threats from a range of sources. It is in the name of the committed public **intellectual** (the engaged intellectual in the Sartrean sense of the term) that Said undertakes the task of speaking truth to power in a spirit of interested disinterestedness: interested in the name of a will to truth that refuses complicity with any form of dominance, dogma, or orthodoxy. Said seems to be fascinated by oppositionality *per se* as though it were a constituency in and by itself. Foucault, for example, is quite similar with his Nietzschean insistence on the perennial sacrifice of the knowing subject in the processes of knowing. Both Said and Foucault, each in his way, are keen on protecting flows of knowledge from premature closure by a gatekeeping political orthodoxy.

Here as elsewhere, Said's strategy is supremely practical. He is not interested in defining and providing a typology of different forms of power: ethical, political, epistemological, and so on. Nor is he interested in making distinctions between good power and bad power, between a power that is properly empowering and the other kind that leads to arrogance, corruption, and ruthless unilateralism. Unlike Foucault, he is not interested in accounting for the ubiquitously productive and capillary nature of power and its micro-physical dimension. He is equally not concerned to get into the complex, interdependent, and contradictory relationships between macro-political and micro-political forms of power. He, to use a couple of popular and effective clichés, goes for the jugular, cuts to the chase, and asks the following question: How does power as a form of inhibition or censorship prevent human critical consciousness from launching its own investigation into the nature of reality? The real issue for Said here is the bugbear of conformism. Like Ralph Waldo Emerson who would declare with magisterial conviction intellectuality that consistency is the virtue of hobgoblins, or Fanon who would cry out from the depths of his racialized and colonized humanity and desire to be forever a questioning body, or Foucault (and Gandhi) whose critical fantasy is never to be the same thinker from one moment to the next, or Noam Chomsky and his brand of political anarchism, or Raymond Williams and his indefatigable "resources of hope" against the heavy odds of system-centric cynicism, pessimism, and nihilism, Said too valorizes non-conformism as an absolute value, even though this very absolute value can only be the product and function of a specific and relative oppositional encounter with a particular dominant regime of truth.

But here again, and this becomes inevitable when one attempts to compare Said with similar-minded thinkers and intellectuals, Said resembles different thinkers for different reasons in different ways. If we took Said away as the common link, the other thinkers in the comparative grid would not belong together in the same room. This point is worth noting, because it shows that Said's freewheeling eclecticism defies conventional classification and makes for non-standard configurations and genealogies.

Said's manifesto of "speaking truth to power" is a critical-utopian plan of action: utopian to the extent that it will not accept any achieved positivity as a definitive arrival that preempts further departures and transformations, and critical in the sense that the ongoing utopian production has to be the result of specific readings against the grain of the powers that be at any given moment in history.

So, how does Said identify and recognize the enemies against whose power truth is to be galvanized? His list would look something like this: **nationalism** and the state, chauvinism, patriotism, religion, **professionalism** and the cult of expertise, essentialism, fundamentalism, cultural nativism, system, tribalism, authoritarianism of any sort or breed, any form of ahistoricism or trans-historicism, messianism, exceptionalism, primordialism, or origin-based thinking. What concerned him most was solidarity before critique, and speaking truth to power was a way of keeping solidarity honest in the name of solidarities to come. The notion of the *avenir* (what was to come) was as precious to Said as it was to Derrida. If speaking truth to power could be considered a micro-political practice, that is, an enunciatory or subject-positional or discursive practice, then the question that follows is: what is the macro-political location (such as class, gender, nationality, sexuality) that underlies such a practice? In other words, for the micro-political practice to be meaningful and well directed, should it emanate from a proper and well-accredited location? Said's answer would be: No, not at all. For Said, speaking truth to power is most effective and credible when it emerges from an exilic location.

Is there any location that in principle is exempt from any kind of prior complicity with Power, or should we say in the lower case, determinate regimes of power? Is there a pure outside from which the critic can launch a war of maneuver (Gramsci); or is what is possible only a passive revolution, a war of strategy (Gramsci again) to be waged from within the system? How "pure" should critical consciousness be before it can arrogate to itself the idealist task of speaking for a truth that has not yet been touched by Power? The fundamental question that comes up here is that of ethical **humanism** and its viability. It is typical of Said that not being a philosophical thinker, he does not invoke the category of the ethical in a significant way in his writings; but ethics is precisely what is at stake in any discussion of speaking truth to power. Said's perennial concern for the other and the other's point of view is quite impeccable. Albert Camus, for one, after the disillusionment with Stalinist communism and its terrorism as well as in the context of France's Algerian Colonialism, elects to be ethical at the expense of the political: a position for which he is squarely taken to task by his erstwhile friend and comrade, Jean-Paul Sartre. Said, while not an ethicist in that tradition, does indeed endeavor to wear the mantle of the political without succumbing to "politics." It is as a reformed humanist, that is, a humanist who has learned with great humility from the egregious errors and crimes committed by humanism, that Said exhorts an exilic critical consciousness to speak truth to power. It is in the name of a radically auto-critical humanism that the Saidian individual-intellectual speaks, non-denominationally in the name of the All.

In different ways, both Foucault and Said resort to the kind of metaphoric play that literature affords. It is no secret that many of Foucault's utopian dreams and fantasies are mediated through literature, and it is equally transparent that Said looks to literature for truly emancipatory possibilities. And of course, there has been a long tradition of writers being persecuted, exiled, and even killed for their antinomian, seditious politics of words: no doubt Rushdie and the *fatwa* come to mind here. The tradition of a literary utopian politics is indeed as long as it is multi-historical. Ethical literary humanism, in its valiant and often unpopular attempts to bridge the actual and the ideal, to launch the "what ought to be" from the inequitable poverty of "what is," has suffered considerable persecution. In his later work, Said makes it clear that he would like to belong to a tradition of ethical humanists, rather than to a family of arid second order theorists who acknowledge neither power nor the world, and instead suffocate in the truths of their hermetically sealed discourses.

If Said sees himself as speaking truth to power, (i) is his politics powerful or empowered? (ii) Is his truth exempt from the hauntings of power? (iii) Is such a truth critically negative or affirmative: does it "aye say" or "nay say"? It is a pity that Said does not address these issues in any conceptually coherent or systematic way, but clearly it does not mean that he is unaware of the profound complications raised by these questions. He just assumes that many of these so-called complications get addressed, though never resolved (and why should they be unless you are a theory zealot or totalizer?), during the moment of practice and performance. On the basis of Said's writings, it is possible to predict his responses. To question 1: his politics is indeed powerful in resistance to the dominant discourse. But Said is not interested in tracing the macro- as well as the micro-political differences between power in its resistant versus power in its affirmative phase, just as he is not interested in the Foucauldian project of studying the phenomenon of "power as such" across the board. Such exercises for Said would represent a kind of theoretical inflation that creates the effect that concepts and categories have a "pure" meaning outside of their contextual applications. To question 2: this should be a crucial question for Said, but his critical orientation, driven by his critical agenda and intentionality, causes him to bypass it. Like Gandhi and other political thinkers who have attempted to tilt the balance, in the phrase "ethico-political," towards the ethical and "purify" politics, but unlike the philosophically or spiritually oriented thinkers, Said does not attempt to differentiate the persuasive power of truth from other phenomenologies of power. (The Gandhi–Tagore debates come to mind here.) I am thinking here of the "powerful" Sanskrit slogan *Satyameva Jayate*, which translates as "Truth alone will triumph," and in this context it is customary for scholars to differentiate the moral power of truth from power as politically hegemonic or dominant. If truth still wins, which means that when truth wins there are losers, how is the win enjoyed by truth different from other victories that participate in a winner-take-all zero-sum dispensation? Is speaking truth to power then inevitably and chronically double-conscious? To question 3: Said would use the term "critical consciousness" to subsume and oversee the critical and the affirmative but would differentiate his operation from deconstruction, which, to Said, is exclusively linguistic and systemic.

In this entire problematic, it is again by resolutely disallowing philosophical formulations of political questions and issues that Said realizes **worldliness**. Whether it is possible to exorcize the philosophical dimension of reality by just not thinking about it is a question too large and complicated to be dealt with here.

specular/border intellectual   This is the eloquent phrase that Abdul JanMohamed uses to describe the specific nature of Said's intellectuality, and it really does justice to the elusive and atypical Saidian model. The most important question concerning Said is this: given his ambassadorial location and sensibility, where does he belong, and what or whom does he represent? Is he a unilateral ambassador, or is he bilateral? Even though ambassadors by definition belong to a home country of which they are the representative (and this should potentially provide them with some sort of ontological consistency), they cannot but be influenced substantively by the context in which they find themselves as ambassadors, in the host country where they are guests. To be efficacious, the voice of the ambassador has to carry a message from the home country and be able to present it in an alien context in a persuasive manner. In other words, like Hermes, the ambassador is also a messenger who needs to be rhetorically alive to questions of reception, the characteristics of the listening culture. The message may have to be massaged, rhetorically finessed, without any basic violation to the original intention. But this ambassadorial situation in itself does not invoke either the mirror (specular) or the border image; there is something more to Said's context.

Said is an interesting instance of a two-way ambassador: he is a Palestinian American living in the diaspora. That is his ontological orientation. He is by professional training an academic deeply immersed in Western literature, culture, and **theory**. That makes him Western, epistemologically speaking. Here is the double twist: he is a hyphenated Palestinian-American who as a diasporic citizen has to do double duty, advocating Palestine here in America, and endeavoring to transform the American perspective to be supportive and understanding of Palestinians living there. At the specialist level, he is not an Arabist, but a Western comparatist modernist seeking to instrumentalize his alien erudition in tune with the non-West. In fact, in a strange way, Said's own point of entry into the non-West is by way of **Orientalist** representations. Said's subject position thus resists all the normal coordinates that govern the politics of one-to-one **representation**, and his sense of belonging is "borderly" and is recalcitrant to the politics of naming. "The specular border intellectual," according to JanMohamed, "while perhaps equally familiar with two cultures, finds himself or herself unable or unwilling to be 'at home' in these societies. Caught between several cultures or groups, none of which are deemed sufficiently enabling or productive, the specular intellectual subjects the cultures to analytic scrutiny rather than combining them; he or she utilizes his or her interstitial cultural space as a vantage point from which to define, implicitly or explicitly, other, utopian possibilities of group formation" ("Worldliness-without-World," 97). JanMohamed's elegantly argued essay raises the border question (Gloria Anzaldua's *Borderlands* comes to mind here; and we are also reminded of Walter Mignolo's work on "border gnoseology") on two levels: existential and epistemological. Said's objective, as JanMohamed points out, is the search for alternatives, for "other" ways of living and knowing that are utopian. From Said's perspective, what is desirable is not the mere juxtaposition of two identities that are both separated and connected by a border, for example, Tex-Mex, but something beyond and utopian that is not reducible to any kind of identity politics or to a formula of hyphenation.

The border, of course, begins to function for Said as a metaphor for restless and mercurial thinking that will not abandon the borderland in the name of security, assimilation, or naturalization. Instead, the border mentality is to be cultivated rigorously to avoid a number of pitfalls: essentialism, mindless homogeneity, either-or identity politics, to name a few. The site of the border also turns into an ideal laboratory where the I–We relationship can be posed as a perennial question. The border individual/intellectual has to be in a state of chronic hyphenation that cannot be resolved or synthesized into a mono-valent belonging. The allegiance of the border is to itself but since the border is a mode of "**between-ness**" it has to do its critical work in response to the two identities that constitute it as border. To Said who has always interrogated the notion of home as identity and heartland, the border becomes an ideal location from which critique can be directed in either direction. In fact, for Said the border functions as close to pure perspective as possible, as a concept metaphor for a mode of intellectual being that can enjoy **worldliness** without the world.

What is the content of Said's critical consciousness? Is he just reflecting (as the term specular would imply) the West back to itself, but in a way that alienates the West from its normative self-recognition? Is Said the spoiler, the insider as outsider? If his mode is that of insider-outsider, is he equally an insider-outsider *vis-à-vis* the non-West as well? Is he reflecting the non-Western world too back to itself from a troubling and unsettling angle? Like the famous Möbius strip that disallows stable notions of insides and outsides, Said's intellectual location too escapes easy coordination. Given his **contrapuntal** orientation in general, his location becomes even more elusive. He is not a card-carrying sovereign citizen of either world, and it is through his critical work at the border that Said breaks down the distinctions between intra- and inter-historical dimensions. Said's primary sense of constituency is not East or West, America or Arab **nationalism**: he is first and foremost a critic whose driving ethic is not to arrive at a canonical identity that has rid itself of borderly problems, but rather to keep open-ended forever the relationship between solidarity/belonging and critique. What is interesting about border intellectuals is that they cannot be "representative" or "representing" voices since borders are the kind of mobile phenomena that beg the very question of representation.

Borders are not sovereign spaces (instead, they are "heterotopic" in Michel Foucault's sense of the term) like nation states that speak with one voice; and border folks are multiply and heterogeneously constituted and therefore cannot be brought under an un-shifting single "I–We" axis. The border is the ideal location where the intellectual can indulge her desire to actualize perennial **oppositionality** as its own politics and constituency, and to realize the existential condition in the intellectual commitment and *vice versa*. That would be closer to Said's agenda. To Said, neither the intellectual nor the individual needs to be ensconced in the heartland of any identity, community, or sovereign regime. That *Out of Place* should be the title of Said's memoirs makes good sense: for example, a border is a perfect example of a place that is out of place, normatively speaking.

style   Quite a stylist himself, as a person–writer–**intellectual**, Said, throughout his career and particularly since *The World, the Text, and the Critic*, and most poignantly in his posthumous work *On Late Style*, was an impassioned defender of "style" and its multiple and multi-layered valences. In a theoretical milieu that privileges system, structure, and discourse, celebrates routinely "the death of the author," parses the author as "author-function," and generally repudiates notions such as "originality," "intentionality," and the "individual" as unfortunate residuals from a dead or moribund **humanism**, Said unabashedly retrieves "style" aesthetically, politically, and theoretically. Of a piece with his advocacy of the individual, **oppositional critical** consciousness, and an imaginative and agential intentionality that steers clear both of the filiative naturalness of Culture and the professional blandishments of System, Said's elaboration of style is both critical and affirmative, polemically antagonistic and protagonistic. In other words, "style" functions in Said's vocabulary both as a way of combating and demystifying high **theory** that works by way of an impersonal discursivity, and as a mode of advancing its own truth claims based on an ever-changing **worldliness** and historical circumstantiality. It is interesting to note that, from *Orientalism* onwards, Said begins to develop, in a theoretically non-fussy manner, a critical repertoire or a combinatorics of terms in active endorsement of his intellectual agenda. Each term, whether a coinage or a creative borrowing or a revisionist renewal of an earlier usage, works both independently and in intimate relationship with the other terms that constitute the constellation: for example, criticism, consciousness, oppositional, invention, originality, secular, performance, **text**, voice, sensibility, form and content, the aesthetic and the political, **virtuosity**, repetition, intentionality, individuality, **exile**, style, **narrative**, presentation, **representation**, worldliness, and so on.

It is only appropriate that "style" should function so centrally for someone who forever sought to enfranchise literature both for its own sake and as a transformative and interventionary point of entry into the world. In Said's critical re-articulation of literary humanism as a pivotal participant in the project of social and political change, "style" is both part of Said's *la langue* as well as his *la parole*. In other words, it takes on both a conceptual-semantic stability even as it becomes available to ongoing transformations through individual performances and performativity. Said's critical use of style has very little to do with style as in ornate display or cosmetic or figurative beautification, or with the branch of study known as "stylistics." Even though not a philosophical thinker or critic, Said deftly "philosophizes" style to reach out and touch on a broad spectrum of issues. Neither a rank amateur expressivity nor a professional compulsion, "style" works in Said's thinking as a way of dwelling critically in the world: as a complex and self-reflexive performance that transcends the theory–practice, the text–world stalemate.

It is quite clear that by style Said does not mean something flamboyantly romantic and iconoclastic that trespasses the integrity of the written text and goes on to do its own anarchic and a-nomic thing. To put it in the context of the age-old distinction, within English literary history, Said's style belongs neither to classicism nor romanticism. The signature of the author is neither its own maverick or idiosyncratic rationale nor a mechanical adherence to an existing mode; the signature of the author is a signature on a pre-existing text. The original integrity of the musical text is repeated non-identically each time an author performs that text with style. Said in a way is invoking the famous philosophical conundrum: If a tree falls in a forest with nobody there, does it still make a noise? To Said, even in the most private, but not solipsistic, context of even a soliloquy, where either total subjectivity or total objectivity is supposed to prevail, there is always a sending and a receiving, and an inevitable repetition intended for reception; and it is in such an immediate, concrete, lively, and contingent context that worldlessness is replaced by worldliness.

It is only germane that Said chooses music and Glenn Gould for his demonstration of style as voice, variation, dialect, idiolect; for music, despite its mathematics-like capacity for symbolic abstraction and notational self-sufficiency, is intended for live performance and live ears. When we talk about a Horowitz or a Gould offering their version of a Bach or a Beethoven text, what we are acknowledging is the real possibility of the same text being rendered different from itself by the "irreducible individuality" of each performer. The impersonal text with its life entombed within the notational parameters of the printed page requires to be "worlded" by the style of the individual performer/player, who, in the very act of applying herself to the "impersonal text," relives it and relieves it of its hermetic loneliness. There are two concerns here for Said: how to neutralize the worldlessness of the text, and how to redeem and recover the performer's "irreducible individuality" with the help of the text. Style is the opposite of silence, which is the same thing after all as identical repetition. If the Beethoven text were so strong, so undeniably and irrefragably itself, that it makes it impossible for a conductor or a performer to produce her own dialectic or idiolectic variation, what we then have is the stunning silence of the perfect acoustic chamber that reduces all repetitions into a state of voicelessness.

In opposition to such a sterile notion of perfection, Said conceptualizes style as a form of double consciousness that renders the already formed text vulnerable to its present historicity: the immediate circumstance where it has to be produced again through artistic labor and application. What is interesting to note is that in Said's usage, style is aligned with vulnerability and historical contingency rather than with marmoreal perfection. When Said invokes voice as covalent with style, the adjective he uses is "transitory." To Said it is crucial that the text be kept alive and not rendered eternal or timeless in the name of formal perfection (the phrase "*mot juste*" comes to mind), and "kept alive" here is the same as "acknowledged as mortal and mutable." Unlike as in Derrida's terminology where "voice" represents a form of humanistic domination over processes of language, that is, phonocentrism, Said employs "voice" to connote historical vulnerability and contingency. Style, in Said's usage, turns into a creative way of honoring the text without at the same time surrendering to the text a life of its own that predetermines individual performance and variation.

It is consistent with Said's own critical style that in his keenly appreciative essays on Jonathan Swift ("Swift's Tory Anarchy," "Swift as Intellectual," in *The World, the Text, and the Critic*), Said makes his case for style even more persuasively than in the more theoretically oriented chapters of *The World, the Text, and the Critic*. In his Swift essays, Said demonstrates, in an act of practical criticism, Swiftian style in action. Rather than read Swift primarily as a writer with a predetermined message, a didactic passion, or a strong political conviction, Said tells us how Swift the writer employs something called style both to craft his arguments and polemical positions and in the process makes his style a representation as well as a representative of his individual intentions. Style here is not merely figurative or tropological: it stands for the author and the author's irreducible individuality. Not only does he read Swift against the grain of contemporary theoretical fads and fashions that do not find Swift an attractive site for their operations, but he also offers us a compelling reason why theory and theorists *à la* Foucault and Derrida bypass what is so unique about Swift's sensibility as author and intellectual. "In general," Said argues, "contemporary criticism has been concerned with authors and texts whose formal characteristics exist in some disjunctive relationship with their ideological or thematic surface: thus the critic's job is to illuminate the disjunction by exposing, or deconstructing, the contradictions woven into the text's formal being." Said goes on to say that it is precisely because "Swift resists this approach" that he becomes so "interesting and challenging a figure." Said's point is that Swift is the kind of writer who "resists any kind of critical approach that does not make his existence, his functioning, and above all his self-consciousness as an intellectual – albeit an intellectual in the special historical circumstances of his cultural moment – the main avenue to approaching him" ("Swift as Intellectual," 87).

In this brief but trenchant passage, Said achieves a double polemical effect: firstly, he rescues, for the right reasons, Swift's "writerly" genius from neglect by high theory, and secondly, he unmasks high theory's unavowed complicity with certain kinds of texts, that is, the nature of its ideological investment. Also, in honoring Swift's style and its organic inherence in the author's intellectual world, Said is taking sides with the author against the theoretically minded critic's gratuitous deconstruction and its obsession with the text's formal being: not that Said denies the formal text its being, but rather that he insists that the text's formal being is "about" the author's intellectual world; in other words, the text has a representational burden. Here again, with very little fuss, Said, by way of his endorsement of style in authorial terms, is taking sides on behalf of "representation" against high theory's claim that representation no longer exists. Style, then, is a linguistic mediation of the author's intent, and as such, relates the author to the world at large, a particular world at a specific historical juncture. Said's solicitude on behalf of style as authorial, intentional, and worldly against a totalizing theory of the text brings to mind the famous dispute between Foucault and Derrida about Descartes' intentionality in the Cartesian text. Whatever his other and major differences with Foucault, Said in his defense of style and its worldly intentionality is on the same side of the debate as Foucault who puts up a thoroughly convincing fight against Derrida's textualization of Descartes' discursive intentions. As Said would say, with Foucauldian methodology it is possible to go into the text and then come out into the world whence one started, whereas with Derrida the critic is immured within the text and unable to get back to the world without.

In his posthumously compiled and published book *On Late Style*, Said comes back to the question of style in the context of his own imminent mortality. Here, too, style becomes the irreducible measure of the human, and of human creativity that refuses to be contained by the closure of aesthetic form. In a way reminiscent of the Dylan Thomas poem, "Do Not Go Gentle into That Good Night," this moving book with the richly suggestive subtitle, *Music and Literature Against the Grain*, adumbrates the thesis of style as a form of urgent recalcitrance that will not accept the solace of closure and presses forward in unquiet clamor in search of something, some value that is forever posthumous *vis-à-vis* temporality. Style becomes the expression of the ineffable not in any mystical sense, but rather with reference to time and temporality. Style, now understood as late style, refers to a mode of dis-accommodated being that resists aesthetic accommodation. Drawing on Theodor Adorno's invocation of "late style" in the context of some of Beethoven's late and musically intransigent texts, Said characterizes style as an a-synchronic and non-synchronizable troublemaker that rebels against closure. Late style is perennially and incorrigibly late not with reference to some objective, calendric event or happening; but rather with reference to itself. Imagine a person saying "I am late" in an intransitive grammar where "late" functions as an ontological predication that comes after the copula and defines the "I." In other words, "late" is neither an adjective or an adverb that further describes an existing situation, entity, or state of being. I am who I am precisely because I am late whereby a constitutive lateness is inscribed as style in my very being. (Here I am reminded of the White Rabbit in *Alice in Wonderland* who is always "late.") Contextually speaking, in the immediate context of his chronic cancer, we can see Said use his literary sensibility to provoke a feeling of "out of home-ness," phenomenologically speaking. To be late is to be in time since lateness itself is marked by time, and at the same time to be late is to have missed the beat of a calendric or programmatic time. Moreover, through late style, the artist seems to be pushing beyond the very "sayability" of her medium towards a form of productiveness that sounds unreasonable, or downright unproductive. "It is this second type of lateness that I find deeply interesting. I'd like to explore the experience of late style that involves a nonharmonious, nonserene tension, and above

all, a sort of deliberately unproductive productiveness going *against* . . ."
(*On Late Style*, 7). Eluding synthesis, subjective and objective at the same
time, processual but resistant to developmental resolution, lacking both in
transcendence and unity, late style is the raging and unruly symptom of a
creativity that "is *in*, but oddly *apart* from the present." It is in short a mode
of dissident dwelling that is embodied as lag in unending reproof of all that
is timely.

More than anything, style becomes serviceable to Said as that rare lived
and individual possibility that bridges the gap between artistic performance
and a theoretical intellectuality: and it is to Glenn Gould again that Said
turns by way of exemplification. In Said's estimation, Gould is that supreme
artist who heals or sutures through his performance the breach between theory and worldly practice. Unlike gung-ho postmodernists who triumphantly
announce the death of narrative and representation and insist on the autonomy of meta-fiction and self-reflexivity, Said honors those practitioners of a
literary, cultural, or musical form in whose performances "the existential,"
to use Ranajit Guha's memorable locution, "tangles with the epistemological." It is the historical or worldly style of the performance that transcends
the binary divide between "the narrow confines of performance" and the
"discursive realm" of "the critique." In other words, with performers like
Gould around, there is no need to conceive of "theory" as a domain over
and above the actual performance of critical consciousness.

Here, as elsewhere, Said is keen on demonstrating, through appropriate
examples from literary and cultural performance, that the valuable activity
of critical consciousness can be achieved directly by writers, musicians, and
critics, that is, without recourse to something called "professional theory."
Unlike the high theorists of poststructuralism, or of postmodernism for
that matter, who seek to realize the radical autonomy of theory and of
theoretical thinking on the other side of "representation," and here I am
referring to the post-representational truth claims of theory, Said is keen
on relating "oppositional critical consciousness" organically to the literary
or the musical work in the form of style. In this sense then, when viewed
from the perspective of high theory, Said remains a willing prisoner of
"representation." In remaining a prisoner to representation, Said avoids
falling into the "art for art's sake" school of Walter Pater and Oscar Wilde.

Style, to Said, accomplished the task of critiquing the limitations of representation from within the realm of representation, whereas high theory
would want a definitive paradigmatic break from the regime of representation: a break that is disingenuous and unreal, that is, purely theoretical and

not worldly, from Said's point of view. Said's ongoing critical affection for **Joseph Conrad** and, in particular, for Conrad's staging of representation in all his fiction, for example, is based on his critical appreciation of how "style" works rigorously and self-reflexively in Conrad's narrative. Unlike his distinguished literary contemporary Chinua Achebe, who has no patience for Conrad's "self-reflexive Eurocentrism," Said grants Conrad's style its own oppositional critical valence within the paradigm that can be recognized as Eurocentrism. Unlike someone like, say, Jacques Derrida who, is committed to the theoretical dismantling of "**centrism** as such" as a precondition for all other historically situated oppositional projects, or Martin Heidegger and his theoretical opposition to "humanism," Said's critical consciousness remains pragmatic within the confines of history. It is in this spirit that Said, in his lecture on Sigmund Freud, condones Freud's Eurocentrism as historically inevitable. It is interesting that both Said and Derrida would contend that criticism (in Said's case) and the critique (in Derrida's case) should be heterogeneous, that is, not be homogeneous and therefore complicit, with its object; and it is even more interesting that they achieve that heterogeneity differently. For Derrida, it was important that the critique have no proper "subject," whereas Said was insistent that the oppositional energy of critical consciousness be played out as a representation of and a representation in the world. What is indeed symptomatic of Said's sensibility is that he has no difficulty defending literary style despite its non-transparent complexity; but he will not grant the same cordiality to the complexity of theory. To Said, style of the first kind is an effective way of being in the world even as it questions the dispensation of that very world. In the final analysis, style to Said represents an inventive possibility, and an openness to contextual improvisation that no textual theory can preempt, anticipate, foreclose, or totalize.

To summarize, in Said's reading, style is not just rhetoric or rhetoricity (as celebrated in theory, particularly by Paul de Man and the Yale School), but a means to a choice, and a type of statement. Style leads to something beyond itself even as it indulges in itself formally, figurally, and performatively. There is also built into the cultural politics of style, the theme of humanistic continuity and the resistance to mechanization, atomization, and a postmodern notion of the medium that becomes the message itself or constructs the human as a mere effect. The emphasis on improvisation is as substantive as it is strategic. The confines of the performance (just as the "Admit All" ticket stub in the book on the cover of Said's book, *Humanism and Democratic Criticism*) lead to a world without, a world full of "motivic mobility," a world where both the composer and the performer count equally. Said is making sure that the text and the performance are in a lively dance together: it is not one against the other in an ideological battle. Finally, the aesthetic results in the elaboration of a rationality that is a stay against disorder and chaos, an elaboration that is an affirmation, a form of aye-saying that Said would argue has been sacrificed in the name of an endless negativity, the negativity of the critique. And this rationale is a communal rationality to be shared and transmitted to all through the agency of the performance. It is all about style in the service not of a ready-made worldliness, but of a worldliness forever in process.

text/textuality   It is not without good reason that the word "text" figures prominently in the title of one of Said's most important books, *The World, the Text, and the Critic*. Textuality is a mode of knowing that is very close to Said's head as well as his heart. Said spent his entire distinguished career with texts, writing texts, explaining texts to his students and a variety of audiences the world over, and sparring and debating with a number of his distinguished contemporaries about the meaning of text and textuality. Text as an epistemological category had been in play well before Said arrived on the scene as the newest star in the literary critical horizon. Texts are as old as civilizations; but the term acquired a special boost for structuralist thinkers, especially after the famous "linguistic turn" inaugurated by Ferdinand de Saussure. The role of language had been redefined philosophically, cognitively, epistemologically. Language was no more a reflection of reality; it was in fact constitutive of reality, a thesis that is quite consistent with the well-known Sapir-Whorf hypothesis, which states that reality is perceived and understood as an epistemological function of a linguistic frame. This hypothesis is very much in consonance with the Saussurean theory of linguistic meaning. Linguistics as a meaning making science had come into its own, and ergo, meaning was no more part of an idealist, neo-platonic superstructure that merely used language as a disposable instrument to establish the realm of semantic content. To get at meaning one had to come to terms with the materiality of language itself; to anticipate the media guru McLuhan, the medium indeed was the message. In the words of Archibald MacLeish, "A poem does not mean, it is." Lévi-Strauss and Roman Jacobson

A Said Dictionary, First Edition. R. Radhakrishnan.
© 2012 John Wiley & Sons, Ltd. Published 2012 by John Wiley & Sons, Ltd.

conducted an excruciating syllable by syllable, phrase by phrase, phoneme by phoneme linguistic analysis of Baudelaire's poem, "Cats," and declared with supreme nonchalance that the meaning of the poem is irrelevant to the success of their analysis.

Structuralism, in its ambitious attempt to bridge the gap between the real and the intelligible, gave the notion of the text inordinate epistemological power. The thesis is that it is in the textualization of reality that reality becomes knowable. For example, Barthes in his attempt to democratize the study of culture would claim that a wrestling match, a soufflé, the Eiffel Tower, a literary work, and a restaurant menu were all texts. In other words, reality itself, in so far as it is intelligible, is constituted like a text. The overall drive is to denaturalize the real and alienate it into its textual readability and meaning. Roland Barthes and Alain Robbe-Grillet got together in intellectual partnership and declared that "the heart of the matter was dead," and in the process announced the demise of **humanism**. The text figured prominently in the ongoing work of Roland Barthes who made sharp distinctions between "the work" that centers around the author and "the text" that is an open and indeterminate field of *jouissance* and intransitive pleasure. All of this culminated in Jacques Derrida's grand claim in *Of Grammatology* that "there is nothing outside the text."

Let us now bring Edward Said to the scene of the text. From the very beginning, which is to say, his initial doctoral work on Conrad's complex and self-reflexive **narrative**, and particularly in his brilliant book, *Beginnings*, Said is concerned with the text, textuality, textual practice, the text and its relationship to the author, the text and the intentionality behind the text, and most importantly, the **worldliness** of the text, that is, the way in which, as a text, it addresses itself to the world and is of the world even as it enjoys its own textual economy. Where Said parts company once and for all from deconstructionists and poststructuralist theorists is in the connection that he establishes between language and the text. As a profoundly secular thinker Said has no difficulty with the thesis that reality is in fact "reality," that it is a construct and not some form of natural presence or Being. He is more than happy to welcome and acknowledge the constitutive role played by language in our perception of reality, but he will not endorse Derrida's claim that there is nothing outside the text. The world may well be a kind of text, that is, textualized by the human *cogito*, but to Said the world is not reducible to mere textuality. On the contrary, (i) there is a constitutive outside to the text, and this is where the worldliness of the text comes in, and (ii) the text is not the pure effect of language as system ("The

Future of Criticism"; "The Text, the World, the Critic"; and "The Problem of Textuality").

It is not at all coincidental that Said creates a triangular relationship among the world, the text, and the critic. The all important middle term here, the text, is the very ground, or perhaps the medium, through which the world and the critic transact. The text operates as the vivified terrain where the worldliness of the world is seen in process, perennially being made and unmade and remade by human history in human history. The critic opens up the literary text to its own contradictory and **contrapuntal** historicity. The text does not turn into a hermetic monad. Said will not allow the text the arrogance to claim that if it did not exist, the world will stop existing as well. The text is a **representation**, not always right and not always wrong, not always just and not always unjust. In being a finite, vulnerable, and contingent representation of the world, the text always points outwards towards "the real." Though Said himself may not appreciate the resemblance, there is something similar between his solicitude for the worldliness of the world and Martin Heidegger's phenomenological care for the Earth and his concern that the Earth not be reduced to mere "standing material" for the anthropocentric positivist project of "worlding." Whereas the Heideggerian project is primarily philosophical and ontological in orientation, and political only in a problematically derivative mode, Said's endeavor is directly historical and political. Unlike Jacques Derrida who is primarily and in fact exclusively a philosopher, Said has no vested interest in the agenda of philosophy and its inconclusively polemical relationship with humanism. Textuality, signification, difference, indeterminacy, the aporia, and many similar terms that are anchored in the discourse of philosophy do not carry any jurisdiction or authority for Said. History is neither allegorical, nor philosophical, nor purely figural or rhetorical for Said. As Ranajit Guha argued recently in *History at the Limit of World-History*, Said too is of the opinion that philosophy rides on the back of history and forces history to become trans-historical. Said has very little patience with high **theory** textualists who take the linguistic turn so seriously as to assume that Mr. Text is ontology personified as well as the epistemology thereof. There still remains something called "reality" to be explained and accounted for by the textuality of the text.

Said's understanding of the economy of the text is inseparable from his critical perception of what literary theory is and what it does. Let us begin with direct life examples. Things, good, bad, and ugly, happen in life; and we keep going with our lives. But when something important happens that requires explanation – a wedding, a birth, a calamity, a divorce – or when we choose to pause to make sense of things, we could be said to be theorizing into intelligibility what has already taken place factually, empirically. Our theorizing could be formal, as in our trying to understand the meaning of a negative situation in terms of God's will or in terms of the laws of economics, or the needs of the nation state; or it could be informal with reference to family, friends, duties, and obligations. When we pause to theorize, we are pausing not just to theorize for the sake of theorizing, but rather, to theorize so as to make sense of the experience. We may resort to a model such as God's will, or the nation's needs, or the rationale of corporate capital; but the models have an obligation to explain something that is anterior to them. In applying the models to our real life situations, we are acknowledging not merely the modal nature of the models but also their worldly accountability, that is, their accountability to those circumstances that warranted understanding and explanation in the first place. In other words, the models of analysis might have made a text of life's circumstances, but the text is not an ontological substitute for those circumstances.

What goes for real life goes for literary theory and its relationship to the text. Something, anything becomes a text when it becomes the object of study. This does not mean that it, whatever it may be – a poem, a feeling, a rose, an event, an experience – did not exist in its own temporality prior to being textualized. When something in reality becomes a text, it gets framed and prepped in a certain way so that it can now be seen in a certain light, from the point of view of a certain gaze. Again, it is not as though prior to being framed in such an explicitly pedagogical, epistemological, institutional, curricular manner, it, whatever it is, was lacking in intelligibility. All that happens when it, whatever it is, becomes a text, is that it is being subjected to a process of **professionalism**, specialization, and, shall we say, disciplinarization. The academic meaning of the poem, and this is Said's emphasis, is still "about" something; that is, it continues to be representational. In other words, just because the poem that was written by someone in a certain set of historical circumstances in response to anything from intimations of dying to the warble of a nightingale, has now become the textual object of study, its meaning does not implode into the text, and in the process sever its organic relationship to history and the changing world of circumstances. The specialized meanings and truths that the literary critic or theorist draws from the text are intimately and organically related to its non- or, shall we say, pre-specialist and generalist location in the world. Specialization, in other words, is not the creation of a new and immanent semantic system that refuses to look "outside" for its validation.

As we look at the historical development of literary theory and its relationship to the text and textuality, we can understand the reasons behind Said's concern and anxiety. Practical criticism turned into literary criticism, which turned into literary theory, which in turn morphed into critical theory, which was re-incarnated as just theory. In this movement, one can easily discern a tendency: the tendency to "autonomize" theory, make it its own subject and object, and radically detach it from its object of explanation, namely, the literary text and its multivalent implication in history and the world of circumstances. The becoming autonomous of theory, strongly inflected by philosophies and philosophers who believe utterly in the "linguistic turn," goes hand in hand with the linguistic fetishization of the text that is now reduced to tropes, rhetoricity, figurality, indeterminacies, aporias, and a whole range of niceties and nuances that are purely intra-lingual. This is exactly the reason why Said defends and admires the complexity of literature as language and deplores the complexity of theory as language.

The crucial difference between the two orders of complexity is that whereas literary linguistic complexity is intensely worldly, theoretical discursive complexity is occlusive of worldliness. What Said would disallow is the claim that the text as conceived of by theory has the right to be autonomously complex just on the basis of its linguistic nature; for language, to Said, is always in the world and worldly, and to think of the linguistic text as though it were a world in itself would be utterly meaningless, even solipsistic. It is one thing to acknowledge happily that language in general is constitutive of reality, and quite another to claim that language *is* reality in and by itself, disburdened of its obligation to represent the very world that it constitutes. It is in this regard that Said's position on the text and textuality is closer to that of Foucault than that of Derrida. Said insists in his essay "Criticism Between Culture and System" that whereas the Foucauldian approach allows the reader to move from the world to the text and then back to the world, Derridean deconstruction traps you within the hermetic interiority of the text with the false claim that reality itself has now imploded into the eminent domain of textuality. There is indeed nothing outside the text since the referent has now been domesticated into a textual function. Though Said has all kinds of disagreement with Foucault on other issues such as Power, the nature of intellectuality, and Eurocentrism, to name a few, he would agree with Foucault that Derrida's theory of reading reduces history and events and discourse to mere "textual traces."

Said uncovers the complicity between the text and a certain theory of reading. According to Said, "textuality is the somewhat mystical and disinfected subject matter of literary theory." He went on to argue that "textuality has therefore become the exact antithesis and displacement of what might be called history." Whereas Derrida would claim over and over again that reading and rigorous practices of reading are the most radical ways of realizing historicity, Said would insist that readings *à la* Derrida had created the false temporality of the text, the temporality of what in literary theory has become famous or infamous as the time of the "always already," and in the process had thoroughly invalidated and domesticated the claims of history on meaning and meaning making, on textuality and text making. Once a certain ideological relationship has not been established between something called the text and a certain practice called reading, the deconstructive critic can prove *ad infinitum* that the meaning of the text is indeterminate, aporetic, and always already undecideable. A theoretically rigorous reading of the text always will demonstrate this indeterminacy, this radical undecidability. The text becomes that joyous field of perennial becoming, and reading becomes that pleasurable activity of *jouissance* that saves the text from semantic closure and finitude.

It would be useful here to recall, from Said's point of view, that early debate between Foucault and Derrida over a certain passage in Descartes. Foucault, in his monumental thesis *Madness and Civilization* had spent just a few pages interpreting a passage in Descartes. Foucault, on the basis of his interpretive reading of Descartes, had concluded that while the Cartesian *cogito* had philosophical/epistemological/cognitive room for the sleeping self and the dreaming self, it had no place for the self that was mad and had in fact exiled it from the realm of reason. In his review of Foucault's text, Derrida obsessively latches on to this brief analysis of Foucault (a few incidental pages in a book that is over 600 pages long), and ferociously disproves Foucault's reading of Descartes. To put it briefly, Derrida's point is that Foucault had entirely mis-recognized and simplified the textuality that was at work in Descartes. Derrida's careful reading would reveal that whatever truth claim Descartes may seem to have made regarding the status of the mad man was already destabilized and deconstructed within the Cartesian text. Had Foucault only been less positivist and historical, had he only paid better rhetorical attention to the economy of the text, he would have realized that the text had "always already" deconstructed itself, with the result that what had seemed a discursive truth claim was a reversible textual effect.

Such a reading of Descartes infuriates Foucault who condemns Derrida's deconstructive reading practice as the last and final flickering of a bourgeois manner of philosophizing that reduces discursive realities into mere textual traces that can be constructed and deconstructed at will. To put it another way, Derrida's "reading" refuses to function as a "reading of" an earlier text, choosing instead a strategy that plays fast and loose with history, and the claims of history on the text. The Cartesian text is deracinated from its own time, and is yoked violently to a textual temporality that is profoundly ahistorical. What both Foucault and Said find disturbing and objectionable in the deconstructionist theory of the text, whatever their other differences, is that the deconstruction happens miraculously and immaculately as an effect of language itself: *sans* agency, *sans* intentionality, *sans* worldly/discursive/historical intervention or consequence ("The Text as Practice and as Idea").

Said's overall intention is to maintain and nurture the text in the world, not as an end in itself, but as a representation of the world. The keyword again is "representation," of something that is already there in the world of history and circumstances. However sophisticated, virtuosic, and formally autonomous the text may be, it can derive its accountability to itself only as a function of its accountability to the world of historical circumstances. The text as representation bears all the marks of the world of history even as it "textualizes" such a world according to rules of stylistic and aesthetic composition. In other words, Said is determined not to allow the text, in the name of its formal self-sufficiency, to wander away into the la-la land of so-called "post-representation," so dear to radical theorists. In all his critical moves against the inflation of textuality as its own sovereign measure, Said is in fact protecting the world from the arrogance of the textual theorist who seeks to master and dominate the world in the name of one theory or another. As a literary critic, Said attends critically to literature on the assumption and the premise that such attention would lead back into the world, rather than immure or closet him inside an enclave called literary theory or literary criticism. Said is no less an indefatigable reader of literary texts than the so-called "pure theorists"; but his readings are intended to keep alive the dynamic connections among literature, language, history, and the world at large. Said would rather be surprised by the world and in the process lose his theoretical hold over the text, than freeze and possess the world as an immaculate text.

theory (or deconstructive theory in the wake of Jacques Derrida) What Said finds particularly objectionable in theory is that under its aegis **textuality** begins its reign in the form of a seamless temporality recognized as logocentrism, phallogocentrism, phonocentrism, **centrism** as such: a temporality that allows no room for history with a lower-case "h," or for discontinuities and diachronic departures and detours and deviations. Like Terry Eagleton, the eminent Marxist cultural critic, Said too has little patience for the famous Derridean dictum that there is no stepping out of the pages of logocentrism: all that is possible is to turn the pages in a certain way. The result is that theory is valorized as the practice of non-intervention. Theory forever justifies *après coup* in the name of a future anterior that is "always already" present in the indefinite and indefinable economy of textuality.

Is this a valid critique of Derridean theory and deconstruction? This is not an easy question to answer. On the one hand, it would appear that Derrida and Said are on the same team. Neither believes in pure epistemological breaks from earlier paradigms. For example, Said argues vehemently that there is indeed no need for a theoretical position known as post-humanism. He is thoroughly confident that a better and more humane and inclusive **humanism** can be practiced in the name of humanism on the assumption that humanism can learn from its past mistakes and reconstitute itself in response to such a learning. Said's strategy here, of not abandoning the *longue durée* of humanism, is quite similar to the Derridean option of staying within, but critically and **oppositionally** within, the jurisdiction of logocentrism. Both Derrida and Said value the importance of an overarching tradition that perennially restructures and re-imagines itself in active response to its own history of good and bad. And yet, when it comes to actual practice and methodology, real differences begin to emerge between the two.

Said contends that "theory" began as an interventionary and insurrectionary possibility in the study of humanities and the human sciences, that is, in conjunction with social movements of change, protest, and revolution, but unfortunately lost this ability and turned into specialist jargon and discourse. The operations of high theory divorce themselves both from circumstantial history and from the burden of **representation**. To bring Raymond Williams into the conversation here, theory, in the name of its self-absorption, forfeits the opportunity of functioning as an institutional "project" in active and sensitive alliance with "movements" taking place in the real world. In becoming a professional, meritocratic "mode of excellence," theory loses its critical edge as well as voice and degenerates into a sophisticated apologist for the status quo. In its most narcissistic form, theory announces the death of the author, of voice and intentionality, and of representation as such, and in doing so writes itself a *carte blanche* for talking about itself in its own sanctioned discourse. Said's trenchant diagnosis is that theory creates and perpetuates a false or pseudo complexity that is not really about anything. Said always makes distinctions between different kinds of complexity: those that are worldly and representative and representational, and those that are the result of spurious fabrications, or just plain obfuscation. Theory, when dominated by unwieldy jargon and rebarbative rhetoric, is much like the emperor with no/new clothes. The grand announcements that theory makes are utterly devoid of content, and its claims are vapid, non-worldly, non-empirical, and thoroughly ahistorical. Raymond Williams's blurb for Said's book, *The World, the Text, and the Critic* is *apropos* in this context. Says Williams of Said, "It is a pleasure to read someone who not only has studied and thought so carefully *but is also beginning to substantiate, as distinct from announcing, a genuinely emergent way of thinking*" (emphasis added). The distinction that Raymond Williams makes between actually substantiating and merely announcing is crucial in Said's critical relationship with theory. What Said looks for but does not find in theory is substantiation and substance; what he finds instead is grandstanding and second order and meta-level pronouncements, that is, mere "vapor-ware," and predictable and formulaic repetitions of system and methodology without any original insight. Also missing from theory are (i) agential thinking and (ii) genuine emergences in the form of alternatives. Theory eventually succumbs to a mindless and mercenary **professionalism** that is only too happy not to address the world at large and to reside instead within its own hermetic enclosure. Said's ultimate verdict on theory is that it is real "in theory" – in other words, in a world of its own and not in the world of real and historical circumstances. If that is what theory has ossified into, Said gladly parts company with it, and champions the cause of an "oppositional critical consciousness" capable of worldly practice and performance.

"Traveling Theory"　　With this influential and well-timed essay, Said was able to clarify a number of issues around "theory," its status, and its truth claims *vis-à-vis* the world and history. Clearly, theory had come from across the Atlantic and had come to stay in the world of literature and literary criticism. Practical criticism had morphed into literary theory; literary theory into critical theory; and finally, theory had come into its own as its own autonomous domain. One of the most crucial questions concerning theory had to do with its origins, its provenance. Is high theory necessarily Western and Eurocentric? Once something is acknowledged and valorized as "theory," does it then become universal, a-contextual, and a-historical? To use that telling colloquialism, "where does theory come from?" and does it matter where it comes from? Is modernity, for example, definitively Western; and if so, how does one evaluate the relevance of modernity to the non-West? Is Foucault French in some inviolable way; or can Foucault's thoughts and findings be made to "travel" to other places in response to local conditions? Is theory static or is it capable of travel in a world constituted by all sorts of reciprocal flows and influences? Is theory modular, or can theory be seriously rethought, originally recast in response to various and varying geopolitical situations and contexts? One of the crucial questions here has to do with the relationship between theory and history. Is theory contingent and circumstantial, or does it transcend history in the name of its own pure truth? What happens when a theory, such as deconstruction or Lacanian psychoanalysis or Barthesian semiotropy, travels far away from its place of origination? Do the wavelengths become weaker and weaker with distance till at some point nothing is heard any more? Is there an exemplary use of theory, or is theory itself no more and no less than a symptom of a certain time and a certain location? Does theory belong somewhere in some authentic manner; or is theory no more than a set of practices that are signified differently in different sites and historical conjunctures? These are the questions that Said seeks to answer.

Said's intentions are crystal clear: to demystify the hermeticism that had grown up around theory and to render theory vulnerable to historical processes as they happen here, there, and everywhere. In other words, the truths of theory are neither sovereign and monolithic, nor are they autochthonous to a particular place that could be identified as their origin. Said's crucial insight here is that all theory travels. It is not as though there are two kinds of theory, one static and the other mobile. Travel, movement, dispersion, dissemination: these constitute our world that is nothing but relational in nature, and theory cannot be an exception to this reality. Poststructuralism may have European origins, but it is by no means constitutively or definitively European. When theory travels, there are no guarantees or safeguards to ensure that its mutations will uphold its origins and remain resolutely centrist with reference to its place of origination. Not only does theory have its own so-called "original" history, but it is also exposed through travel to other histories and realities that are in the world in their own way.

Said unpacks the travel into different **narrative** moments: "a point of origin," the "distance traversed," then "a set of conditions ... which then confronts the transplanted theory or idea, and finally, "the now full (or partly) accommodated (or incorporated) idea ... transformed by its new uses, its new position in a new time and place" (*The World, the Text, and the Critic*, 226–7). This way of looking at theory is of particular salience to **postcolonial** critics who typically are painfully aware of their own "derivative" condition and to minority and subaltern **intellectuals** in general who feel stultified by the formula of having no tools of their own. In generalizing the motif of travel, influence, borrowings, and acknowledgments across and beyond the master–slave and the colonizer–colonized divide, Said is looking towards a world that is multilateral and multidirectional through and through. Said, in the process, is also mobilizing different locations, none of which is a *tabula rasa*, in response to one another within an ongoing process of change, re- and trans-formation.

It is quite clear that Said is interested not in offering a comprehensive theoretical definition of "traveling theory," but rather in putting the concept to use intentionally, argumentatively, and pragmatically to further one set of interests and counter or critique an opposing platform. To begin with, Said insists on historicizing theory: in other words, theory is not an autonomous constituency by itself. Theory is, to resort to that useful cliché, but what theory does; and what theory does can only take place in a world of changing circumstances. Theory is not to be quarantined, in its own cocoon of ideality, from the world and its many protean and contradictory flows and energies. In insisting that the agenda of theory is itinerant, even peripatetic, Said ensures that theory does not take root in any one soil, resisting transplantation in the name of nativism, autochthony, essentialism, or some theory of natural or divine inherence. Theory is worldly and of the world; and since the world is ubiquitous, that is, here, and there, and somewhere else in perennially different ways, theory too is in a state of constant change and self-transformation. In other words, no one person or group or school of thought owns theory as their own normative practice or system. If anything, Said would argue that it is precisely through its transformations in other locations and sites that theory attains its real and effective history.

When theory travels from one history to another set of circumstances, it repeats itself, to use a phrase from Deleuze, non-identically. The travel itinerary of the concept or the theory makes us aware both of what is common and what is not common between the two situations. Moving against both the crude distinction between pure theory and applied theory, and a programmatic understanding of "application" as a mechanical instantiation of theory, Said understands theory as an integral part of history and of the historical "worlding" of the world. In a classic conjunctural reading of Georg Lukacs and Lucien Goldmann, Said demonstrates how the meaning of theory changes as it travels from one historical situation to another. Said is not suggesting for a moment that Lukacs's theory is right and proper and Goldmann's wrong and fallen, or the other way around, but rather that the two theoretical situations stand as testimonies to two different historical contexts ("Traveling Theory Reconsidered," in *Reflections on Exile*).

Vico, Giambattista   A constant and abiding philosophical and political presence in Said's work. Throughout his publishing career, whenever he is in doubt or whenever he needs to make an important point by way of grounding his political practice in a philosophical position or conceptual framework, Said invariably turns to Vico and his work *The New Science*. It is from Vico that Said derives his profound and non-negotiable conviction that humankind makes its own history and that history, unlike nature, is never a "given." History is made, unmade, begun, completed, re-imagined, done and then undone by human beings historically, that is, in history. The truths of history are many and heterogeneous, and moreover, the truths of history are the results of historical labor and not the immaculate manifestation of an idea or of a primordial covenant between divinity and its chosen constituency ("Vico: Autodidact and Humanist").

It is in his work ***Beginnings*** that Said makes extensive use of Vico and *The New Science* to understand the epistemology of "beginnings" both as practice and as **theory** and the relationship of "beginnings" to history, historiography, and historicism. What Said gets from Vico is that there are no guarantees, promises, or categories that are trans-historical: no essences, no providential imperatives that guide processes of history. Later in his work Said would connect Vico to secular **humanism**. In Vico's formulation of history and self-making, both at the individual and the collective level, Said finds a rare combination of inventiveness, originality, **style**, and a complex and protean accountability to the "livedness" of history. In Vico's theatre of

A Said Dictionary, First Edition. R. Radhakrishnan.
© 2012 John Wiley & Sons, Ltd. Published 2012 by John Wiley & Sons, Ltd.

thought, the thinking and acting human being, the *cogito* if you will, comes alive both as subject and as agent of its own immanently exfoliating history. Often, in a polemical vein, Said contrasted the liveliness of the Vico's historical imagination, on the one hand, with messianic historiographies and their reliance on the mystique of fervently held but historically non-demonstrable notions of sacred origins, and on the other hand, with discursively and theoretically inflated formulations (by and large poststructuralist) of history that debilitate and "always already" negate human agency in the name of structure/system and a theory that will not engage with history on the ground. "With the discrediting of mimetic representation," writes Said, a "work enters a realm of gentile history, to use Vico's phrase for secular history, where extraordinary possibilities of variety and diversity are open to it but where it will not be referred back docilely to an idea that stands above it and explains it." For example, Said would exhort the Israeli state and its people not to allow the idea of **Zionism**, trans-historical to the core, willfully to misrecognize the Israeli–Palestinian reality on the ground.

Said's essay "On Repetition" captures most of his appreciation of what is unique in Vico's historical imagination. Clearly, Vico is neither the first nor the only thinker to focus on history as human. So, what is so special about Vico's formulation of history? Said's understanding is that Vico is one of those rare thinkers who means by history "the realm of unadorned fact." It is quite fascinating how in a hermeneutic sort of way Vico, from a different and much earlier time period, offers comfort and hope for Said who comes much later in history at a time when history is either being preempted by theory or constantly side-staged by meta-history, historiography, and other fancy discursive systems. In other words, Said in his own time is witnessing a systematic repudiation and etiolation of history by forces and discourses that claim to know more and know in more sophisticated ways than the bare bones modality of history. It is revealing, almost symptomatic, that in an essay that ascribes "repetition" as a methodology that is unique to Vico in his project of honoring history, Said is in fact "repeating" Vico into his essay powerfully to make his point.

The "realm of unadorned fact," Said asserts has its own meaning and significance before it is made sense of either by **philology** *à la* Erasmus, Cartesian rationality, Hegelian world-historical phenomenology, or any other schematic endeavor to render history meaningful by rescuing it from the realm of unadorned fact. Clearly Said has something in common with philosophers like Deleuze and Guattari who too are keen to rescue history as singular event from falsifying historiographies such as positivism, historicism, empiricism, and phenomenology. Deleuze too philosophizes "repetition" into conceptual respectability, but for him it is all about phantasmal non-identical repetition. Said's path is different. He does not reach out and backward to Vico across the centuries to seek a theory of history, or to announce radical breaks from histories of the *longue durée* such as humanism. Said's intentions are clear as he makes the following statement as a paraphrase of what he has learned from Vico: "Human history is human actuality is human activity is human knowledge." This is a fascinating sentence that effects a series of quick, almost spontaneous, and therefore not self-conscious, equations as displacements in synonymy. What in fact is a series of mediations is being claimed by Said as truths in the realm of unadorned fact. The adamant assertion of each "is" denies and aggressively rejects the need for a meta-code or meta-discourse. In Vico, Said finds a historical way of validating and rendering history meaningful. Repetition, epistemologically speaking, avoids the need for divine originality. History is neither something gratuitous to be forced into meaning, nor a mechanical realization of a foregone meaning.

It is in the context of such an unadorned understanding of history as meaningful that Said maintains that "repetition takes place inside actuality." Repetition in Vico, according to Said, achieves the following effects. First, repetition makes for an incremental accumulation of meaning from past to present, generationally, dynastically, periodically. The theme of continuity is crucial. This does not mean that sons and daughters merely repeat the history of their parents. The repetition motif renders one generation meaningful in terms of the other. Out of this comes the construction of traditions and canons, which also means the elaboration of counter-traditions and counter-canons. Said has never, in the name of theoretical radicality, anathematized canonicity or traditions: on the contrary. Said would be more in agreement with the T.S. Eliot of "Tradition and the Individual Talent" than poststructuralist/theoretical bashers of tradition and canonicity as such. Secondly, repetition functions as a framework for the working out of meanings, agreements, and contestations over meanings and valences. The framework itself can be renegotiated, restructured, re-coordinated, re-imagined: but repetition ensures that the framework is maintained. Thirdly and finally, repetition endows the scholar with the responsibility of historical consciousness; it is a responsibility, not a mere fad or a whimsy or a fetish. In *Humanism and Democratic Criticism* Said argued that humanism indeed does have a spotty and even a culpable record, but that is no reason to dismiss it altogether; for that way lies historical amnesia.

Here is a summary of the many wide-ranging comments that Said makes to his interviewer when he is asked about Vico's influence on his work (*Power, Politics, and Culture*, 78–9). Vico's *The New Science* is about self-making, and the various stages of self-making, as in Marx and Ibn Khaldun. Vico also uses the mode of literary analysis, rather than ornamental methodologies or philosophy, to bring home this truth about history as a developing story of self-styling at various levels. It is the literary element that addresses the unadorned realm of meaning as the realm of meaning-making and brings out the inherent themes of education and development. And what is astonishing is that Vico manages all this without having to be professional, methodological, or a card-carrying practitioner of a particular guild or "-ism." He is an **oppositional** thinker who can carry on his interpretive secular work outside of boxes such as Cartesianism, Erasmian philology, rationalism, and Catholicism.

virtuosity   Here is a concept that Said develops brilliantly in his essay, "The virtuoso as intellectual," a chapter in his posthumously published book, *On Late Style*, with the suggestive and predictable sub-title, *Music and Literature against the Grain*. The hero in this essay is the brilliant and controversial Canadian pianist Glenn Gould: an exemplary character, who, like **Vico, Conrad**, and **Auerbach**, figures often in Said's narrative as a theorist, performer, stylist, and powerful teacher. The title of the essay pretty much announces Said's agenda: an agenda that is qualitatively elitist even as it is uncompromisingly democratic in its zeal to admit quality and the qualitative appreciation of value into the life of the all. Said is aware that folks like him are the custodians of high culture, but this does not induce guilt in him. Why not? Because he is a teacher, and teachers are not hoarders or monopolists, but democratic disseminators and broadcasters and educators, who spread the appreciation of quality and complexity among the populace without succumbing to the seduction of easy populism on the one hand, and to the temptation of **professionalism** on the other. The **intellectual** as teacher, as the sub-title makes abundantly clear, is interested not in abstract theory but in music and literature, domains that are of affective interest to all; and if even music and literature are considered elitist, the intellectual as teacher is devoted not to apologistic or apostolic readings of the great, canonical **texts**, but in readings against the grain. In other words, virtuosity is intellectual *and* democratic.

Here is why Said finds Gould's virtuosity persuasive. In Said's own words: "Unlike the digital wizardry of most others of his class, Gould's virtuosity was not designed simply to impress and ultimately alienate the listener/spectator but rather to draw the audience in by provocation, the dislocation of expectation, and the creation of new kinds of thinking based in large measure on his reading of Bach's music" ("The Virtuoso as Intellectual," 117). It is clear that virtuosity is not formal pyrotechnics that dazzles in an arid way, resulting in alienation. It is not about the medium or about the artist's enviable and unique mastery of the medium, but about the relationality between the humanity of the artist and that of the audience: a humanity mediated by music, the musical text, and the openness of the text to new meanings and musical possibilities. It is easy to see how in Said's context music itself is set up both as a means and as a means to an end. Ultimately, it is about renewing perennially the relationship between the performing artist and his audience through artistic provocation. Expectations are foregrounded so that they can be left behind for newer pastures. The register here is of a daring and persuasive intellectual didacticism very much in the spirit of Gramsci's characterization of the intellectual as "permanent persuader." What is noteworthy is that the Bach text is crucially and fundamentally involved in the transformation of the artist–audience relationship. And yet, the composer and his/her inaccessible authority is not what it is all about. It is rather the availability of the composer to the performing artist who is committed to his experiential rendezvous with her audience. If there is no "elitist" text, then there can be no democratization. Democratization in the name of the all is taking place in the concert hall, in and through the elevated pleasure of the listening experience. It must also be added that in Said's reading, "the virtuoso, is after all, a creation of the bourgeoisie and of the new autonomous, secular, and civic performing spaces (concerts and recital halls, parks, and especially built palaces of art to accommodate precisely the recently emergent performer and not the composer) that had replaced the churches, courts, and private estates that had once nurtured Mozart, Haydn, Bach, and in his early years Beethoven" ("The Virtuoso as Intellectual," 118).

Another invigorating aspect of Gould's virtuosity is its extra-mural orientation. It is multi-locational and will not be confined within a single discourse of expertise or a single realm of production. Many of those who learned from Said, one way or another, remember his exhortation: Write, and publish in a variety of contexts; write on many registers and wavelengths. Gould's work is against the grain. He wrote, produced radio documentaries, "stage-managed his own video recordings," and much else. Also, he taught through his performances and not the way conventional intellectuals teach, that is, by way of the meta-language of **theory**. In Said's evaluation, virtuosity *à la* Gould forever deconstructs the distinction between life within the world music and life without. Gould uses negation to question music as system and that negation results in inventiveness. Said quotes thus from Gould himself to help us understand what he means by inventiveness and invention: "that replenishment of invention upon which creative ideas depend, because invention is, in fact, a cautious dipping into the negation that lies outside system from a position firmly ensconced in the system" ("The Virtuoso as Intellectual,"123).

The virtuosic pedagogy of Glenn Gould makes many important points: that music is a human, secular construct. In other words, it is not something natural. As the exemplar of human rationality, music uses sound or musicality to combat all the ambient senselessness. Gould rescues musical taste and appreciation from mere consumerism, and offers instead possibilities of the analysis of music in and through music. That is precisely why as a virtuosic teacher he focuses not on mechanical details of practicing and reproducing the score with obedient fidelity. His focus is elsewhere: how to produce a mode of rigorous musical analysis in and through the performance. The performance is both a performance and a performance of: immanent and transcendent, **representation** as well as a critique of representation, critical as well as affective, epistemological as well as existential, theoretical as well as situated and historical. Said uses an expressive phrase to sum up his endorsement of what Gould does – "motivic mobility" – and here is how it figures in Said's passage: "Gould's virtuosity first of all expanded the confines of performance to allow the music being rendered to show, present, reveal its essential motivic mobility, its creative energies, as well as the processes of thought that constructed it by composer and performer equally" ("The Virtuoso as Intellectual," 132). Virtuosity as performance is simultaneously a *mise en scène* as well as a *mise en abyme* whose objective is to break barriers and constrains rationally, analytically, and rigorously. Motivic mobility functions as a creative form of restlessness that in its very accountability to *motif* renders it mobile, protean, itinerant. It is ceaseless movement and creativity that Said is after, and the virtuosic performer captures and embodies that mercurial temporality in the name of a worldly music.

voyage in   So, why are *they* here? Why do we hear Urdu and Hindi resound in Southall, London? Why is there a successful proliferation of balti restaurants in various sections of London? Why do Bhangra beats pulse through

First World youth culture, and when did Islamic chants and "costumes" become part of metropolitan culture? Why are England, France, Holland, and Italy subjected to forms of multiculturalism that are not indigenous to *us*? Why are we, a sovereign, integral nation and culture, being contaminated by *their* customs, rationale, smells, clothes and colors, their dialects and *patois*? Of course the obvious and correct answer is: They are here because you once were there as colonizer. The phenomenon I have been referring to could be called the "voyage in," a process by which the ex-colonized Third World becomes part of the First World, the metropolitan center. The voyage in begins to deconstruct the borders between the worlds of the ex-colonizer and the ex-colonized, creating in the process a different cartography of relationality, of distance and proximity, of belonging and non-belonging, of citizens and non-citizens, immigrants, exiles, and a whole range of unassimilable "others."

It is not coincidental that Edward Said published an influential essay entitled "Voyage In," reincorporated as part of his book, *Culture and Imperialism*. This essay deals with the intellectual trajectories that constitute the voyage in from the colonies to the heart of the metropolis: and he is dealing in particular with the work of four significant thinkers: C.L.R. James, George Antonius, Ranajit Guha, and S.H. Alatas. The voyage in for Said is not neutral and passive; on the contrary it is identified as "the emergence of opposition." Focusing on the amazing work being done in what used to be the colonies, Said talks about a new phenomenon: "a spiral away and extrapolation from Europe and the West." He is also paying special attention to a process that "begins most productively in peripheral, off-center work that gradually enters the West and then requires acknowledgment." Let us hear Said directly as he valorizes the significance of the "voyage in." "*The voyage in*, then, constitutes an especially interesting variety of hybrid cultural work. And that it exists at all is a sign of adversarial internationalization in an age of continued imperial structures. No longer does the logos dwell exclusively, as it were, in London and Paris" (*Culture and Imperialism*, 292).

There are a number of questions here which Said does not address. Why does it even matter that these works enter the West? Would they not matter if they chose not to address the West, not to enter the West? Why should they require acknowledgment and recognition from the West? What if no acknowledgments were forthcoming from the West, and what if the West in the very act of acknowledging them in fact mis-recognized them? The picture delineated by Said of these critics is one where the non-Western intellectual is still cast in the role of a supplicant awaiting benefaction by foreign currency. Real power lies in acknowledgment and not in the work itself, and this model makes sure that the power is vested in the receiving West. Rather than provincialize the West, to borrow from the eminent subaltern historian and theorist Dipesh Chakrabarty, the "voyage in" model reconfigures the Western metropolis as "where it is all at." This model barely seems interested in wanting to know what the valences of these works might be in their own respective regions. It seems to assume rather naively that acknowledgment in the West would be in seamless harmony with acknowledgments elsewhere. Is this because Said is himself a metropolitan by location? The larger geopolitical question then is: why should the non-West realize itself as a dynamic of resistance to the West rather than its form of affirmation and aye-saying? The ultimate criticism would be that the voyage in model leaves the in/out, the West/non-West, center/periphery model in tact and un-deconstructed.

Supporters of Said have a different vision of the world, and this vision is hybrid, diasporic, disseminated, borderless, anti-nationalistic, anti-identitarian, cosmopolitan, and open-ended. Said would argue that the metropolis, whether it be London, Paris, or New York, does not have to perform a chronic *mea culpa* just because it is metropolitan. No location is by definition or *ipso facto* culpable or wrong. What matters is what happens or is allowed to happen in that location. **Postcolonial** Paris and London are not and cannot be the same as they were during the halcyon days of colonial modernity. It is precisely because, as Salman Rushdie would have it, the real history of the colonizing powers happened overseas in the colonies, that the location called the metropolis has the obligation to involve itself conscientiously in all matters and transformations postcolonial. London and Paris have the moral and political obligation to redefine and re-recognize and re-write their histories in total response to the so-called problem of immigrants from the ex-colonized countries. Said has no patience with Third World diehards who maintain from a position of absolute political correctness that the Third World is *there* and not *here*. Postcoloniality, to Said, is a perspective, and not a fixed or static geopolitical territory. Postcolonial projects and performances are as valid and relevant in the heart of the metropolitan West as they are in the cities and villages of African and Asian nations.

The voyage in, as narrativized by Said, has the potential to make crucial intellectual, cultural, and symbolic connections between work being done "there" and projects being accomplished "here." What Said is hoping to achieve here, like a number of other scholars of diasporic dissemination such as Stuart Hall, Paul Gilroy, Arjun Appadurai, Rey Chow, Lisa Lowe, and others, is a horizontal spatialization of history, that is, history that is so inured to being vertical, dynastic, mono-radical or mono-rooted, just plain historicist. Said's hope, in valorizing the work of Guha, Antonius, Alatas, and James, is not to patronize them or submit them to the avant-garde prestige of metropolitan recognition, but rather to initiate a vitally different geopolitical cartography that permits and validates the recognition of forms of sympathy, empathy, fellow feeling and thinking, critical solidarity along axes that have been forbidden in the name of empire, the nation state, religion, or filial identity. The work of these four intellectuals, and clearly they are not the only ones, represents a different political imaginary that runs counter to regnant cartographies. Work like this needs to travel and not get rooted to its provenance in the name of indigeneity, nativism, or autochthony. It must also be conceded to Said that he does not use the four names interchangeably, and he does not lump them together indivisibly under the rubric the "the voyage in." Quite to the contrary, he is careful to differentiate them on the basis of style, methodology, and intentionality. Each of these works is related to a specific historical moment. The works of James and Antonius emanate from within a national movement towards independence and were at the same time works of great erudition, but erudition in a political cause that was also intended for a general audience. Guha's work is solidly archival and deconstructively archeological and Alatas' work deals with the collusion between capital and colonialism in the context of the so-called "lazy native." Even as he subsumes the directions of these four writers under the rubric "the voyage in," Said has no problem locating them and evaluating them within their original contexts.

But there is something else about these thinkers that instantly appeals to Said's intellectual and critical sensibility: none of the four is a separatist from the West and none of them shuns the West on doctrinaire or ideological grounds. As Said himself puts it: "There is no sense in their own work of their standing outside the Western cultural tradition, however much they articulate the adversarial experience of colonial and/or non-Western peoples. Well after *negritude*, Black nationalism, and the nativism of the 1960s and 1970s, James stubbornly supported the Western heritage at the same time that he belonged to the insurrectionary and anti-imperialist moment which he shared with Fanon, Cabral, and Rodney" (*Culture and Imperialism*, 248). This is exactly the kind of inclusive attitude for which Said was excoriated by Aijaz Ahmad: "metropolitan ambivalence" is how Ahmad characterized Said's desire to have it all, to have it both ways, not to make painful either–or choices. Perhaps because he is a cultural critic Said has no difficulty separating what is wonderful, and moving, and profound in the Western heritage from the implication of that very culture in the histories of Imperialism and Colonialism. Every nerve in Said's being cries out against reductive, visceral, polemically shrill either–or choices. In the end, it is likely that Said cannot but be influenced by his own position as ambassador between two cultures, the Western world and the Arab world, and hence his genuine solicitude for scholars who act as emissaries between cultures. In addition, Said is also saying that there is no "outside the whale" of modernity, to use Salman Rushdie's phrase. The ubiquity of modernity is hardly to be contended, but what are possible are other, discrepant, alternative significations of modernity from locations all over the world. In the all-important project of identifying and recognizing "modernity" as "colonial modernity," and finding sumptuous evidence for this in the very heart of the metropolitan West, Said's essay "Voyage In" continues to play a stellar role.

worldliness Sure enough, we all know there is a world out there whose objectivity is beyond all doubt. It is also well known that human beings, and all that they are and all that they do on various levels and registers, are part of the world as well. So, what is worldliness, a word that has a special fascination for Edward Said? We know the word "worldly," as in worldly-wise, a phrase that runs counter to other-worldly or impractical or impossibly ideal, theoretical or abstruse. To be worldly-wise is to be pragmatic, street smart, opportunistic, trained in the ways of the bustling, practical, material world. But worldliness? Where does worldliness belong or inhere? To maintain that the world is characterized by worldliness sounds awkwardly tautologous. What is Said's special perspective on this term? In a way, Said could be seen as responding to the implicit dualism in the Cartesian dictum: *Cogito, ergo sum*. The question to ask is this: Is the "I" in the "I think" the same as the "I" in the "I am?" Unlike an animal, the human being has the capacity, the cognitive obligation to thematize, that is, to reproduce the lived world as an understood world, the world as "world." Now, there are two worlds: the world as real, empirical, messy, contradictory, contingent, crisscrossed and crosshatched by uneven flows of power; and then there is the world rendered as intelligible discourse within the human epistemological model. Does the model make sense of the world by way of an aseptic procedure that cleanses the world of its worldliness, prep the body of the world so that it may be understood ideally within the controlled conditions of the laboratory, the aesthetic conventions of the literary **text**;

A Said Dictionary, First Edition. R. Radhakrishnan.
© 2012 John Wiley & Sons, Ltd. Published 2012 by John Wiley & Sons, Ltd.

or does the model allow itself to be contaminated, controverted, rubbed against the grain by the clamor and the worldliness of the world? When humans begin to devise expert systems that make sense of the world, and what comes to mind here immediately is the structuralist drive to make the "real" "intelligible," they begin to believe that the worlding of the world takes place within their epistemological models and structures. The casualty of such an extreme **professional** attitude is the notion of a "constitutive outside." "There is nothing outside the text," Derrida would declare, and in the process textualize reality *tout court*. If something is in the world, but not in the text, then, the verdict is that effectively such a thing does not exist. This is the "wall to wall discourse" predicament that Said deplores.

Said's critical thesis is that professional **intellectuals** and academicians are particularly prone to lose sight of the fact that their experiments, procedures, modes of analysis, and trajectories of expert analysis are not events in another world of pure thought and ideation. As Said himself puts it in an interview: "Worldliness originally meant to me, at any rate, some location of oneself or one's work, or the work itself, the literary work, the text, and so on, in the world, as opposed to some extra-worldly, private, ethereal context. Worldliness was meant to be a rather crude and bludgeon-like term to enforce the location of cultural practices back in the mundane, the quotidian, and the secular" (*Power, Politics, and Culture*, 335–6). Said intends the term to be an instance of Brechtian *plumpes Denken*: a form of "crude" and polemical intervention. Culture does not constitute an ideal order; on the contrary, it is deeply implicated in empire and imperialism. Arguing strongly against the ivory tower intellectual and the art for art's sake artiste, Said makes the case that in its very special, subtle, and sophisticated formal and structured being, culture as art, literature, music, and aesthetics is in the world, partakes of the world, and is constituted by the ideological, political, and power flows of the world. It is not one or the other. To be finely tuned as Art is to carry the worldliness and testify to that worldliness in a certain way. The thesis is **Culture *and* Imperialism**, and not Culture *or* Imperialism.

To Said, worldliness is not a bland, fact-driven, empirical given. It has to be produced through creative labor in the arts, in literature, in the field broadly known as the Humanities. There is Said the individual who lives his life in the world non-professionally, non-academically, in ways that are non-expert. Then there is Said the superbly trained and credentialed scholar–intellectual–critic–theorist who dwells and labors in the specialized fields of literary and cultural study. All that Said is asking for, to put it simply, is an organic connection between these two realms. Professionalism also has to be a way of life, and not an arid practice within the closed classrooms of academia. This is indeed a crucial concern. Let us take a simple example. Let us say I identify myself as a postmodernist, or a New Historicist, or a deconstructionist critic. Would this make a difference to the way I live my life, to my politics, to the choices I make as a conscientious democratic citizen, to the affiliations that I cultivate in my life, to the constituencies and interests I choose as mine and for which I am prepared to fight and struggle, to my critical vision of how the world is and should be? Said is asking the following all important questions. What makes us who we are, and how do we go about assuming accountability for such a determination? Do we view the world through our professional lenses, and if so, what are the consequences? Or, do we maintain the position that the world and reality at large have very little to do with the vision and the focal length afforded by our professionalism?

If I have taught myself to read Jane Austen, Shakespeare, Virginia Woolf, George Eliot, and other great writers in a highly specialized way, does such an expert training have any bearing on the way in which I live my life, and make my choices in my life at large? Or, is there no viable connection between the two realms: the one professional-specialist, and the other lived and every day? To cultivate worldliness for Said is to find that missing organic connection between our general quotidian lives and our professional practice. His point is that we are not just wearing different hats. There is just one general hat, and being an expert Shakespeare scholar comes under the rubric of the general hat. Whereas the narrow professionals are just happy to hold forth on and on within their little fiefdoms, the professionals who are also public intellectuals are deeply committed to the task of bridging the gap between the world as lived and the world as reproduced as a specialist domain of knowledge and expertise.

Said was fond of telling the younger generation of literary critical practitioners, "Write for larger, broader, more general audiences," something that he himself scrupulously did throughout his career. Worldliness is intimately related to democracy. Worldliness should be profound but not esoteric; it should be complex but not hermetic, worthy of analysis but not cabbalistic or cultish. Worldliness becomes a mark of democratic **humanism** that ensures (i) that whatever is said is being said for the All and not the few, and (ii) that the expert in the humanities in staying in touch with her special field does not lose the common touch. In the ultimate analysis, our interlocutor has to be all of humanity and not just specialized discursive communities that speak one argot or jargon or the other. In this respect, Said reminds us of Ralph Waldo Emerson, who also bemoaned the tragedy of specialization and constantly defended "Man thinking" against "the philosopher," or for that matter D.H. Lawrence, who in his own eccentric way lamented the loss of life's vitality in mechanized ways of knowing and knowledge-seeking.

One of the moves that Said makes is that worldliness is a language in and of itself and therefore does not require jargon to ennoble it or inflate it into meaning. If anything, it is the specialized intellectual who has to unlearn her precious discourse in the name of worldliness. Said is not suggesting that worldliness is something numinous or unmediated, but rather that it exists much like the signified to which the signifier should refer. With the linguistic turn, and alongside it the arrogance of systemic thinking, worldliness has been abandoned in the name of reality as the object of theory. Said makes a direct connection between the thinker as generalist and the worldliness of the world. The world may well be a text, but the reader has to be the democratic citizen, and the job of expert readers like Said is to help the lay reader understand not how the book as object is a counter-system to the world, but rather, how it is the valuable site where the world may be seen in process, that is, where it may be seen as worlding. Said here is also contending against the aestheticist tradition that celebrates the *mot juste*, the epiphanic moment in the text, and other such idealized states of being in the text.

Worldliness becomes a way of submitting these other-worldly privileged moments to a genealogical analysis that demonstrates (i) that moments in the literary text had to be moments in lived life first, and (ii) that even the epiphany was the result of worldly circumstances. In this entire polemic, Said uses the term "other-worldly" to indicate something non-circumstantial, metaphysical, mysterious, mystical. Other-worldliness is a form of bad faith. In insisting that literature and works of art are worldly through and through, Said is also advancing the thesis that they have a *savoir faire*, that "they make their way in the world." In other words, works of art and literature are not marooned in some never-never land of idealism. Even the most recondite, romantic literary imagination is advancing its particular perspective in the world. Literature is not a private realm realized in opposition to the public realm. Even the world of a Jane Austen, however private and apolitical it may seem, is connected to Empire, to the colonies, to the colonialist–modernist–nationalist practices of England, and so on. Though he does not quite put it that way, worldliness resides as a symptom in the very heart, fiber, and being of all cultural, literary, and aesthetic texts; and the symptoms could be good or bad, healthy or pathological, progressive or retrogressive. Literary works, just because they are superbly wrought and formally virtuosic, are not transcendent of the symptomatic condition. They are not at peace with themselves in an ideal realm that has gone beyond the horizon of the worldly with all its imperfections, contradictions, glories, and horrors. The same text that is resplendent along one axis could be thoroughly culpable and reprehensible along another. Said warmly applauds Walter Benjamin's profound diagnosis that every document of civilization is equally a document of barbarism.

In positing "worldliness" as a common circumstance that undergirds, informs, and subtends all human experience, Said seeks to question and destabilize the canonical distinction between specialization and "generalism," between professional knowledge and lay–amateur–commonsensical understanding. Siding with Antonio Gramsci who in the very act of valorizing the category of the "intellectual" commits the intellectual to an accountable organic relationship, Said, unlike Michel Foucault and Gilles Deleuze, invests strongly in the politics of **representation** that binds the intellectual to the *demos*. The intellectual, in the act of performing as an intellectual, is a citizen too; and the question of course is: citizen of what, the country, the nation, the world, the planet, the ecosystem? Lest he be misunderstood or oversimplified, it must be strongly stated on behalf of Said that worldliness to him is not something that is felt immediately and spontaneously, or sensed proximally. Worldliness is heavily and intensely mediated by way of disciplines, ideological apparatuses, institutions, canon formations, rigorously formed tastes and sensibilities, and much else. Said acknowledges and honors the relative autonomies of these mediations and at the same time insists that all these forms and formations are mediations *of* and *into* something "real," that is, worldliness. Professional thinkers in their passion to stay loyal to their disciplines, or fiefdoms as Said would term them, entirely overlook the representative and mediatory functions of their respective disciplines.

What lies behind Said's powerful advocacy of intellectual worldliness (and here I am reminded of the term that Ralph Ellison invents on behalf of his nameless antagonist in *Invisible Man*, "thinker-tinker") is his concern that in their hyper-extended zeal to be professionals and specific intellectuals, academics have marginalized themselves beyond belief. They have lost the general public not unintentionally, not inadvertently, but in the name of expertise and specialization. Rather than stay with worldliness and explain to the lay public, and share with them, the amazingly complex, protean, and contradictory ways in which the "world worlds" differently and differentially in genres such as poetry, the novel, the short story, drama, and so on, academic critics and professional theorists have turned their back altogether on worldliness. They even presume that their second order formulations are more real than the worldliness of the world. Some of the finest demonstrations of Said at work in his project of worldliness are his essays and reviews of music, that most abstract and symbolic and self-referential form of art. Whether he is writing about opera or Glenn Gould's particular mode of performing, or reviewing a particular concert on a particular day at Carnegie Hall, Said brings together, within the same critical thought, insights about the composition, the quotidian conducting of that piece by that particular conductor during that particular performance, the performance of the different sections that comprised the orchestra, the determinate variations and interpretations deployed by the conductor on that particular day with larger speculations about the historicity and the context of the composition, the composer and his/her aesthetic ideology, the synchronic-diachronic variances in the reception of the piece, the critical relationship of the music as public rhetoric to a particular populace, and so on (for example, in *Musical Elaborations*, and *Music at the Limits*). In these analyses, Said convinces the reader that though it is permissible to dream of an ideal composer, an ideal conductor, and an ideal listener, what we actually have on hand is the history of the piece and its reception in a series of empirically and historically specific contexts and aegis: for example, a certain New York City audience responding to a particular piece of exciting but nationalist music after 9/11. In its very endeavor to transcend the specificities of time and place, the music as performance returns to history, returns to temporality, returns to the human calendar as it reenacts its worldliness time and again in different milieus. The cultural/aesthetic politics of the music, its reception, production, circulation, and distribution under different systems of patronage and dissemination: these characteristics constitute a certain worldliness that is inscribed in the musical text and its circumstantial performability. When one reads Said's essays on music, whether one agrees with Said's perspective and evaluation or not, the reader is persuaded that it is indeed possible and desirable to consider music as form and world, as structure and intention, as necessary and contingent, as specialized and public, as intimate and subjective and as impersonal and objective: all at the same time. Whatever one does or is doing and in whatever capacity, as Said would have it, "the world is never too much with us."

Zionism   "Zionism from the Standpoint of its Victims" is a classic essay by Said: an essay that had difficulty getting published since it offended different constituencies for different reasons. It is a classic Said essay for the simple reason that in this essay Said showcases his unique capacity to be partisan without being unilateral, to be a strong and unflinching advocate of a particular case and at the same time make room for multilateralism, to initiate reciprocity through recognition even when that very reciprocity is mired in chronic antagonism. The title of the essay aptly dramatizes the dilemma of the Palestinian subject and the Palestinian intellectual. Given the **contrapuntal** history of the Israeli–Palestinian conflict, the Palestinian cannot fail to take into account the historical reality of Zionism and its all too real impact on the history of an emerging Palestine. And yet, taking into account the significance as well as the salience of Zionism in the Palestinian context should not be construed as acquiescence to the claims of Zionism. Zionism, in this essay, is both acknowledged as historically real and valid and at the same time fundamentally problematized from the Palestinian/Arab standpoint. Said does not hesitate admitting into the history of the Palestinian subject the history of Zionism: a movement and a political philosophy that by very definition negates the possibility of a Palestinian national emergence. Said is contrapuntally aware that there is a flip side to this: that there is a radical Palestinian point of view that will not accept or honor the existence of the state of Israel. The irony in this situation is that recognition has to be gained from one's dire antagonist through rational and coeval persuasion: and coeval means the obligation to read the history

A Said Dictionary, First Edition. R. Radhakrishnan.
© 2012 John Wiley & Sons, Ltd. Published 2012 by John Wiley & Sons, Ltd.

of any one people not in isolation but in terms of the history of another people: in this case, two peoples locked together hopelessly in an ongoing antagonism where neither party will consider the ideological givens and compulsions of where the other party is coming from. Said understands that a Palestinian state recognized by Palestinians alone and not by Israel cannot exist, is in fact not real. In the same way, Israel has to be recognized by the Palestinian gaze in order to be legitimate ("Identity, Negation, and Violence"; "An Ideology of Difference").

Said's critical perspective on Zionism tells the Zionist things about Zionism that she herself is not aware of, or aspects she has suppressed: things she needs to hear. Like Jacqueline Rose's brilliant book, *The Question of Zion*, which functions as an insider's or Jewish critique as well as a symptomatic reading of Zionism and its collective unconscious, Said's essay exhorts and implores the Zionist to understand his doctrine contrapuntally. This is not an easy thing to do. For this to happen, the Zionist has to acknowledge the reality that in his history the Palestinian is necessarily implicated as the victim. There would be no Zionist historiography without the victimization of the Palestinian. What is progressive and transformative about Said's project is that it does not remove Zionism from the agenda just because it is a problem for the Palestinian. But by the same token, and as a counterpoint, he does not desist from producing an **oppositional** reading of Zionism just because such a reading would seem to violate and alienate the Zionist. A two-state solution requires as a prerequisite a thorough and comprehensive recognition between the two parties in conflict. Said's tendency, somewhat compatible with the ways in which the eminent political theorist Chantal Mouffe tries to push democracy beyond its anemic and often content-less obsession with mere "procedure," and towards a genuine pluralism and a democratic politics of difference, is to insist that each party not just understand where the other is coming from (the mealy-mouthed motto, "I don't agree with you, but I will defend to the death your right to have your point of view"), but acknowledge and internalize the reality that the other's claim actively intervenes in and complicates the legitimacy of one's own claims. The result may not be a harmonious mutual capitulation: but at the very least, the accord reached will have sincerely taken into account all the relevant historical factors and genealogies.

Said's reading of Zionism brings home to the gung-ho Zionist the unpleasant truth that Zionism, in spite of its Semitic heritage, remains deeply **Orientalist** in its ethical and epistemological orientation. This is corroborated by the differential treatment meted out within Israel to Sephardic,

Mizrahi, and Ashkenazi Jews; the discrimination based on their Eastern or European origins. What is most galling to the Zionist is Said's diagnosis that Zionism has close ties to European Colonialism, and in fact replicates it in its assumption of rational superiority over Eastern political cultures. That the state of Israel is recognized as Western is no coincidence; nor is it fortuitous even now, as the people's uprising in Egypt continues at the time of writing, that the United States considers Israel its staunch Western ally against pan-Arabic turmoil and unrest in the Middle East. The troubling question of course is: Is Zionism a form of racism? Referring to the United Nations resolution of 1975 that declares that "Zionism is racism," and the outcry against the declaration in the West, Said has this to say: "*Racism* is too vague: Zionism is Zionism. For the Arab Palestinian, this tautology has a sense that is perfectly congruent with, but exactly the opposite of, what it says to the Jews."

As he engages critically with the genealogy of Zionism, Said is keen to make two fundamental points. The first is that the Palestinian people have been condemned to the utterly unconscionable and ironic fate of being oppressed by a people who had been the oppressed till recently. His second point is that a secular Palestinian struggle is obligated to take into account the history of Zionism and its successful culmination in the formation of the state of Israel in 1948: celebratory independence for one people, and mourning for the other. The Palestinian struggle, in the name of the purity of its cause, cannot disregard or refuse to acknowledge the reality of a history that has already happened. Palestinian subjecthood is unavoidably double-conscious, just as Israeli subjecthood should be. But unfortunately, the dominant Israeli subject refuses the rigor of a contrapuntal reading. Zionism believes that it is exclusively about its chosen people with a guarantee of return. It is willfully and doctrinally unmindful of the historical reality that the return of one people is congruent and coextensive with the stark dis-accommodation, the un-homing, of another people. The reading from the other side, the contrapuntal reading, is totally denied. The other people have no permission to narrate their story. At best, their intentional un-homing is perhaps a form of collateral damage. The Israeli state's point of view has no place for the Palestinian perspective. The Palestinian is turned into a pure and irrational enemy by Zionist paranoia. The Palestinian on the other hand is obliged to take into account the reality of his placement in Israeli history. From the point of view of Israel, since Palestine supposedly has no history whatsoever, it becomes absurd even to raise the question of how to locate Israel in Palestinian history.

It seems appropriate to end with Said's words as he concludes his essay, a conclusion that takes the Palestinian through Zionism and beyond: "Zionism from the standpoint of its victims." "But just as no Jew in the last hundred years has been untouched by Zionism, so too no Palestinian has been untouched by it. Yet it must not be forgotten that the Palestinian was not simply a function of Zionism. His life, culture, and politics have their own dynamic and ultimately their own authenticity, to which we must now turn."

Bibliography

Books by Edward Said

1966. *Joseph Conrad and the Fiction of Autobiography.* Cambridge, MA: Harvard University Press; London: Oxford University Press.

1975. *Beginnings: Intention and Method.* New York: Basic Books.

1978. *Orientalism.* New York: Pantheon Books; London: Routledge and Kegan Paul.

1979. *The Question of Palestine.* New York: Times Books.

1980. Editor. *Literature and Society.* 1978 Selected Papers from the English Institute. With an introduction by Said. Baltimore: Johns Hopkins University Press.

1981. *Covering Islam: How the Media and the Experts Determine How We See the Rest of the World.* Pantheon: New York; London: Routledge and Kegan Paul.

1983. *The World, the Text, and the Critic.* Massachusetts: Harvard University Press.

1986. *After the Last Sky: Palestinian Lives.* Photographs by Jean Mohr. New York: Pantheon; London: Faber.

1988. Editor with Christopher Hitchens. *Blaming the Victims: Spurious Scholarship and the Palestinian Question.* London: Verso.

1988. *Yeats and Decolonization.* Field Day Pamphlets, Series 5, Nationalism, Colonialism, Literature. Field Day.

1991. *Musical Elaborations.* New York: Columbia University Press.

1991. *Peace in the Middle East.* Open Magazine Pamphlet Series, 13. Westfield, NJ: Open Media.

1993. *Culture and Imperialism.* New York: Knopf/Random House.

A Said Dictionary, First Edition. R. Radhakrishnan.

© 2012 John Wiley & Sons, Ltd. Published 2012 by John Wiley & Sons, Ltd.

1994. *The Pen and the Sword: Conversations with David Barsamian.* Monroe, ME: Common Courage Press.

1994. *The Politics of Dispossession: The Struggle for Palestinian Self-Determination, 1969–1994.* New York: Pantheon Books.

1994. *Representations of the Intellectual: The 1993 Reith Lectures.* New York: Pantheon Books.

1995. *Peace and its Discontents: Essays on Palestine in the Middle East Process,* with an Introduction by Christopher Hitchens. New York and London: Vintage.

1999. *Out of Place: A Memoir.* New York: Knopf.

2000. *The Edward Said Reader,* edited by Moustafa Bayoumi and Andrew Rubin. New York: Vintage.

2000. *The End of the Peace Process: Oslo and After.* New York: Pantheon Books; London: Granta.

2000. *Reflections on Exile and Other Essays.* Massachusetts: Harvard University Press.

2001. *Power, Politics, and Culture: Interviews with Edward W. Said,* edited with an introduction by Gauri Viswanathan. New York: Pantheon Books.

2002. With Daniel Barenboim. *Parallels and Paradoxes: Explorations in Music and Society.* New York: Pantheon Books.

2003. *Freud and the Non-European.* London and New York: Verso.

Posthumous publications

2004. *Humanism and Democratic Criticism.* New York: Columbia University Press.

2006. *On Late Style: Music and Literature Against the Grain.* New York: Pantheon Books.

2008. *Music at the Limits.* New York: Columbia University Press.

Edward Said's essays: a selective bibliography

1967. "Labyrinth of Incarnations: The Essays of Maurice Merleau-Ponty," *Kenyon Review* (January 1967), 29(1): 54–68.

1967. "The Totalitarianism of Mind," Review of Claude Lévi-Strauss' *The Savage Mind. Kenyon Review* (March 1967), 29(2) (114): 256–268.

1967. "Vico: Autodidact and Humanist," *Centennial Review* (Summer 1967), 11(3): 336–352.

1968. "Beginnings," *Salmagundi* (Fall 1968), 2(4): 36–55.

1969. With Maire Said. Translator and Introduction. Eric Auerbach's "Philology and *Weltliteratur*," *Centennial Review* (Winter 1969), 13(1): 1–17.

1969. "Swift's Tory Anarchy," *Eighteenth-Century Studies* (Fall 1969), 3: 48–66.

1970. "Narrative: Quest for Origins and Discovery of the Mausoleum," *Salmagundi* (Spring 1970), 12: 63–75.

1970. "Notes on the Characterization of a Literary Text," *MLN* (December 1970), 85(6): 765–790.

1971. "Abecedarium Culturae: Structuralism, Absence, Writing," *TriQuarterly* (1971), 20: 33–71.

1971. "Linguistics and the Archeology of Mind," *International Philosophical Quarterly* (March 1971), 11(1): 104–134.

1971. "Molestation and Authority in Narrative Fiction," in J. Hillis Miller, ed., *Aspects of Narrative: Selected Papers from the English Institute*, pp. 47–68. New York: Columbia University Press.

1971. "What Is Beyond Formalism?" *MLN* (December 1971), 86(6): 933–945.

1972. "Michel Foucault as an Intellectual Imagination," *boundary2* (Fall 1972), 1(1): 1–36.

1973. "On Originality," in Monroe Engel, ed., *Uses of Literature*, pp. 49–65. Harvard English Studies, 4. Cambridge, MA: Harvard University Press.

1973. "The Text as Practice and as Idea," *MLN* (December 1973), 88(6): 1071–1101.

1974. "Conrad: The Presentation of Narrative," *Novel* (Winter 1974), 7(2): 116–132.

1974. "An Ethics of Language." Review of Michel Foucault's *The Archeology of Knowledge and the Discourse on Language*. *Diacritics* (Summer 1974), 4(2): 28–37.

1975. "Chomsky and the Question of Palestine," *Journal of Palestine Studies* (Spring 1975), 4(3): 91–104.

1975. "Contemporary Fiction and Criticism," *TriQuarterly* (Spring 1975), 33: 231–256.

1975. "The Text, the World, the Critic," *Bulletin of the Midwest Modern Language Association* (Fall 1975), 8(2): 1–23.

1976. "Interview with Diacritics," *Diacritics* (Fall 1976), 6(3): 30–47.

1976. "On Repetition," in Angus Fletcher, ed., *The Literature of Fact: Selected Papers of the English Institute*, pp. 135–158. New York: Columbia University Press.

1976. 'Raymond Schwab and the Romance of Ideas," *Daedalus* (Winter 1976), 105(1): 151–167.

1976. "Roads Taken and not Taken in Contemporary Criticism," *Contemporary Literature* (1976), 17: 327–348.

1978. "The Idea of Palestine in the West," *Middle East Research and Information Project (Merip Reports)*, September 1978, 8(7)(70): 3–11.

1978. "The Problem of Textuality: Two Exemplary Positions," *Critical Inquiry* (Summer 1978), 4(4): 673–714.

1979. "An Exchange on Deconstruction and History," *boundary2* (Fall 1979), 8(1): 65–74, with Marie-Rose Logan, Eugenio Donato, William Warner, and Stephen Crites.

1979. "Reflections on Recent 'Left' Literary Criticism," *boundary2* (Fall 1979), 8(1): 11–30.

1979. "The Text, the World, the Critic," in Josue Harari, ed., *Textual Strategies: Perspectives on Post-Structuralist Criticism*, pp. 161–188. Ithaca: Cornell University Press.

1979. "Zionism from the Standpoint of Its Victims," *Social Text* (1979), 1: 7–58.

1980. "Islam Through Western Eyes," *Nation* (April 26, 1980), 230(16): 488–492.

1980. "The Palestine Question and the American Context," *Arab Studies Quarterly* (Spring 1980), 29(2): 127–149.

1981. "Reflections on the Palestinians," *Nation* (December 5, 1981), 233: 601–605.

1982. "Opponents, Audiences, Constituencies, and Community," *Critical Inquiry* (September 1982), 9(1): 1–26. Also in W.J.T. Mitchell, ed., *The Politics of Interpretation*, pp. 7–32. Chicago: University of Chicago Press, 1982.

1982. "Traveling Theory," *Raritan* (Winter 1982), 1(3): 41–67.

1983. "The Music Itself: Glenn Gould's Contrapuntal Vision," *Vanity Fair* (May 1983), 46(3): 97–101, 127–128.

1983. "A Response to Stanley Fish," *Critical Inquiry* (December 1983), 10(2): 371–373.

1983. "Secular Criticism," *Raritan* (1983), 2(3): 1–26.

1984. "The Future of Criticism," *MLN* (September 1984), 99(4): 951–958.

1984. "Michel Foucault, 1927–1984," *Raritan* (Fall 1984), 4(2): 1–11.

1984. "Permission to Narrate – Edward Said Writes about the Story of the Palestinians," *London Review of Books* (February 16–29, 1984), 6(3): 13–17.

1984. "Reflections on Exile," *Granta* (Autumn 1984), 13: 159–172.

1985. "An Ideology of Difference," *Critical Inquiry* (Autumn 1985), 12: 38–58.

1985. "Orientalism Reconsidered," *Cultural Critique* (Fall 1985), 1: 89–107, and *Race & Class* (Autumn 1985), 27(2): 1–15.

1986. "Foucault and the Imagination of Power," in David Couzens Hoy, ed. *Foucault: A Critical Reader*, pp. 149–155. Oxford: Blackwell.

1986. "Intellectuals in the Post-Colonial World," *Salmagundi* (Spring–Summer 1986), 70–71: 44–64.

1987. "Interpreting Palestine," *Harper's Magazine* (March 1987), 274(1642): 19–22.

1987. "Interview," in Imre Salusinszky, *Criticism in Society: Interviews with Jacques Derrida, Northrop Frye, Harold Bloom, Geoffrey Hartman, Frank Kermode, Edward Said, Barbara Johnson, Frank Lentricchia and J. Hillis Miller*, pp. 120–148. New York: Methuen.

1987. "Irangate: A Many-Sided Crisis," *Journal of Palestinian Studies* (Summer 1987), 16(4): 27–49.

1988. "American Intellectuals and the Middle East," (Interview) *Social Text* (Fall 1988), 19: 37.

1988. "Identity, Negation, and Violence," *New Left Review* (September–October 1988), 171: 46–60.

1988. "Spurious Scholarship and the Question of Palestine," *Race & Class* (Winter 1988), 29(3): 23–39, the introduction to *Blaming the Victims* (1988).

1989. "Representing the Colonized," *Critical Inquiry* (Winter 1989), 15(2): 205–225.

1990. "Narrative, Geography and Interpretation," *New Left Review* (March–April 1990), 180: 81–100.

1990. "Third-World Intellectuals and Metropolitan Culture," *Raritan* (Winter 1990), 9(3): 27–50.

1992. "Palestine, Then and Now," *Harper's Magazine* (December 1992), 285(1711): 47–55.

1992. "Peace and the Middle East," *Journal of Communication Inquiry* (Winter 1992) 16(1): 5–19.

1993. "Nationalism, Human Rights, and Interpretation," *Raritan* (Winter 1993), 12(3): 26–51.

1994. "Gods that Always Fail," *Raritan* (Spring 1994), 13(4): 1–13.

1995. "Symbols Versus Substance: A Year After the Declaration of Principles," *Journal of Palestine Studies* (Winter 1995), 24(2): 60–72. Interview conducted by Mouin Rabbani.

1998. "Daniel Barenboim and Edward Said: A Conversation," *Raritan* (Summer 1998), 18(1): 1–30.

1998. "Edward Said Talks to Jacqueline Rose," *Critical Quarterly* (Spring 1998), 40(1): 72–89.

1998. "The Panic of the Visual: A Conversation with Edward W. Said," *boundary2* (Summer 1998), 25(2): 11–33, interview conducted by W.J.T. Mitchell.

2001. "The Clash of Ignorance," *Nation* (October 22, 2001), 273(12): 11–13.

2001. "The Public Role of Writers and Intellectuals," *Nation* (September 17, 2001), 273(8): 27–28, 31–32, 34–36.

Selected works dealing with Edward Said's thought and work

Amin, Samir. *Eurocentrism.* New York: Monthly Review Press, 1989.

Afzal-Khan, Fawzia and Seshadri-Crooks, Kalpana. Eds. *The Pre-Occupation of Postcolonial Studies.* Durham: Duke University Press, 2000.

Ahmad, Eqbal. *Confronting Empire: Interviews with David Barsamian.* Cambridge, MA: South End Press, 2000.

Ahmad, Aijaz. *In Theory: Classes, Nations, and Literatures.* London: Verso, 1992.

Ali, Tariq. *Conversations with Edward Said.* London: Seagull, 2006.

Anidjar, Gil. "Secularism," *Critical Inquiry* (2006), 33: 52–77.

Apter, Emily. "Saidian humanism," *boundary2,* (Summer 2004), 31(2): 35–53.

Ashcroft, Bill. *Postcolonial Transformations.* London: Routledge, 2001.

Bhabha, Homi K. *The Location of Culture.* London: Routledge, 1990.

Brennan, Timothy. *At Home in the World: Cosmopolitanism Now.* Cambridge: Harvard University Press, 1992.

Bhabha, Homi and Mitchell, W.J.T. *Edward Said: Continuing the Conversation.* Chicago: University of Chicago Press, 2005.

Bove, Paul. *Intellectuals in Power: A Genealogy of Critical Humanism.* New York: Columbia University Press, 1985.

Bove, Paul. Ed. *Edward Said and the Work of the Critic: Speaking Truth to Power.* Durham and London: Duke University Press, 2000.

Bove, Paul. "Mendacious Innocents, or the Modern Genealogist as Conscientious Intellectual: Nietzsche, Foucault, Said," *boundary2* (Spring/Fall 1981), 9/10: 359–388.

Chakrabarty, Dipesh. *Provincializing Europe.* Princeton, NJ: Princeton University Press, 2007.

Cheah, Pheng and Robbins, Bruce. Eds. *Cosmopolitics: Thinking and Feeling Beyond the Nation.* London and Minneapolis: University of Minnesota Press, 1998.

Chomsky, Noam. *The Fateful Triangle: The United States, Israel, and the Palestinians.* Boston: South End Press, 1983.

Diacritics (Fall 1976), 6(3), Issue devoted to Said's *Beginnings* with articles by J. Hillis Miller, Hayden White, Joseph N. Riddel, and Eugenio Donato, with an interview with Edward Said.

Gandhi, Leela. *Postcolonial Theory: An Introduction.* New York: Columbia University Press, 1998.

Gourgouris, Stathis. "Transformation, not Transcendence," *boundary2* (2004), 31: 55–79.

Hussein, Abdirahaman. *Edward Said: Criticism and Society.* London: Verso, 1992.

Iskandar, Adel and Rustom, Hakem. Eds. *Edward Said: A Legacy of Emancipation and Representation.* Berkeley, CA: University of California Press, 2010.

Karavanta, Mina and Morgan, Nina. *Edward Said and Jacques Derrida: Reconstellating Humanism and the Global Hybrid.* Newcastle: Cambridge Scholars Publishing, 2008.

Kennedy, Valerie. *Edward Said: A Critical Introduction.* Cambridge: Polity Press, 2000.

Kumar, Amitava and Ryan, Michael. Eds. Special Issue of *Politics and Culture*, no. 1 (2004).

Lambropoulos, Vassilis. *The Rise of Eurocentrism.* Princeton and Oxford: Princeton University Press, 1992.

Lazarus, Neil. *The Postcolonial Unconscious.* Cambridge: Cambridge University Press, 2011.

Loomba, Ania. *Colonialism/Postcolonialism.* London and New York: Routledge, 1998.

Lowe, Lisa. *Critical Terrains.* New York: Cornell University Press, 1991.

MacClintock, Anne. *Imperial Leather.* New York: Routledge, 1995.

Marrouchi, Mustapha. *Edward Said at the Limits.* Albany: State University of New York Press, 2004.

Marrouchi, Mustapha. "The Critic as Dis/Placed Intelligence: The Case of Edward Said," *Diacritics* (Spring 1991), 21(1): 63–74.

Marzec, Robert. *An Ecological and Postcolonial Study of Literature; From Daniel Defoe to Salman Rushdie.* New York: Palgrave, 2007.

Mitchell, W.J.T. "Secular Divination: Edward Said's Humanism," *Critical Inquiry* (2005), 31: 462–471.

Mufti, Aamir R. "Critical Secularism: A Reintroduction for Perilous Times," in Aamir R. Mufti, ed., *Critical Secularism, a special issue of boundary2* (2004), 31(2): 1–9.

Nandy, Ashis. *The Intimate Enemy: Loss and Recovery of Self under Colonialism.* Bombay: Oxford University Press, 1983.

Nixon, Rob. *London Calling: V.S. Naipaul, Postcolonial Mandarin.* Oxford: Oxford University Press, 1992.

Porter, Dennis. "Orientalism and its Problems," in Patrick Williams and Laura Chrisman, eds., *Colonial Discourse and Postcolonial Theory*, pp. 150–161. London: Harvester, 1993.

Radhakrishnan, R. *History, the Human, and the World Between.* Durham, NC and London: Duke University Press, 2008.

Radhakrishnan, R. "Edward Said's Literary Humanism," *Cultural Critique* (Fall 2007), 67: 13–42.

Robbins, Bruce. "Deformed Professions, Empty Politics," *Diacritics* (Fall 1986), 16(3): 67–72.

Robbins, Bruce. *Secular Vocations.* New York: Verso, 1994.

Rose, Jacqueline. *The Question of Zion.* Princeton, NJ: Princeton University Press, 2005.

Shohat, Ella and Stam, Robert. *Unthinking Eurocentrism.* London and New York: Routledge, 1994.

Spanos, William V. *The Legacy of Edward W. Said.* Urbana-Champaign: University of Illinois Press, 2008.

Spanos, William V. *America's Shadow.* Minneapolis and London: University of Minnesota Press, 2000.

Sprinker, Michael. Ed. *Edward Said: A Critical Reader.* Malden and Oxford: Blackwell, 1993.

Varadharajan, Asha. *Exotic Parodies: Subjectivity in Adorno, Said, and Spivak.* Minneapolis: University of Minnesota Press, 1995.

Viswanathan, Gauri. *The Masks of Conquest.* New York: Columbia University Press, 1989.

Young, Robert. *Postcolonialism.* Oxford: Blackwell, 2001.
Young, Robert. *White Mythologies: Writing, History, and the West.* New York and London: Routledge, 1991.

Selected reviews of Edward Said's books, alphabetically listed

After the Last Sky (1986)

Armanazi, Ghayth N. *Arab Affairs* (Winter 1986–87), 1(12): 137–140.
Brand, Laurie A. "Palestine and Palestinians," *The Middle East Journal* (Spring 1988), 42(2): 315–316.
Easton, Celia A. *Southern Humanities Review* (Winter 1988), 22(1): 67–69.
Gilsenan, Michael. "Picturing the Palestinian Experience," *Times Literary Supplement* (June 12, 1987), 4393: 629–630.
Rushdie, Salman. "Books: If I Forget Thee . . . ," *Guardian* (September 19, 1986): 11.

Beginnings (1975)

Arac, Jonathan. *Comparative Literature* (Spring 1978), 30(2): 185–189.
Bruns, Gerald L. *Philological Quarterly* (Spring 1978), 57(2): 255–265.
Culler, Jonathan. *Modern Language Review* (July 1978), 73(3): 582–585.
Choice (March 1976), 13(1): 54.
Fletcher, Angus. "The Interpretation of Beginnings," *boundary2* (Winter 1977), 5(2): 615–628.
Gelley, Alexander. *Nineteenth-Century Fiction* (June 1977), 32(1): 16.
Hillis Miller, J., "Beginning with a Text," *Diacritics* (Fall 1976), 6(3): 2–7.
Riddel, Joseph N. "Scriptive Fate/Scriptive Hope," *Diacritics* (Fall 1976), 6(3): 14–23.
Tanner, Tony. "Points of Departure," *Times Literary Supplement* (August 20, 1976), 3884: 1026.
Watkins, Evan. *Journal of Aesthetics and Art Criticism* (Fall 1978), 37(1): 100–101.
White, Hayden. "Criticism as Cultural Politics," *Diacritics* (Fall 1976), 6(3): 8–13.

Covering Islam (1981)

Berg, Richard. *Theatre Journal* (October 1982): 417–418.
Geertz, Clifford. "Conjuring with Islam," *New York Review of Books* (May 27, 1982), 29(9): 28.
Howard, Anthony. "Reporters and a Critic," *New York Times Book Review* (July 28, 1981), 7: 18–19.
Lippman, Thomas W. *Middle East Journal* (Autumn 1981), 35(4): 646–647.

Culture and Imperialism (1993)

Bove, Paul A. *boundary2* (Summer 1993), 20(2): 266–272.
Brantlinger, Patrick. *Victorian Studies* (Summer 1994), 37(4): 583–585.
Gellner, Ernest. "The Mightier Pen?" *Times Literary Supplement* (February 19, 1993), 4690: 3–4.
Jehlen, Myra. *William and Mary Quarterly* (October 1994), 51(4): 783–787.
Leonard, John. *Nation* (March 22, 1993), 256(11): 383–390.
Polan, Dana. "Art, Society, and 'Contrapuntal' Criticism," *Clio* (Fall 1994), 24(1): 69–79.
Wood, Michael. *New York Review of Books* (March 3, 1994), 41(5): 44–47.

Orientalism (1978)

Arac, Jonathan. *Clio* (Spring 1980), 9(3): 465–468.
Asad, Talal. *English Historical Review* (July 1980), 95(376): 648–649.
Buttigieg, Joseph A. *Structuralist Review* (1980), 2(1): 135–141.
Chambers, Ross. "Representation and Authority," *Comparative Studies in Society and History* (July 1980), 22(3): 509–512.
Choice (April 1979), 16(2): 210.
Clifford, James. *History and Theory.* (May 1980), 19(2): 204–223.
Greene, Thomas M. "One World, Divisible," *Yale Review* (1979), 68: 577–581.
Manzalaoui, Mahmoud. *Modern Language Review* (October 1980), 75(4): 837–839.
Meyers, Jeffrey. "Under Western Eyes," *Sewanee Review* (Spring 1980), 88(2): xlv–xlviii.

The Question of Palestine (1979)

Ahmad, Eqbal. *Nation* (March 22, 1980), 230: 341–343.
Najjar, Fauzi. "The Question of Palestine," *Review of Politics* (October 1980), 42(4): 604–610.
Robbins, Bruce. "Homelessness and Worldliness," *Diacritics* (Fall 1983), 13(3): 69–77.

Reflections on Exile (2000)

Nussbaum, Martha C. "The End of Orthodoxy," *New York Times Book Review* (February 18, 2001): 28.

Representations of the Intellectual (1994)

Khalidi, Rashid. *Journal of Palestine Studies* (Spring 1995), 24(3): 96–98.
Walzer, Michael. *New Republic* (November 7, 1994), 211(19): 38–40.

The World, the Text, and the Critic (1983)

Cain, William E. "Criticism and Knowledge," *Virginia Quarterly Review* (Winter 1984), 60(1): 181–188.

Carroll, David. *Comparative Literature* (Spring 1986), 38(2): 187–190.

Conley, Tom. *Sub-Stance* (1985), 46: 98–102.

Donoghue, Denis. "An Organic Intellectual," *New Republic* (April 18, 1983): 30–33.

Hutcheon, Linda. "A Poetics of Modernism?" *Diacritics* (Winter 1983), 13(4): 33–42.

Lodge, David. "Adventures among Master-Theories," *Times Literary Supplement* (May 4, 1984), 4231: 487.

Weales, Gerald. *Kenyon Review* (Fall 1983), 5(4): 122–125.

Williams, Raymond. "Ours and not Ours," *Guardian* (March 8, 1984): 10.

Wright, Iain. *Times Higher Education Supplement* (April 13, 1984): 20.

Other works cited

Aijaz, Ahmad. *In Theory*. London and New York: Verso, 1994.

Anzaldua, Gloria. *Borderlands/La Frontera*. San Francisco: Aunt Lute Books, 1990.

Appiah, Kwame Anthony. "Is the Post- in Postmodernism the Post- in Postcolonial?" *Critical Inquiry* (1991), 17(2): 336–357.

Auerbach, Eric. *Mimesis: The Representation of Reality in Western Literature*. Fiftieth Anniversary Edition. Trans. Willard Trask. Princeton: Princeton University Press, 2003.

Benda, Julien. *La trahisons des clercs*. Grasse: Les cahiers rouges, 2003.

Benjamin, Walter. "Theses in the Philosophy of History," in *Illuminations*, trans. Harry Zohn, pp. 253–264. New York: Schocken, 1969.

Conrad, Joseph. *Heart of Darkness*. London: Penguin, 2007.

Derrida, Jacques. *Of Grammatology*, trans. *Gayatri Chakravorty Spivak*. Baltimore and London: Johns Hopkins University Press, 1976.

Disraeli, Benjamin. *Tancred*. London: Henry Colburn, 1847.

Du Bois, W.E.B. *The Souls of Black Folk*. New York: Bantam, 1903.

Durrell, Lawrence. *Alexandria Quartet*. London: Faber and Faber, 1957–60.

Eliot, T.S. "Tradition and the Individual Talent," in *The Sacred Wood: Essays on Poetry and Criticism*. New York: Alfred A. Knopf, 1921.

Eliot, T.S. *The Waste Land*. New York: W. W. Norton, 2001.

Ellison, Ralph. *Invisible Man*. New York: Random House, 1952.

Forster, E.M. *A Passage to India*. London: Penguin, 2005.

Foucault, Michel. *Madness and Civilization*. Abingdon: Routledge, 2001.

Foucault, Michel. *The Order of Things*. London: Tavistock Publications, 1970.

Foucault, Michel. "What Is an Author?" in *Language, Counter-Memory, Practice*, pp. 124–127. Ithaca: Cornell University Press, 1977.

Ghosh, Amitav. *The Shadow Lines*. London: Bloomsbury, 1988.

Gorimer, Nadine. *Burger's Daughter*. London: Jonathan Cape, 1979.

Guha, Ranajit. *History at the Limit of World-History*. New York: Columbia University Press, 2003.

Heidegger, Martin. "Letter on Humanism," in *Basic Writings*, pp. 213–266. San Francisco: Harper, 1993.

Hong Kingston, Maxine. *The Woman Warrior*. New York: Vintage, 1989.

Huxley, Aldous. *Point, Counter-Point*. London: Vintage, 2004.

Ishiguro, Kazuo. *The Remains of the Day*. London: Faber and Faber, 1989.

JanMohamed, Abdul. "Worldliness-without-World, Homelessness-as-Home: Toward a Definition of the Specular Border Intellectual," in *Edward Said: A Critical Reader*, ed. Michael Sprinker, pp. 218–241. Oxford: Blackwell, 1992.

Marx, Karl. *The Eighteenth Brumaire of Louis Bonaparte*. Chicago: Charles H. Kerr, 1907.

Mufti, Amir. "Secular Criticism: A Reintroduction for Our Perilous Times," *boundary2* (special issue edited by Amir Mufti) (2004), 31(2): 1–9.

Ngugi wa Thiong'o. *A Grain of Wheat*. Oxford: Heinemann, 1986.

Radhakrishnan, R. "Ethnic Identity and Poststructuralist Difference," in *The Nature and Context of Minority Discourse*, ed. A. R. JanMohamed and D. Lloyd, pp. 50–71. New York: Oxford University Press, 1990.

Rahn, John. *Music Inside Out: Going Too Far in Musical Essays*. Amsterdam: G+B Arts International, 2000.

Rushdie, Salman. "Outside the Whale," *Granta* (1984) 11: 125–138.

Rushdie, Salman. *The Satanic Verses*. New York: Viking, 1988.

Spivak, Gayatri Chakravorty. "Can the Subaltern Speak?" in *Marxism and the Interpretation of Culture*, ed. Cary Nelson and Lawrence Grossberg, pp. 271–313. Urbana, IL: University of Illinois Press, 1988.

Vico, Giambattista. *The New Science*, trans. Thomas G. Bergin and Max H. Fisch. Ithaca: Cornell University Press, 1968.

Viswanathan, Gauri. *The Masks of Conquest: Literary Study and British Rule in India*. New Delhi: Oxford University Press, 1989.

Viswanathan, Gauri. *Outside the Fold: Conversion, Modernity, and Belief*. Princeton: Princeton University Press, 1998.

Viswanathan, Gauri, ed. *Power, Politics, and Culture: Interviews with Edward W. Said*. New York: Vintage, 2002.

Index

academia 82
Achebe, Chinua 19, 72, 124
Adorno, Theodor 35, 122
Africa/n 17, 19, 22, 27
Ahmad, Aijaz 28, 88, 146
agency 62, 75, 139
Alatas, Syed Hussein 144
Algeria 26, 89
Almayer's Folly 22
Althusser, Louis 30, 35, 43, 45, 58, 60
alienation 35, 39
"always already" 131
America/n, USA xii, xvi, 2, 8, 13, 27, 38, 39
ambivalence 20, 28, 31
anarchism 70
Anderson, Perry 57
Anglophone 76, 89
anthropology xiii
Antonius, George 144
Anzaldua, Gloria 116
aporia 13, 130
Appadurai, Arjun 146
Appiah, Anthony 88
a priori 11, 52, 59

Arab xii, 2, 3, 14, 154
Arafat, Yasser xii, 64, 72, 111
Asad, Talal 67, 105
Asia, 51
asymmetry xiii, 58, 59
Austen, Jane 26, 30, 31, 42, 77, 150
authenticity 2, 88, 107
authority 2
author-function 118
avant-gardism 33

Bach, Johannes Sebastian 42, 142
Bachelard, Gaston 11
Bakhtin, Mikhail 56, 103
Baldwin, James 103
Balibar, Etienne 64, 68, 108
Barthes, Roland 30, 43, 55, 127
Barenboim, Daniel 91
Baudelaire, Charles 30, 127
Beethoven, Ludwig van 51, 120, 142
Being 11
belonging 2
Benda, Julien 51, 102
Benjamin, Walter 26, 152
Bharucha, Rustum 67, 105

A Said Dictionary, First Edition. R. Radhakrishnan.
© 2012 John Wiley & Sons, Ltd. Published 2012 by John Wiley & Sons, Ltd.